Just About Managing?

Effective management
for voluntary organisations
and community groups

by Sandy Adirondack
Illustrations by Steve Simpson

London Voluntary Service Council

356 Holloway Road, London N7 6PA

July 1992

Registered charity 276886

British Library Cataloguing-in-Publication Data

A catalogue record for this book is available
from the British Library.

ISBN 1 872582 80 X

Typeset from disk by Sue Dransfield.

Printed by Spider Web, 14 Sussex Way, London N7 6RS.

Foreword

Since *Just About Managing?* was first published in 1989 it has become an increasingly important aid to all those involved in the management of voluntary organisations.

Many trainers have also used it as a reference in developing and delivering training for managers of voluntary organisations.

In deciding to produce this new edition, LVSC took account of the continuing importance for voluntary organisations to develop good management practices and the need to include guidance on matters such as contracts, planning and evaluation which more and more affect the management of voluntary organisations.

I am particularly grateful to BP for sponsoring this new edition. I would also like to thank Sandy Adirondack for her efficient work in updating the publication, members of LVSC staff who advised on the new edition, and voluntary organisations which gave such positive feedback on the first edition.

Dee Springer
Director, LVSC
June 1992

Production sponsored by
British Petroleum

Contents

Introduction

Voluntary organisations and community groups of all types and sizes are facing a bewildering range of new challenges.

- Changes in the pattern of local authority and central government expenditure are keeping grant-aided voluntary organisations under constant threat, and forcing them to compete within the 'contract culture' or look elsewhere for funding.

- Local authorities, health authorities and other statutory bodies will no longer directly provide many services, but will buy in services from the 'independent sector'. This includes commercial (profit-making) enterprises, not-for-profit organisations and voluntary organisations. In some cases voluntary groups will step in, perhaps without financial support, to fill the gaps.

- There is increasing emphasis on a 'new philanthropy', based on volunteering and charitable fundraising.

- The creation of the European single market is likely to mean the further marginalisation of disadvantaged groups within Britain and Europe, new regulatory frameworks for charities and other voluntary organisations, access to new sources of funding, and competition for contracts from European organisations.

- The pace of change appears to be accelerating, and every year significant new legislation affects the voluntary sector. Voluntary sector management committees and managers, especially in small organisations, are hard-pressed to keep up with it all.

The basic assumption of this book is that good management enables organisations to achieve what they set out to do and to retain their most important values while responding to changing needs and circumstances. The guidelines here will help management committees, managers, staff and volunteer workers manage effectively, in a way which recognises and builds on the strength of the voluntary sector in general and each individual organisation.

Who are the managers?

Even in organisations which have no one called 'manager', people manage. In this book 'manager' refers to anyone, paid or volunteer, who has responsibility for organising, coordinating or making decisions about an organisation, team, department or project. This includes:

- the management committee;

- a person employed as a senior manager (who might be called a chief executive officer, director, coordinator, project leader, or something similar);

- middle managers or line managers (who might be called head of department, project leader, team leader, supervisor or something similar);

- workers in a non-hierarchical organisation, where managerial responsibilities are shared among all workers;

- anyone, paid or volunteer, who organises activities for the organisation.

Just about managing?

The title of the book has three meanings:

- Are you muddling through, making do, just about managing? This book will help you manage in a planned, coherent way that will increase the effectiveness of the organisation and its management committee, managers, staff and volunteers.

- It will help you be just about managing, dealing with management issues and problems with a concern for justice, fairness, respect and individual commitment.

- And it is just about managing. It covers many topics, ranging from teamwork to training, but they are all directly related to good management.

Just About Managing? is a companion to *Voluntary But Not Amateur: A guide to the law for voluntary organisations and community groups*, also published by London Voluntary Service Council.

Voluntary sector managers who came to rely on the first edition of *Just About Managing?* will find in this new edition all the good bits, plus new material on policy development, strategic planning, technical aspects of service agreements and contracts, performance indicators, staff reviews, and more.

Acknowledgements

The voluntary and community groups with which I have worked and the people I have trained may recognise in these pages their problems and their solutions. I am grateful to all these groups and individuals for their commitment and insight, and for letting me share their experience.

I especially want to thank Sheila Francis Ramdular, Aidan Merritt and Ian Duncan, and all those who offered helpful comments on the first edition. David Green, Caroline Hopper, Alan Lawrie, Shirley Otto, Gill Roberts, Cristine Smalligan, Sandra Vogel, Adrian Williams, Jo Woolf and Steve Wyler provided advice on individual chapters. Jacki Reason remains a supportive editor, and although Steve Simpson's original cartoons still make me laugh, the new ones are even better.

Sandy Adirondack
June 1992

Chapter 1:

Managing in the voluntary sector

Although the principles of good management are the same in organisations of any size or type, the voluntary sector has particular problems which arise from its history, development and ways of working.

This chapter looks at:

● typical voluntary sector management problems;

● what management is, with definitions of relevant terms and concepts;

● functions of management, and which chapter deals with each function;

● a checklist of information needed for good management, and a basic booklist.

THE VOLUNTARY SECTOR

Many voluntary and community organisations start as **volunteer groups**, with like-minded people coming together for a particular purpose: to share a common interest, organise activities, help or support each other, perform a service to the community, or campaign for or against something. In these small informal groups there are shared philosophies and politics, and differences are smoothed over in the interests of getting on with whatever the group has set itself up to do. If differences become irreconcilable people leave or the group splits; this can be traumatic but the effects are generally short-lived.

Decision-making in volunteer groups is in the hands of any members who want to attend meetings, and activities are carried out by the members on a voluntary (unpaid) basis. Money for activities typically comes from members' subscriptions, donations, fundraising events such as fetes or jumble sales, and grants from trusts or local businesses.

Many organisations which are now very large started in this way.

Two factors change a volunteer group into a **voluntary organisation**. One is if the group becomes too large for all members to be involved in decision-making. The members appoint or elect a committee which becomes (whatever it is actually called) a management committee. Or the group receives a grant which requires the money to be paid to a formally constituted body, usually called a management committee or something similar, which will take legal responsibility for ensuring funds are properly spent.

Decision-making is no longer in the hands of all the members, but is done on their behalf by a committee. In the early stages of this transition the organisation's work may still be carried out by volunteers, but later paid staff may be hired (sometimes initially to organise the volunteers).

Even when the work is done by paid staff these groups are still called 'voluntary', partly because of their connection to volunteer groups and partly because they are managed by voluntary (unpaid) management committees.

The difficulties now faced by many voluntary organisations have their roots in an unplanned or badly planned transition from a one-tier organisation (members or volunteers) to a three-tier or four-tier organisation (members/committee/paid staff/volunteer workers) and then to an organisation with yet another tier (a manager) between the committee and staff, and perhaps a tier of subcommittees between the committee and manager.

The voluntary sector is not in any way homogeneous. It encompasses the small group of local women coming together to support each other through a miscarriage, and international agencies such as Save the Children or Greenpeace; groups with annual incomes ranging from a few pounds to many millions; groups with no paid workers and others with hundreds of employees; groups committed to collective and cooperative working arrangements and those with rigid hierarchies; groups ranging politically from far right to far left – and everything in between.

It includes groups which primarily provide a service, those which primarily campaign, and those which do both; groups engaged in research or action or both. And it covers an incredible range of sectors: arts, children, disability, education, elderly, employment, environment, health, housing, human rights, peace, prison reform, sport, welfare, and dozens of others.

There is considerable dissatisfaction with the term 'voluntary sector'. On the Continent the term **social economy** is used. But social economy includes workers' cooperatives, mutual aid societies and other organisations which in the UK would not be considered part of the voluntary sector.

Some people argue that voluntary sector organisations are more accurately defined by their purpose, and we should refer to **social purpose** or **common benefit** organisations.

TYPICAL PROBLEMS

The voluntary sector's history, its breadth and the inherent contradictions make it difficult to develop a broad management perspective. Nevertheless certain problems appear in voluntary organisations of all shapes and sizes:

● lack of clarity about or an unwillingness to set long, medium and short term objectives and priorities;

- confusion about the boundaries and relationships between management committee, subcommittees, managers, staff, volunteers and users;

- unconfident and/or overcommitted management committee members;

- unconfident and/or overcommitted managers;

- a misfit between the organisation's ideals and its day to day reality;

- badly planned, badly run and badly minuted meetings;

- unclear decision-making and management structures within the staff group;

- unclear job descriptions and job expectations for staff and volunteers;

- unclear or inadequate procedures for dealing with unsatisfactory work performance or behaviour;

- haphazard administrative systems which hinder rather than help effective running of the organisation;

- inadequate procedures for financial management and control;

- unwillingness to recognise or deal with disagreements or conflict within the organisation;

- unwillingness to look after each other, thus contributing to stress and burnout;

- unwillingness to address any of these problems, or inadequate procedures for dealing with them.

This book provides guidelines for dealing with these situations. They can only be broad and will have to be adapted for different types of groups, but there should be something for nearly every voluntary organisation. Most of the book is also relevant for cooperatives and community businesses.

WHAT IS MANAGEMENT?

Good management is a tool to ensure people give the best to and get the best from any organisation, and to ensure the organisation can do what it wants and needs to do, without wasting precious time, energy or money.

There is a mystique around management: it is seen as something people can only do if they are highly trained, super intelligent or extremely efficient. In fact, nearly everyone is involved in high-level management all the time. Anyone who can get three children dressed, breakfasted, washed and off to school *and* get to work on time despite having to rely on public transport is a superb manager. Anyone who can plan and produce a dinner for 12 can manage complex administrative and task functions. Anyone who can survive on social security is a financial manager. People simply need the confidence to transfer these skills to other situations.

At its most basic, management can be defined as **ensuring an organisation makes the most effective and efficient use of resources in order to achieve agreed objectives.**

Within this statement lie the rudiments of good management:

- a perception of management as relevant to everyone involved in the organisation, not just the management committee or paid managers;

- a shared **vision**: a clear understanding of why the organisation exists and its overall aims or **long term objectives**;

- **shorter term objectives** or goals which are clear and shared;

- a good understanding of the **resources** available (people, money, time, premises, equipment, materials);

- an ability and willingness to **plan, organise** and **coordinate** the use of these resources to meet the objectives;

- clarity about how the organisation will know when it has met its objectives;

- an ability and willingness to set and monitor **expectations** and **standards**;

- **flexibility** to change plans or objectives when circumstances change.

Other basics of good management lie in being clear about:

- who has responsibility for making decisions or taking action;

- the information required for effective and efficient decision-making or action;

- who deals with situations if things go wrong.

What needs managing?

It is helpful to distinguish between:

● responsibility for managing the **organisation** (setting and monitoring long and medium term objectives, and developing policies);

● responsibility for **day to day management** of the organisation's work (what the organisation does, how it does it, and how well the work is done), the people who do the work, and resources;

● responsibility for managing a team, department or project;

● people's individual responsibility for managing their own work.

The chart illustrates these divisions.

WHO MANAGES?

The governing body

Every organisation has a governing body which is legally and financially responsible for the organisation. In most organisations this body will also make major management decisions, but sometimes the governing body (for example a board of trustees) might delegate management responsibility to a separate management committee. In this book, the governing body is generally referred to as the management committee. When very specific legal and financial responsibilities are being considered, the phrase 'management committee or other governing body' is used.

Broadly, the committee is responsible for ensuring the organisation knows what it is supposed to be doing, has

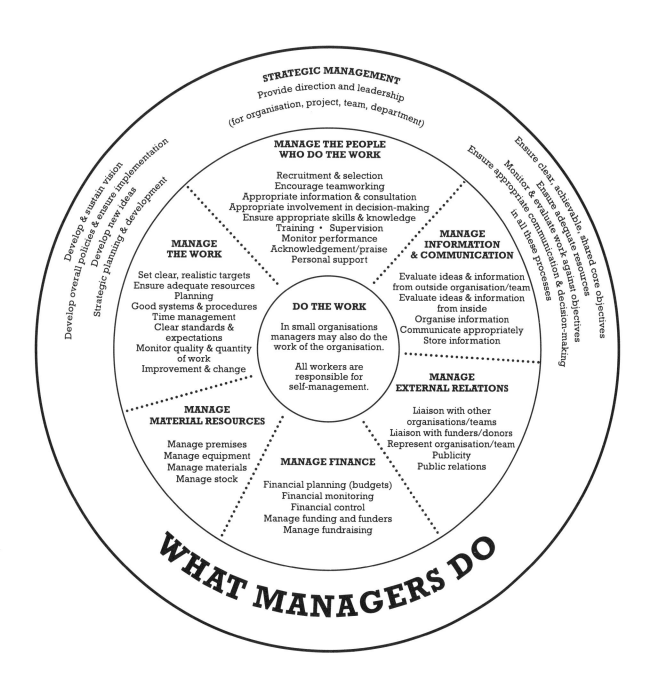

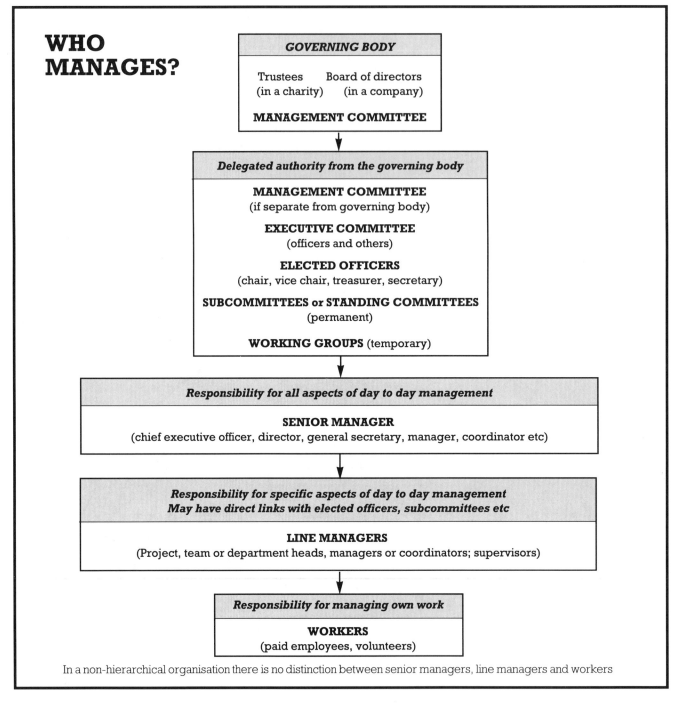

WHO MANAGES?

GOVERNING BODY

Trustees   Board of directors
(in a charity)   (in a company)

MANAGEMENT COMMITTEE

Delegated authority from the governing body

MANAGEMENT COMMITTEE
(if separate from governing body)

EXECUTIVE COMMITTEE
(officers and others)

ELECTED OFFICERS
(chair, vice chair, treasurer, secretary)

SUBCOMMITTEES or STANDING COMMITTEES
(permanent)

WORKING GROUPS (temporary)

Responsibility for all aspects of day to day management

SENIOR MANAGER
(chief executive officer, director, general secretary, manager, coordinator etc)

Responsibility for specific aspects of day to day management
May have direct links with elected officers, subcommittees etc

LINE MANAGERS
(Project, team or department heads, managers or coordinators; supervisors)

Responsibility for managing own work

WORKERS
(paid employees, volunteers)

In a non-hierarchical organisation there is no distinction between senior managers, line managers and workers

enough people and money to do it, and does it well. It must ensure the functions in the outer circle on the 'What managers do' chart are carried out.

Chapter 2 looks in more detail at the responsibilities of governing bodies and management committees. *Voluntary But Not Amateur* provides information about legal structures and charitable status.

Subcommittees and working groups

As management becomes more complex it may be helpful to set up subcommittees to deal with specific aspects of the organisation's work: personnel, finance, fundraising, project development etc. Or there may be a need to set up short term working groups to focus on specific tasks, such as planning a tenth anniversary event, developing an equal opportunities policy, or drawing up guidelines for

contractual funding arrangements. Each subgroup should have clear terms of reference stating what sort of decisions and actions it can take and how it is expected to report back to the main committee.

Committee officers

The organisation's constitution may set out the minimum responsibilities of elected officers. As with subgroups, it is important to be clear about what sorts of decisions and actions officers can take on their own and how these get reported back to the main committee, and what must be referred back to the committee for final decision or action.

The manager

In a very small organisation the management committee may be involved in managing the organisation, managing the day to day work, and actually doing the work. With a very small staff group, one staff member (or some or all of them) might be delegated responsibility for day to day management, with the committee retaining overall management responsibility. As the staff group gets larger it is likely that a manager will be appointed with explicit responsibility for day to day management.

This manager (who might be called director, managing director, chief officer, chief executive, general secretary, coordinator, leader) is in a key position: the pivot between the management committee with its subgroups and officers, and the staff and volunteers who carry out the work of the organisation. Management can only be effective if there is a good working partnership in both directions: between the manager and the committee, and between the manager and other workers.

Chapter 3 looks in more detail at the role of the manager in voluntary organisations.

Line managers

If the staff group gets larger or the work of the organisation becomes more differentiated or compartmentalised, line managers may be appointed to manage specific teams, departments, sites or projects. They will take on more of the day to day management responsibility, and the senior manager is likely to become more involved in overall (strategic) management. At this point the relationship between the management committee and the senior manager can become very confused.

Self-management

Nearly all workers have some responsibility for managing their own work: deciding priorities, managing their time, and setting and monitoring standards. Problems can arise if there is confusion about the extent to which individuals can manage their own work and how much it is managed by others. Good managers ensure individual workers have as much autonomy as possible, but within clear boundaries and with regular supervision.

MANAGEMENT FUNCTIONS

Fostering teamwork and involvement

People in the voluntary sector spend a lot of time talking, but are not always very good at communicating. Nor are they always very good at working in groups, making decisions or implementing decisions when they are made. **Chapters 4, 5 and 6** look at ways to improve verbal and written communication, teamwork and decision-making and make meetings and reports more effective.

Developing and implementing policy

When organisations are new or very small there is often an implicit assumption that everyone agrees about what the organisation should be doing, why and how. As organisations get older or larger these assumptions need to be made explicit and tested against reality. **Chapter 7** looks at the process of developing, implementing and reviewing the organisation's policies, and ensuring they remain consistent with the organisation's vision and values.

Setting and achieving objectives

Compared with the statutory sector, the voluntary sector has been able to respond relatively quickly to new needs and demands. This can be a great advantage, but it can also lead to overwork or to unplanned activities which waste energy. In this situation planning is an essential step in good management.

Increasingly voluntary organisations are being asked by funders to produce three-year or five-year plans. The idea of long term strategic planning or development planning is still quite strange for many organisations, and is often seen as directly contradictory to a view of the voluntary sector as responsive and flexible.

Monitoring and evaluation ensure the organisation actually does what it is supposed to be doing, whether its plans are long term or shorter term. Monitoring and evaluation can, as some people fear, be used as a means of control in an authoritarian, repressive way, and can be used by funders to justify cuts to ineffective organisations. But properly used, monitoring and evaluation can enable an organisation to show how much it is achieving in both qualitative and quantitative terms. **Chapters 8 and 9** clarify the steps in setting objectives, planning, implementing the plans, monitoring, and evaluating work. Terms of reference for a development subcommittee and an outline for a strategic plan are included.

Managing change

Any change in organisational direction, policies or procedures represents both an opportunity and a threat. The management of change – maximising opportunities and reducing the negative effects – is a key factor in enabling organisations to grow and develop. **Chapter 10** gives some basic guidelines for enabling organisations to cope smoothly with change and difficult situations.

Effective use of time

There is no point in having clearly defined objectives if there is simply not enough time to achieve them. Time management is an essential part of good management; **chapter 11** provides some hints on how to use this irreplaceable resource more effectively.

Managing new funding relationships

For many grant-funded organisations, the most important change in the early and mid-1990s will be the shift away from grants to service agreements and contracts. **Chapters 12 and 13** look at some of the legal, financial, personnel, management and service aspects of this change.

Personnel management and development

Even if objectives and tasks are well defined, they will not be achieved if the people who are supposed to do the work are unsure of what they are meant to do or feel unsupported. **Chapter 14** looks at personnel management and development in general, and includes terms of reference for a personnel subcommittee. **Chapter 15** sets out the recruitment process as the cornerstone of good personnel practice. **Chapter 16** covers procedures for staff and volunteer supervision, support and formal reviews and **chapter 17** looks at training.

Personnel problems

In any group, differences are inevitable. Good management lies in recognising these differences, using them creatively to develop new approaches or activities, and ensuring people can work together towards shared objectives even if they disagree quite fundamentally about other issues. **Chapter 18** provides guidelines for working with people with differing ideas, avoiding destructive conflict and dealing with it if it does erupt.

If an organisation is not properly managed – if clear and realistic goals are not set, people do not understand what is happening around them or disagreements are not dealt with – the organisation and the individuals within it will eventually suffer from stress and burnout. This leads to sickness and absenteeism which puts even more stress on the other people involved in the organisation. This 'stress cycle' and what can be done to prevent it is the topic of **chapter 19.**

Managing money

'Community Group Cash Probe' screams the headline in the local newspaper as yet another group succumbs to the difficulties of managing large sums of money without adequate guidelines, training or support.

This book does not cover financial management in detail but **chapter 20** looks at some of the basics, including the role of the treasurer, terms of reference for a finance sub-committee, and how to prepare for audit.

Creating systems for management

Management is sometimes confused with administration. To some extent they overlap, especially in small organisations. But management involves making broad decisions and ensuring appropriate systems and procedures are set up to implement those decisions, while administration involves the day to day work of running the systems.

As an example, the management committee decides the organisation should monitor the number of people with a disability using its services. Someone, who might be from 'management' or 'administration', sets up a system to keep track of service users, whether they have a disability and what type of disability. The worker responsible for administration keeps the records, ensures they are up to date, and makes the information available. The 'manager' interprets the information and makes proposals for changes based on the data.

Administration without management is inefficient because paperwork is done unnecessarily (because it is not needed), or inappropriately or inadequately (because the workers responsible for administration are not sure what is needed or how it will be used, so they cannot set up appropriate systems).

Management without administration is ineffective because managers will not have the information needed to make good decisions, and decisions will not be implemented because there is no one to provide the day to day backup.

Chapter 21 looks at ways to define and clarify administrative functions and manage information systems.

Managing the managers

A book such as this can only be a starting point for management committee members or managers. Further training is important; time to look at management issues within each organisation is essential. **Chapter 22** looks at management training and self-consultancy, and provides guidelines for deciding when and how to use an outside consultant. It also provides suggestions for dealing with managers who are not as competent as they should be – and don't realise it.

INFORMATION FOR MANAGEMENT

Anyone responsible for managing a voluntary organisation, whether as a management committee member, manager, or member of a collective, must have solid information about management in general and about the organisation. Good intentions are not enough.

What committee members should know

Management committee members often know remarkably little about the organisations for which they have responsibility. To manage effectively they should have, or have access to, the following information.

Background information

● Current leaflets or other **publicity materials.**

● Most recent **annual report.**

● Current **newsletter.**

● Brief **history**: why, when and how the organisation was set up, its main accomplishments, major changes, major problems.

● Possibly not the whole **constitution**, but at least a summary of the main points, including aims and objectives, procedures for general meetings, election of committee members, election of officers, how committee meetings are called.

Policies and activities

● Copies or summaries of **major policies**, such as equal opportunities, and policy decisions taken in the past year.

● Summary of the organisation's **current work** and who uses the services or activities.

● Summary of future **development plans.**

Structures and procedures

● **Organisational structure and procedures**: how the organisation as a whole is structured (membership, management committee, subcommittees etc) and where the management committee fits in.

- Outline of the **committee's major responsibilities** (employment, finance, policy, planning and prioritising, premises).

- **Committee structure and procedures**: information (perhaps a diagram) about how the management committee is structured, and terms of reference for the committee and its subcommittees or working groups. This helps people know whether subgroups can make decisions or if decisions have to be made by the whole committee. Brief summaries of the role of officers and other committee members with specific responsibilities.

- **Expectations**: what is expected of committee members (attendance, apologies if they can't attend, reading papers in advance, participating in subgroups etc), and what they can expect of the organisation (induction, ongoing training, good information provided in advance of meetings, management experience).

- Names, addresses and phone numbers of **committee members**: when they were elected or co-opted and how long their term as a committee member lasts; whether they are on the committee as individuals or represent a group or organisation.

- **Dates** of committee, subcommittee and other meetings for the next six months or year.

- **Minutes** of the last two or three committee meetings.

Personnel

- **Staff and permanent volunteers**: job title, brief (one paragraph) job description, and brief biographical information for each worker.

- **Staff structure**: diagram or description of how the staff work together (who is accountable to whom or how they work collectively); and a brief description of how the staff make decisions.

- Copy or summary of **contract of employment**, including disciplinary, grievance and redundancy procedures.

Finance and funding

- Outline of **funding** sources, how much, what for, when it expires, and prospects for continuation.

- **Financial reports and information**: latest annual accounts, most recent monthly or quarterly financial report, and current year's budget.

- Addresses, phone and fax numbers of the organisation's **premises**, who works there, very brief details of lease or mortgage arrangements.

'HELP!!' you scream, 'how can I cope with so much information?'

And the only reply can be, 'How can you cope as a management committee member *without* it?'

What staff and volunteers should know

Staff should have the same basic information as management committee members. They will also need to know far more about their particular area of work. Chapter 15 includes an outline for an induction programme for new workers.

There is a common tendency to assume workers low in the staff hierarchy do not need or want background information about the organisation. While it is important to avoid overwhelming people with unnecessary detail, it is also important to recognise that people work more effectively if they understand how their job fits into the overall organisation and if they know what others are doing and why.

Each organisation has to decide how much information to pass on to volunteer workers. Volunteers who receive too much may feel overwhelmed; on the other hand if they are told virtually nothing about the organisation they may quickly feel alienated, no matter how great their commitment to its aims. Another reason to keep volunteers well informed is because they are often asked to serve on the management committee; they are more likely to feel confident about this if they have a clear idea of what the organisation is and does.

Putting it together

For management committee members and senior staff it may be appropriate to provide a management handbook – a ring binder divided into sections for:

- current committee minutes;

- current subcommittee and working group minutes (separate section for each group);

- constitution, general background and policy documents;

- committee structure, procedures and members;

- services/activities: information about what the organisation does;

- personnel: staff structure, staff members, contracts;

- finance: financial reports and information;

- premises.

If each section is numbered, future documents can include the relevant section number at the top, with a note indicating they should be filed in the management handbook. All such documents should be clearly dated in the top corner of the front page, and should indicate if they are replacing an existing document.

For other staff and volunteers a shorter staff/volunteer handbook is a good idea. This might also be a ring binder or clip binder, or might be printed as a booklet. The advantage of providing a binder is that information can easily be updated or new pages added; the disadvantage is that pages go missing.

ESSENTIAL READING

As well as information about the organisation, people responsible for management also need a basic awareness of legal requirements and good practice relating to voluntary organisations. Most books on management are oriented towards business, industry or public services. Those intended for local authorities or small businesses may be of some use to voluntary organisations, but must be carefully used to ensure approaches are not transferred inappropriately from one sector to another.

Fortunately, there are now many books about voluntary sector management. The most useful are:

● *Voluntary But Not Amateur: A guide to the law for voluntary organisations and community groups*, 3rd edition, by Duncan Forbes, Ruth Hayes and Jacki Reason (London Voluntary Service Council, 1990; 101 pages; ISBN 0 901171 95 6; £7.95 + £1 p&p from LVSC, 68 Chalton Street, London NW1 1JR). Absolutely essential.

● *Planning Together: The art of effective teamwork* by George Gawlinski and Lois Graessle (Bedford Square Press/National Council for Voluntary Organisations, 1988; 88 pages; ISBN 0 7199 1202 4; £11.95 + £1.50 p&p from Plymbridge Distributors Ltd, Estover Road, Plymouth PL6 7PZ). Exercises to help groups and teams clarify and achieve their objectives.

● *Getting Organised: A handbook for non-statutory organisations* by Christine Holloway and Shirley Otto (Bedford Square Press/National Council for Voluntary Organisations, 1985; 70 pages; ISBN 0 7199 1162 1; £5.95 + 75p p&p from Plymbridge Distributors, as above). Exercises and checklists to improve teamwork and decision-making, especially for staff groups.

● *Understanding Voluntary Organisations* by Charles Handy (Penguin, 1988; 180 pages; ISBN 0 14 022491 2; £3.99 from bookshops). Looks at how staff communicate with and influence each other in voluntary organisations, and at organisational cultures and structures.

● *Croner's Management of Voluntary Organisations* (Croner Publications, 1989; 450 pages plus quarterly updates; £47.40 including first year's updates, then £22 per year for updates from Croner Publications Ltd, Croner House, London Road, Kingston upon Thames, Surrey KT2 6SR). Intended primarily for larger or national organisations; good sections on fundraising and publicity.

● *Managing to Advise* by Christine Thornton (Federation of Independent Advice Centres, 1989; 278 pages; ISBN 1 871181 01 1; £4.50 for FIAC members and £6.95 for others from FIAC, 13 Stockwell Road, London SW9 9AU). Intended primarily for advice agencies but useful for other organisations.

The following are not specifically oriented towards the voluntary sector, but may be useful.

● *A Guide for New Managers*, 2nd edition (HM Stationery Office, 1990; 58 pages; ISBN 0 11 560019 1; £3.80 from HMSO Books, Freepost, Norwich NR3 1BR or HMSO bookshops). Published for HM Treasury, which is about as far as you can get from the voluntary sector, but a little gem with lots of basic common sense.

● *The Industrial Society Handbook of Management Skills* (Industrial Society, 1990; 422 pages; ISBN 0 85290 903 9; £33 from Industrial Society, Robert Hyde House, 48

Bryanston Square, London W1H 7LN). Disappointing for the price, but it's a chunky hardback that looks impressive on the bookshelf and it does contain a fair amount that is useful for voluntary organisations. A reasonably priced paperback version would be welcome.

● *Organizational Behaviour: An introductory text* by David Buchanan and Andrzej A Huczynski (Prentice/Hall International, 1985; 488 pages; ISBN 0 13 641069 3; £13.95 from bookshops). A big book but easy to read, for those interested in theoretical perspectives on organisations and management.

Other books are mentioned in the relevant chapter.

Two newsletters which regularly include articles on voluntary sector management and which review new publications for voluntary organisations are *Voluntary Voice* (from London Voluntary Service Council, 68 Chalton Street, London NW1 1JR) and *NCVO News* (from National Council for Voluntary Organisations, Regents Wharf, 8 All Saints Street, London N1 9RL).

Local councils for voluntary service and other umbrella organisations, coordinating bodies or networks often publish newsletters, and may have guidelines on various aspects of management practice.

BS5750

BS5750 is a British standard which seeks to ensure 'quality management'. Originally designed in the 1960s by the Ministry of Defence and subsequently adopted within manufacturing industry, it is now being used within the public sector and other service sectors. It covers 20 areas where there must be policies, procedures and defined practices. The basic requirements are:

● clear objectives and 'mission' for the whole organisation;

● service requirements, with success criteria;

● process for achieving requirements;

● system for monitoring and recording success or failure;

● system for monitoring records;

● auditing process;

● corrective action if the quality system fails;

● reviewing system.

This book sets out good practice which fits into the BS5750 framework. While relatively few voluntary organisations are likely to want to apply for a British Standards Institute kitemark, BS5750 outlines the ideal towards which voluntary sector managers may want to aspire.

Information about BS5750 and its applicability to the voluntary sector is available from the Management Development Team, National Council for Voluntary Organisations, Regents Wharf, 8 All Saints Street, London N1 9RL (tel 071 713 6161).

Chapter 2:

Management committees

THE GOVERNING BODY

Every organisation has a **governing body** whose members have legal and financial responsibility for the organisation. The governing body is usually, but not always, the same as the management committee.

- In a membership organisation without any committee, the governing body will be **all the members.**

- In a membership organisation with an **elected or appointed committee**, this committee (usually called a management committee or something similar) is the governing body. Committee members are assumed in law to be acting as agents of the organisation's members. The committee is usually elected at the annual general meeting although in reality it might be made up of anyone who volunteers, or people invited to join by the current committee members. If the organisation has a constitution it will say how the committee is chosen; the procedures set down in the constitution must be strictly followed.

- If the organisation is registered as a charity the **charity trustees** are the governing body. The charity trustees are sometimes called **managing trustees**. Depending on the charity's constitution the charity trustees might be appointed or might be elected in the same way as a committee. In most charities the trustee body is the same as the management committee. Even if the committee is not called a board of trustees and members are not called trustees, they have the legal responsibilities of charity trustees. However some charities have a board of trustees who delegate considerable management authority to a separate body, often called a management committee or something similar; in this situation the trustees, not the management committee, have ultimate legal responsibility.

- If the organisation is registered as a company limited by guarantee, the **company directors** are the governing body. These will be elected at an annual general meeting. In most voluntary sector companies the board of directors is the same as the management committee. Even if the committee is not called a board of directors and committee members are not called company directors, they have the legal responsibilities of company directors. However some voluntary sector companies have a board of directors who delegate considerable management authority to a separate body, often called a management committee or something similar; in this situation the company directors, not the management committee, have ultimate legal responsibility.

The same principles apply to directors of friendly societies and industrial and provident societies.

A voluntary organisation which is both a company and a charity is called a **charitable company**. It has only one governing body, with the same people as both company directors and charity trustees. In this case people on a management committee who may think they are 'only' committee members may find they are also company directors and charity trustees.

If an organisation has a board of directors or board of trustees, that will be the governing body. A committee, management committee, steering committee, council of management, general council, council, executive committee or body with a similar name will be the governing body **if there is not a separate board of directors or board of charity trustees.**

It is sometimes not clear who the governing body is, for example with branches of national organisations, (semi-) autonomous projects within larger organisations, organisations with complex management structures, or consortia made up of several organisations. In this situation it is essential to clarify who has the ultimate responsibility *before* disputes arise about how the organisation should develop, it gets into debt or something else goes wrong.

In this book the term 'management committee' refers to the body with responsibility for making major decisions about the organisation and its work. The management committee will usually be the governing body, but to avoid any confusion about legal liability the term 'management committee or other governing body' is used when referring specifically to legal responsibilities.

Throughout this book it is assumed the organisation has a constitution and is committed to operating within it. Informal groups not accountable to funders or members and not registered in any legal way can choose not to have a constitution or not to abide by it if they do have one. But for most organisations, a constitution is a set of rules which must be followed.

This chapter includes:

- reasons for having a management committee;

- responsibilities of members of the committee or other governing body, and where to find out more about them in this book, *Voluntary But Not Amateur* or other books;

- ways to limit the legal liability of members of the management committee or other governing body;

- responsibilities of a company secretary;

- what charitable status means;

- officers and what they do;

- the role of subcommittees or link people;

● some ideas on how to get the best from a management committee.

WHY HAVE A COMMITTEE?

Groups have management committees:

● to ensure the organisation meets the needs of its members, its users or clients, and/or the community it serves;

● to ensure the organisation is accountable to its members, its users or clients, the community it serves and/or its funders;

● to draw on people's experience or expertise in making decisions about the organisation;

● because donors or funders want to know financial and other decisions are being made properly, and not just by one or two people;

● because organisations registered as trusts, friendly societies, industrial and provident societies, companies and/or charities are required to have a governing body.

Managers and staff in voluntary organisations sometimes feel a management committee is more trouble than it is worth and say committee members constantly interfere with their work or, at the other extreme, never show any interest in the organisation. Committee members, on the other hand, may feel paid workers do not have a long term view of what the organisation is about or are more interested in their careers than in the community or campaign. If a voluntary organisation is to function effectively, it is essential for staff, managers and committee members to see themselves not as adversaries but as **partners working together** to achieve the organisation's goals.

Delegation

Although the ultimate responsibility for running a voluntary organisation rests with the management committee as a whole, specific responsibilities may be delegated to elected officers (either individually or jointly), other committee members, subcommittees or working groups, the manager, staff, or other individuals or groups.

Confusion can arise if it is not clear exactly what is being delegated. Can the officer, committee member, subcommittee, manager or staff member actually make the **final decision**, are they being asked to put forward **proposals** or **recommendations** to the whole committee, or are they simply being asked to provide **information** to enable committee members to make a decision? Clarifying these points means drawing up **terms of reference** for various areas of responsibility.

Good communication between the management committee and the body or person with delegated authority is essential, otherwise members of the committee could find themselves being held responsible for something they didn't even know about.

Note that the ultimate legal responsibility for what the organisation does cannot be delegated. Members of the management committee or other governing body remain responsible even if they were not aware of what was being done by the organisation.

MAIN RESPONSIBILITIES OF THE COMMITTEE

The main responsibilities of the management committee or other governing body are:

● to maintain a long term overview of the organisation and all its work;

● to make strategic and major decisions about the organisation's objectives, policies and procedures;

● to ensure the needs and interests of relevant people and bodies are taken into account when making decisions;

● to ensure adequate resources (especially people and money) to carry out the organisation's activities;

● to monitor progress towards objectives, and other work;

● to take legal responsibility for the organisation and all its actions (or inaction). **If the organisation gets into legal or financial trouble, members of the management committee or other governing body can in many cases be held personally liable.** This is explained in more detail later in this chapter.

LEGAL RESPONSIBILITIES

The legal responsibilities of the management committee or other governing body can be divided into 10 main areas.

Constitutional objects and powers

The management committee or other governing body is responsible for ensuring the organisation carries out its objects (aims or purposes) and operates within its powers according to the constitution, so committee members must know what the objects and powers are and understand what they mean. If the constitution is written in incomprehensible legal jargon try to find someone who can draw up a simple explanation of the legal language.

A committee carries out this responsibility by:

● ensuring people within the organisation are clear about why the organisation exists, its overall objects or purposes, and constitutional or legal limits on what it can do;

● setting policy, and ensuring it is implemented;

● setting strategic or long term objectives (what the organisation wants to achieve over, say, five to seven years for a large national organisation or three to five years for a smaller local group), and ensuring they fit into the organisation's objects;

● setting medium and short term objectives and priorities, and ensuring they fit into the organisation's policies and long term objectives;

● deciding whether to undertake new projects or activities, and making policy relating to them;

● interpreting or adapting policy when existing activities change;

● helping the manager, staff and volunteers determine how the organisation should carry out its activities;

- ensuring there are proper procedures for monitoring and evaluating provision and use of activities, services and facilities.

A good committee will always consult users, managers, staff and volunteers before making decisions of this type. Chapters 7, 8 and 9 look in more detail at how to set policy, objectives and priorities and how to monitor and evaluate an organisation's work.

If an organisation with charitable status operates outside its objects or powers, the Charity Commission can require the charity trustees personally to pay back to the charity any money used for these activities.

Procedures and accountability

The management committee or other governing body is responsible for ensuring the organisation carries out its business according to its constitution and good practice. Part of the constitution relates to why the organisation exists and the type of activities it is supposed to carry out; a constitution also defines *how* the organisation is supposed to conduct its business. It is the committee's responsibility to ensure these rules are followed. Specific responsibilities include:

- serving as a well informed, interested, supportive committee;

- maintaining democratic procedures and accountability;

- holding meetings regularly, and ensuring members have the information needed to make decisions;

- calling the annual general meeting and ensuring elections and other essential items are dealt with as required;

- ensuring adequate communication between the committee, subgroups, managers, staff, volunteers, and the organisation's users, members, clients, residents or other people served by the organisation.

In addition to its constitution, an organisation may have other rules or standing orders which set out how meetings are to be run, how decisions are made, when and how subscriptions are set or other procedural matters. These rules should be kept with the constitution and if necessary the appropriate section of the constitution should be cross-referenced to the rule.

Chapters 4, 5 and 6 look in more detail at communication, decision-making, meetings and reports.

Legal obligations and undertakings

Statutory obligations exist in law and must be met: for example having to register under the Data Protection Act if the organisation keeps information about recognisable living individuals on computer, or having to give contracts of employment to staff who work 16 or more hours per week. It is the responsibility of the management committee or other governing body to ensure the organisation meets these obligations.

Legal undertakings are legally binding commitments which the organisation chooses to enter into: for example renting premises, hiring staff, leasing a photocopier or entering into a contract to provide services. It is the respon-

sibility of the committee or other governing body to ensure the organisation can and does meet the terms of any such undertaking.

If the organisation is incorporated as a company limited by guarantee or an industrial and provident society (IPS) it can enter into legal undertakings in its own name. If it is not a company or an IPS it cannot enter into a legally binding agreement in its own name, so this will have to be done by individuals, usually the organisation's elected officers, acting on behalf of the organisation. (See the section on incorporation of charity trustees, later in this chapter, for an exception to this rule.) Anyone who signs a legal document must be authorised to do so, by a proper decision made by the committee, and must clearly indicate she or he is **signing on behalf of the organisation.**

To protect themselves as well as the organisation, members of the management committee or other governing body should be satisfied the organisation is meeting its legal obligations with respect to:

- contracts of employment and employment legislation;

- equal opportunities legislation (Race Relations Act, Sex Discrimination Acts, Disabled Persons Acts);

- lease, licence or tenancy agreements;

- Health and Safety at Work Act, Offices, Shops and Railways Premises Act and other health and safety legislation;

- insurance requirements;

- financial record-keeping and information, income tax, national insurance, other taxes, VAT;

- bank accounts, loans, overdrafts;

- fundraising and grants;

- work done by the organisation under a service agreement or contract;

- Data Protection Act;

- Companies Acts and Charities Acts.

There is more information about these responsibilities throughout this book and in *Voluntary But Not Amateur.* Increasingly European legislation will apply to voluntary organisations; it is sensible to keep up to date by reading newsletters from relevant umbrella organisations or local councils for voluntary service.

Financial responsibility and accountability

The management committee or other governing body is responsible for ensuring the organisation has enough money to carry out its work, meets its financial obligations when they are due, accounts for all its financial dealings and does not get into financial trouble. This includes not only the payment of bills but also ensuring proper records are kept and the organisation's money is spent in the correct way. This means the management committee or other governing body has ultimate responsibility for:

- wages, tax, national insurance, statutory sick pay and maternity pay, pensions, redundancy pay, and any other pay or benefits due to workers under legislation or the terms of their contracts;

- mortgages, rent, rates;

- insurances;

- all other bills;

- ensuring the organisation will have enough money to meet any financial obligations when they come due;

- ensuring all grants or other funds received for specific purposes are spent as specified;

- ensuring the organisation is being paid enough for any services it is providing under a service agreement or contract;

- ensuring the organisation's funds are wisely invested;

- ensuring the organisation keeps accurate and comprehensible financial records, accessible to management committee members and authorised members of staff;

- receiving regular financial reports in a form which committee members can understand;

- ensuring annual accounts are drawn up and audited in accordance with the constitution and, where relevant, funders' requirements and/or legislation.

Financial responsibilities are covered in detail in chapter 20 and in *Voluntary But Not Amateur* chapter 7.

Fundraising is not included in this book. An excellent guide is *The Complete Fundraising Handbook* by Sam Clarke (Directory of Social Change, 1992; 256 pages; ISBN 0 907164 65 X; £9.95 from DSC, Radius Works, Back Lane, London NW3 1HL). The Directory of Social Change publishes a very wide range of other books on all aspects of funding and fundraising. Another source of information is the Institute of Charity Fundraising Managers (1 Nine Elms Lane, London SW8 5NQ; tel 071 627 3436).

Employment and volunteers

In most voluntary organisations the management committee or other governing body is legally the employer, with responsibility for hiring, supporting and if necessary firing staff. This can cause all sorts of problems, especially if the committee is made up of users or clients who receive services from the staff whom they hire, or people who are not very aware of what the organisation is doing.

Even if some aspects of employment are delegated to staff or a personnel subcommittee, the committee as a whole is responsible for ensuring the organisation has appropriate procedures to:

- draw up and regularly update job descriptions;

- ensure adequate funding to pay staff;

- advertise appropriately, shortlist, interview and select staff;

- issue and abide by contracts of employment;

- ensure there is appropriate induction, training, supervision, support, and ideally a regular review/assessment procedure for staff;

- deal with moans and grievances;

- undertake disciplinary and redundancy proceedings.

If some or all of the organisation's work is carried out by volunteers the committee has legal responsibility for them and their work. The committee should ensure they are adequately inducted and supported and there are appropriate disciplinary and grievance procedures.

If a staff member or volunteer acts negligently, for example by giving incorrect advice to a client or not looking after a child properly in a community nursery, members of the governing body could be found negligent if the organisation does not have and enforce proper procedures for recruiting and training staff, setting standards, monitoring work and maintaining a safe environment.

Employment responsibilities are covered in chapters 14 to 17 and in *Voluntary But Not Amateur* chapters 2 and 3.

Equal opportunities

It is the responsibility of the management committee or other governing body to ensure the organisation complies with equal opportunities legislation (Race Relations Act, Sex Discrimination Acts, Equal Pay Act, Disabled Persons Acts). But good practice goes far beyond the legislation. If the organisation is concerned about equal opportunities (and all voluntary organisations should be) it is the committee's responsibility to ensure the organisation has a clear statement of intent on equal opportunities and a workable code of practice setting out how it will make its statement a reality, and to ensure the code of practice is implemented and monitored.

The statement of intent and code of practice should cover:

- staff recruitment and selection;

- conditions of employment;

- volunteer recruitment, selection and placement;

- access to training;

- membership;

- provision of the organisation's activities, services and facilities;

- guidelines and procedures for dealing with direct or indirect discrimination, harassment, victimisation and racism, sexism or other personally abusive behaviour.

It is good practice to state any exceptions to the equal opportunities statement, for example services or facilities not available to people below or above a certain age or with certain disabilities, or jobs not open to people with convictions for certain offences.

Good management is an essential tool for the promotion of equal opportunities, because it ensures information and skills are appropriately shared and people are involved in decisions affecting them.

Some aspects of equal opportunities are covered in chapters 7 and 15. The issue is covered in detail in *Voluntary But Not Amateur* chapters 1 and 2.

Premises and equipment

A management committee or other governing body generally has overall responsibility for the use, safety and security of premises used by the organisation and must ensure they are properly and legally managed and used. This includes:

- making decisions about major change of premises use. Day to day decisions about use (for example bookings) might be delegated to staff or volunteers but are still the ultimate responsibility of the committee;

- ensuring adequate finance and insurance;

- setting conditions for bookings, hire of premises, licences and similar requirements;

- developing and implementing a health and safety policy covering all aspects of the organisation's work;

- ensuring the organisation meets public health and fire regulations and precautions;

- ensuring adequate security for premises, equipment and people;

- approving alterations, repairs and renovations;

- ensuring planning and building regulations are met.

Responsibility for premises is covered in *Voluntary But Not Amateur* chapter 4, with further information in *Managing your Community Building* by Peter Hudson (National Federation of Community Organisations, 1992; ISBN 0 900787 15 5; £13.95 from NFCO, 8-9 Upper Street, London N1 0PQ).

If the organisation is unincorporated (that is, if it is not registered as a company or an industrial and provident society) it will not be able to own property in its own name. Any property will be held on behalf of the organisation by **holding trustees** who have ultimate responsibility for the property. (See the section on incorporation of charity trustees, later in this chapter, for another way of dealing with this.) The relationship between the holding trustees and the organisation should be clearly set out. Note that **holding trustees are not the same as charity trustees**. Holding trustees have no responsibility for the organisation as a whole.

Insurances

Insurance tends to get overlooked; no one is certain who should deal with it, so no one does. But the management committee or other governing body is responsible for ensuring all insurances are taken out and paid. To prevent mistakes, it is good practice for the committee to appoint one committee member and one staff person or volunteer to oversee all insurances and be sure they are kept up to date. They should report to the management committee at least once a year and ensure committee members have the necessary information to make decisions about changes.

The committee should be clear about the terms of any lease or mortgage and should be aware of the implications if their premises, whether leased, mortgaged or owned, remain uninsured or underinsured.

Some insurances are **compulsory:**

- employer's liability insurance must be held by any organisation with paid staff, and the certificate of insurance must be prominently displayed at the organisation's office;

- public liability insurance covers injury, loss or damage caused to any person (including volunteers and management committee members) as a result of the organisation's negligence;

- if an organisation has vehicles it must have third party insurance, which covers injury or death caused to other people;

- buildings insurance and/or plate glass windows insurance are not required by law but might be required by the terms of a lease or mortgage.

Other insurances are **discretionary:**

- if buildings or plate glass windows insurances are not explicitly required or if the organisation owns its premises these insurances are discretionary;

- contents insurance covers items within premises and can be extended to include contents when they are away from the building;

- insurance can be taken out against failure of major equipment, for example boilers and lifts;

- discretionary road traffic insurances include vehicle theft, vehicle fire or comprehensive insurance covering other damage to the vehicle;

- the organisation can take out fidelity insurance against dishonesty, covering employees and/or management committee members who handle large amounts of cash or sign cheques;

- professional indemnity insurance protects groups that give advice against claims of negligence for incorrect advice;

- accident and medical insurance covers the cost of paying sick pay to staff;

- trustees' liability insurance covers members of the management committee or other governing body against personal liability for the organisation's losses or negligence.

Further information is available in *Voluntary But Not Amateur* chapter 5 and *Insurance Protection: A guide for voluntary organisations* (£5 from Advice Development Team, National Council for Voluntary Organisations, Regents Wharf, 8 All Saints Street, London N1 9RL). Organisations which use volunteers should consult *Protecting Volunteers: Guidelines for volunteer organisers in voluntary and statutory agencies*, 2nd edition by Cressida Wasserman (£1 from Volunteer Centre UK, 29 Lower King's Road, Berkhamsted, Herts HP4 2AB). Insurance to protect committee members is discussed in more detail below, in the section on limiting committee members' liability.

Legal status

The management committee or other governing body must ensure the organisation meets its legal obligations if it is a company limited by guarantee, an industrial and provident society, a friendly society and/or a registered charity.

Any organisation registered under the Companies Acts, the Friendly Societies Act or the Industrial and Provident Societies Act *must* meet the requirements of the relevant Act. Organisations which fail to do so can face heavy fines, as can individual members of the management committee or other governing body. Responsibilities include:

- preparing annual accounts and balance sheet, having them audited and submitting them to the Registrar of Companies or Registrar of Friendly Societies;

- holding the annual general meeting as required by the constitution, electing directors (management committee) and submitting annual returns to the Registrar;

- notifying all changes of director to the Registrar.

In charities the charity trustees (usually the same as the management committee, but not necessarily) have responsibility for:

- preparing annual accounts, having them audited as required (see chapter 20) and submitting them to the Charity Commission and Inland Revenue;

- filing an annual report and annual return, as specified in regulations under the Charities Act 1992, with the Charity Commission;

- ensuring all the organisation's activities fall within the charity's objects and are charitable as defined by law;

- indicating on all the charity's documents, invoices, cheques and publications that it is a registered charity.

Voluntary But Not Amateur chapter 1 covers the legal structures available to voluntary organisations. Later in this chapter responsibilities of company secretaries are outlined, and sources of further information about legal structures and charitable status are listed. Audits are covered in chapter 20.

Everything else

Last but not least, the management committee or other governing body is responsible for any other legal or moral responsibilities which might apply. This could include, for example:

- conditions imposed by funders;

- legislation applicable to certain types of work, such as housing associations, work with children or people considered vulnerable, work with dangerous machinery or equipment, food handling, lotteries or public events. Many of these requirements are covered in *Voluntary But Not Amateur*.

DON'T QUIT YET!

Obviously no one in their right mind would take on these responsibilities – or would they? People get involved in management committees because they are committed to the organisation and what it is doing. They then have these responsibilities whether they know it or not. The responsibilities can seem frightening but they can nearly all be handled with the right information, common sense and enough time to absorb and think.

Remember:

- Each individual member of the management committee or other governing body does not have to *do* all these things, although they do have to *ensure*, individually and as a group, that someone does them and reports back at appropriate intervals to the committee. The 'someone' might be an elected officer or other

committee member, members of a subcommittee or working group, a manager, another staff person, or someone from outside the organisation.

- Committee members should feel able to ask other committee members, managers or staff for necessary background information and for help in understanding the information.

- If information is presented in a way committee members don't understand, they should ask for it to be explained and ask for the presentation to be simplified next time. This applies especially to financial information. (Don't worry about looking stupid; if one person does not understand, probably many of the others on the committee don't either.)

- A good organisation will provide books (like this one and *Voluntary But Not Amateur*) for its committee members, and will build up a library committee members can use.

- A good organisation will provide training for its committee members. This might include induction sessions about the organisation and about the committee's responsibilities, in-house training on specific topics, and attendance at courses run by a council for voluntary service or other local development agency, relevant umbrella organisation, training organisation or funder.

- There are ways of limiting the potential personal liability of members of a management committee or other governing body (see below).

Members of the management committee or other governing body are generally legally responsible for what the organisation does only if they have the right to vote on the committee. So co-opted members or representatives of other bodies without voting rights would not usually have any liability for what the organisation does. (Shadow directors of a company are the exception; see below under 'Incorporated organisations'.) If an individual who represents another body has voting rights on the committee any legal liability rests with the individual, not the organisation which she or he is representing.

LIMITING LIABILITY

The legal liability of members of the management committee or other governing body is determined by the legal status of the organisation. This depends on whether the organisation is unincorporated or incorporated.

Unincorporated organisations

An unincorporated organisation does not have a legal identity of its own. In law, it is simply a collection of individuals.

Unincorporated organisations cannot officially enter into contracts or other legal agreements in their own name. If they want to rent property, employ people, borrow money or take legal action, this has to be done (or will legally be assumed to have been done) by individuals acting on behalf of the organisation. If they want to own property, the property will be legally held by individuals (**holding trustees**) on behalf of the organisation.

Albert Scroggins, Committee Member, your subject is: WHAT REALLY GOES ON at Crumbley Mansions Community Centre?

MASTER MIND

Some unincorporated organisations are registered as friendly societies or trusts, but most are unregistered associations. An **unregistered association** is not accountable to anyone except its own members and funders.

If an unincorporated organisation gets into debt or has other legal problems, the people who have responsibility for the organisation (the management committee, if there is one, or all the members) can be held personally responsible for the difficulties. They have **legal liability** for whatever mess the organisation gets itself into.

Ways to limit individual liability

There are several ways to reduce the risk to individual members of the management committee or other governing body.

● Members of the governing body must always act **sensibly and responsibly** in making decisions about the organisation. This means getting proper information from staff or professional advisers, discussing issues fully, and not taking on obligations they know the organisation might not be able to fulfil.

● Individuals who sign legal or financial undertakings should make it clear, in writing, they are **signing on behalf of the organisation** rather than as individuals. If possible, they should indicate that their liability 'is limited to the extent of the assets of the organisation'.

● If an individual committee member thinks a decision is irresponsible, she or he can be **publicly disassoci-**

ated from it. If this disassociation is properly minuted, the individual will not be held responsible for any liability arising from the decision. The section on voting in chapter 5 explains the procedure for this. Disassociating oneself from a vote is a very serious matter, indicating a lack of confidence in one's colleagues on the committee.

● The organisation should have all legally required **insurances** and sufficient other insurance to cover possible claims.

● It is possible to get insurance to indemnify (repay) committee members for any personal liability they incur on behalf of the organisation. Details are available from St Olaf Insurance Brokers, tel 071 739 7234.

● If the organisation hires several staff, owns premises, or has other long term financial commitments, it should consider **incorporation.**

Incorporated organisations

'Incorporated' comes from the Latin word *corpus* which means body. 'Incorporate' means 'make into a body'. An incorporated organisation has an existence of its own, as a legal body separate from its individual members. The organisation can, in its own name, rent or buy property, hire workers, borrow money or take legal action. This is sometimes referred to as having **legal personality**.

There are several types of incorporated organisation, which are explained in more detail in *Voluntary But Not Amateur* chapter 1.

- In a **company limited by shares** members (shareholders) invest money in the company in order to make a profit. This structure is not appropriate for voluntary organisations but is sometimes used for trading subsidiaries.

- An **industrial and provident society** (IPS) is a genuine cooperative, or a business or industry 'acting for the benefit of the community'. A community business, housing association or voluntary organisation involved in producing and selling goods or other trading activities can become an IPS.

- A **company limited by guarantee** is a group which exists for a social or political reason and puts any profits back into the group. Most voluntary or community groups which incorporate become companies limited by guarantee.

For any organisation which is, or is thinking about becoming, a company limited by guarantee it is important to read *A Practical Guide to Company Law for Voluntary Organisations* by Bev Cross (Directory of Social Change in association with Sheffield Law Centre, 1991; 48 pages; ISBN 0 907164 73 0; £5.95 from Directory of Social Change, Radius Works, Back Lane, London NW3 1HL).

Advice on incorporation as a company or IPS and on registering as a charity (see below) is available from:

- Legal Department, National Council for Voluntary Organisations, Regents Wharf, 8 All Saints Street, London N1 9LR (tel 071 713 6161);

- ICOM Legal and Registration Services, Vassalli House, 20 Central Road, Leeds LS1 6DE (tel 0532 461737);

- InterChange Legal Advisory Service, 15 Wilkin Street, London NW5 3NG (tel 071 267 9421);

- local councils for voluntary service, rural community councils or other local voluntary sector development agencies.

Extent of individual liability

The members of a company limited by guarantee will **guarantee** (promise) to pay a small amount, usually £1 or £5, if the organisation gets into financial trouble. Their liability is limited to this amount.

Members of the company might be all the current members of the organisation, the founding members, or some or all of the members of the management committee or other governing body. This will be set out in the constitution, which is called the **memorandum and articles of association**. The memorandum sets out the organisation's objects and what it can do (its powers); the articles set out its rules and procedures.

The liability of company directors (usually the same as the management committee) is limited in the same way. However **company directors can lose this protection** if it can be shown that they have acted **negligently** (irresponsibly) or **fraudulently** (dishonestly). And under the **Insolvency Act 1986** company directors can be held personally liable in cases of **wrongful trading**. This is where a company continues to operate when the directors know, or could reasonably have been expected to know, that it does not have a reasonable hope of being able to meet its financial obligations when they come due.

If the company is also a charity, the company directors will also be charity trustees. As trustees they can be held personally liable (even though the organisation is incorporated) if the charity's funds are used for purposes which are outside its objects or powers.

To a large extent incorporation reduces the risk of members of the management committee (or separate board of directors, if there is one) being held personally liable if the organisation gets into debt or gets into other trouble. But **there is still considerable risk if the committee operates irresponsibly**.

If the committee regularly relies on professional advice from people who are not company directors, for example managers or other staff, or non-voting members of the committee, the non-directors could also be held personally liable, on the basis that they were acting as **shadow directors.**

The company secretary

Every company limited by guarantee must have a company secretary who is appointed by the directors. Company secretary is not an elected position.

The company secretary can be a member of the governing body, a staff person, or someone from outside the organisation. The post may be paid or unpaid (except for someone who is also a charity trustee of the organisation, since trustees cannot usually be paid).

The company secretary is legally responsible for carrying out certain statutory requirements. These include:

- maintaining the organisation's registers and keeping them up to date (the law requires a register of members, register of directors and register of company secretaries; a register of treasurers is optional);

- ensuring an annual general meeting is held within 18 months of incorporation and then at least every 15 months; ensuring proper notice is given and business is transacted according to the constitution;

- calling other general meetings as required, and ensuring proper notice is given and business is transacted according to the constitution;

- keeping the minute books for general meetings and directors' meetings;

- submitting an annual return to the Registrar of Companies when it is due each year;

- ensuring an income and expenditure account and balance sheet are prepared and properly audited;

- submitting the income and expenditure account, balance sheet, auditor's report and directors' report (management committee report) to the Registrar of Companies within ten months of the end of the organisation's financial year;

- keeping copies of all annual returns and annual accounts;

- notifying the Registrar of Companies within 14 days of all changes of directors and any changes in directors' home addresses;

- notifying the Registrar of Companies within 14 days of any change in the organisation's registered address;

- ensuring the certificate of incorporation is prominently displayed at the registered office;

- ensuring the organisation's stationery shows the name under which the organisation is registered, the registered address, the fact that it is a registered company and its registration number (and, if applicable, its charity registration number and/or VAT number);

- ensuring all legal agreements or contracts are properly discussed and agreed by the directors;

- having custody of the company seal (if there is one), ensuring it is properly used, and keeping the sealing register (list of documents on which the seal has been used).

Penalties for companies which do not fulfil the statutory requirements are severe: £2000 fine for failing to complete and send the annual return to the Registrar of Companies when it is due, £2000 fine for failing to hold an AGM, £2000 fine for failing to notify the Registrar of any change in directors or company secretary, £400 fine for failing to notify the Registrar of a change in registered address. These fines apply to the company directors and company secretary.

CHARITABLE STATUS

Any organisation in England and Wales, whether unincorporated or incorporated, can register as a charity with the Charity Commission if *all* its aims and objects are charitable and *all* its activities are 'charitable' or are allowed under charity law. Charitable organisations are not obliged to register with the Commission, but those which are not registered are less likely to be able to get the tax and other advantages of charitable status.

However, some charities have the benefits of charitable status without registering with the Charity Commission. Places of worship, Scouts, Girl Guides and very small charities are **excepted** from having to register. Organisations with charitable purposes registered as friendly societies or industrial and provident societies are **exempt** from having to register. In Scotland and Northern Ireland charitable organisations apply to the Inland Revenue for charitable status.

There are only four types of charitable activity. They are:

- **relief of poverty**: helping people who are 'poor, ill, disabled or aged';

- **advancement of education**: education or research for the benefit of the public, including arts and sports facilities;

- **advancement of religion**: religious activities which benefit the public (not just members of the church or religious group);

- **other purposes beneficial to the community**: other activities, such as providing public recreation and leisure facilities or promoting racial harmony.

All registered charities must have **charity trustees** (sometimes called **managing trustees**) who have ultimate responsibility for the organisation. In some charities the trustees delegate some management responsibilities to another body, which might be called a management committee but does not have ultimate responsibility. In this situation the relationship between the two groups must be clearly set out in terms of reference. Serious problems can arise if the trustees and a subsidiary committee do not know what each other is doing or disagree about what the organisation should do.

Charity trustees cannot 'profit' from the charity. This means they cannot be employed by the organisation, even for part-time or temporary work. Conversely, employees of a charity cannot be trustees and cannot be voting members of the committee if the committee is also the trustee body. (Employees can, of course, attend meetings and participate, if the trustees so wish.)

If the charity wants to give grants or financial benefits to individuals who are on the trustee body (for example, an AIDS charity giving a grant to a person who is HIV positive who is a trustee of the charity), advice should be sought first from the Charity Commission.

Most charities must submit their accounts each year to the Charity Commission (see chapter 20), and to the Inland Revenue if they want to claim the tax benefits which charities enjoy.

Under the Companies Act 1989 a charity which is also a company, and which does not have the word 'charity' or 'charitable' in its name, must indicate that it is a registered charity on its business letters, notices, cheques, orders, invoices, receipts and all other official or financial documents. The Charities Act 1992 extends this obligation to charities which are not companies.

Voluntary But Not Amateur chapter 1 lists the advantages and disadvantages of charitable status. For more comprehensive information read *Charitable Status: A practical handbook*, 3rd edition by Andrew Phillips (InterChange Books, 1988; 106 pages; ISBN 0 948309 05 9; £5.95 from Directory of Social Change, Radius Works, Back Lane, London NW3 1HL). Information about the Charities Act 1992 is available from the National Council for Voluntary Organisations, Regents Wharf, 8 All Saints Street, London N1 9LR (tel 071 713 6161).

Responsibilities of Charity Trustees is a free nine-page booklet from the Charity Commission; charities should distribute this to all trustees. The Commission has a wide range of other free materials on all aspects of charity registration and administration. The Commission's addresses are:

- St Alban's House, 57-60 Haymarket, London SW1Y 4QX (tel 071 210 3000) for national charities and charities in London, the Southeast and East Anglia;

- Graeme House, Derby Square, Liverpool L2 7SB (tel 051 227 3191) for charities in the Midlands, Wales and the North;

- Woodfield House, Tangier, Taunton, Somerset TA1 4AY (tel 0823 321102) for charities in Southern and Southwestern counties.

The Charity Commission can advise on any aspect of charity registration or charity law, and should be contacted if there is *any* doubt about what a charity can and cannot do.

Incorporation of charity trustees

It is possible for a charity to incorporate its trustee body, while not incorporating the organisation as a whole. This enables the organisation to own property and enter into contracts or other legal arrangements in its own name, rather than through individuals acting on behalf of the organisation. This type of incorporation does not, however, limit the personal liability of the trustees in any way. Further information is available from the Charity Commission.

OFFICERS AND WHAT THEY DO

Although there are broad similarities, the exact role of the elected officers is different in every organisation and at different times within the same organisation.

The organisation's constitution may set out officers' basic responsibilities. But how they carry these out and what additional responsibilities they take on will depend on a number of factors including the individuals involved, the sort of work the management committee does, and whether there are paid staff.

It is important that everyone on the committee understands what officers are supposed to do in *this* organisation.

The chair

The chair's role has two separate parts:

● planning and running meetings, being sure everything is covered and decisions are made when required, keeping order, helping the group to deal with differences of opinion and conflicts, being sure everyone who wants to has a chance to speak;

● ensuring the organisation as a whole sets and sticks to its policies and priorities, serving as a spokesperson for the group, making essential or emergency decisions between committee meetings, helping workers deal with difficult situations.

The first role (**meetings chair**) can be rotated, although it is good practice to give everyone two or three meetings in a row, rather than just one, so they can learn from their mistakes. Sometimes a meetings chair is called a **facilitator**.

Chapter 4 looks at decision-making and problem-solving, chapter 5 gives guidelines on chairing meetings, and chapter 18 provides ideas on dealing with differences and conflicts.

The second role (**organisation chair**) should be taken for at least one year by a person elected at the annual general meeting or chosen in some other formal and democratic way. It is not good practice to rotate or change the organisation chair at intervals of less than one year. A constitution or rules may limit the chair's tenure to a fixed number of years, to be sure no one stays in the post too long.

If urgent decisions must be made between meetings, the organisation's constitution or rules usually give the chair the right to take **chair's action**. This should be used only for decisions which genuinely cannot wait, and if the organisation's policy on an issue is not clear the chair should consult with the vice-chair or others before proceeding. Any action taken under chair's action must be reported to the next meeting of the relevant group.

Chapters 7, 8 and 9 cover the processes of setting policy and objectives, prioritising, planning, monitoring and evaluating.

The vice-chair

The vice-chair stands in for the chair and helps with difficult decisions between meetings. Sometimes the chair deals with the 'organisational' and policy side of chairing, and the vice-chair with the meetings side.

The chair should liaise regularly with the vice-chair and ensure she or he knows enough about current issues within the organisation to be able to stand in at short notice.

The secretary

The secretary's role also has two distinct aspects:

● helping the chair plan meetings, ensuring they are held according to the constitution, ensuring notices of meetings or agendas are drawn up and sent out in advance if required and members receive all necessary information, taking and distributing minutes, helping the chair ensure decisions are made when required;

● dealing with correspondence, ensuring the appropriate people are notified of correspondence, sending out publicity or other information about the organisation.

The roles can be divided so a **minutes secretary** deals with meetings and a **correspondence secretary** deals with letters.

Some or all of this work may be done by staff. It is important to be clear about what the secretary is expected to do and what staff are expected to do. Unless the constitution requires it, it is not necessary for an organisation to have an elected secretary.

If the organisation is a company limited by guarantee it will have a **company secretary** whose duties are defined in law (and are outlined on page 16). An organisation with a company secretary does not have to have an elected secretary as well, but can do. The division of responsibilities between company secretary, minutes secretary, correspondence secretary and staff must be absolutely clear. An industrial and provident society also has a secretary with defined duties.

Chapter 5 covers agendas and minutes and chapter 6 includes an outline for presenting verbal or written reports to meetings.

The treasurer

The treasurer must ensure the group spends its money correctly, pays all its bills and does not get into financial trouble. The treasurer must also ensure the committee receives regular financial reports and has enough information to make decisions about finance.

If a staff member deals with day to day finance, the treasurer should be sure the work is done properly and should advise on any difficult situations (for example prioritising expenditure if there is not enough money to go round). The treasurer also coordinates grant applications and fundraising activities.

Chapter 20 includes a detailed checklist on the responsibilities of a treasurer.

Other officers

Other officers might include a **meetings host** (see chapter 5), **social secretary**, **press secretary**, **fundraising officer**, or any other positions the organisation decides to establish. These positions do not need to be included in the constitution unless the organisation wants to formalise them permanently.

SUBCOMMITTEES AND WORKING GROUPS

Management committee members sometimes become frustrated or alienated because they feel they are expected to know and do too much, or because staff or elected officers are doing everything and committee members feel they are simply rubber-stamping decisions already made.

When a group is small, everyone on the committee can be involved in every decision. But when an organisation becomes large or complex, it is unreasonable to expect everyone on the management committee (or everyone on the staff) to be an expert in all aspects of the organisation's management. One way to get around this problem is to set up subcommittees to deal with specific areas of management responsibility. Permanent subcommittees are sometimes called **standing committees.** Typical subcommittees are:

● personnel, which might be called employment or staffing;

● volunteer recruitment and support;

● finance, funding and fundraising, which might be one subcommittee, two or even three;

● premises;

● development, which might be one subcommittee, or two or more to deal with specific aspects of the organisation's work;

● equal opportunities;

● publications;

● publicity and media.

If subcommittees are short term rather than permanent they may be called working groups. Working groups might be set up, for example, to draw up a draft equal opportunities policy and submit it to the whole committee for approval, develop a training policy, organise the annual general meeting or a specific fundraising event, or undertake similar time-limited tasks.

Having subcommittees and working groups means:

● there is less pressure on the chair and other officers;

● managers, staff and volunteer workers feel better supported and less isolated, because they can refer to the relevant subgroup for support or advice;

● the organisation can build up and draw on areas of specific expertise;

● committee members only need to have substantial knowledge about one or two areas of management responsibility;

● committee members' specific interests and skills can be recognised and used;

● gaps in committee knowledge or experience can more easily be identified;

● people from outside the organisation with specific expertise who would not want (or be allowed) to serve on the management committee can be involved;

● new committee members can work with more experienced members;

● individuals can participate more, because most of the work is done in small groups;

● meetings of the whole committee are shorter and more effective, because information can be collected by the subgroup and presented to the committee in an accessible form.

Drawing up terms of reference

It is essential for every subcommittee and working group to have clear **terms of reference**. These should state:

● the purpose of the subgroup;

● who is on the subgroup, how they are appointed and how long they serve;

● how often the group meets;

● who services the group (calls meetings, draws up the agenda, takes minutes);

● what topics or issues the group covers;

● what sorts of decisions or action the group can take on its own (**delegated powers**), and what needs to be referred back to the main committee for decision or action;

● how often the subgroup reports back to the main committee and whether this has to be in writing;

● how the group is funded, and how its expenditure is authorised;

● whether the group is intended to be permanent or time-limited, and if the latter, how it will be wound up.

Most importantly, the terms of reference should be explicit about how much authority the subgroup has to make and implement decisions. There is a big difference between:

● a subgroup which is expected only to collect information about a problem or project, sift through it, discuss it, and extract the most important elements for discussion by the whole committee;

● one which is expected to make proposals or recommendations to the committee;

● one which is able to make and implement decisions and simply report them back to the whole committee.

Serious problems can arise if these expectations and limits are not absolutely clear.

Sample terms of reference are given in chapter 8 for a development subcommittee, in chapter 14 for a personnel subcommittee, and in chapter 20 for a finance and fundraising subcommittee.

Link people

In many voluntary organisations, there simply are not enough people on the committee to have subgroups. In this case it may be more appropriate to have link people who take responsibility for a specific area of management responsibility, performing the information-gathering role of subcommittees or working groups.

Just as a treasurer has overall responsibility for ensuring the financial management is properly carried out, so link people have responsibility for ensuring the management functions relevant to their particular area are appropriately undertaken. This does not imply the link person does the work (although she or he might); it means she or he is responsible for seeing the work is done and the management committee has the information it needs to make decisions about that area of work.

As with subcommittees, it is essential to have clear terms of reference for link people, to ensure they do not do work which should be done by staff or by the committee as a whole. The terms of reference checklists in chapters 8 and 14 would be useful for link people as well as for subcommittees.

MAKING THE MOST OF THE COMMITTEE

A good committee, good staff, good volunteer workers: all have an essential role in ensuring the organisation can do its work well. Yet too often the committee is seen as irrelevant or even a liability.

The organisational structure

In many organisations a negative view of the committee is an almost inevitable result of the organisational structure (the way the organisation is set up).

The committee may be an august body made up of 'the great and the good': people committed to the organisation and its work, but very far removed from the day to day reality of workers and the organisation's users or beneficiaries. In this case it might be a good idea to set up a users forum or similar group which could send representatives to committee meetings.

At the other extreme the committee might be made up solely of members or service users primarily interested in what the organisation can provide for them now, rather than in its long term development. Here it might be useful to widen the committee to include outside people with particular skills or experience, to give a wider perspective.

The structure may be difficult because of its circular nature: the committee is the employer of staff who supervise volunteers who are on the committee which is the employer of the staff ... or the committee is the employer of staff who provide services to users who are on the committee which

is the employer of the staff ... and so on. Circular structures of this type require particular skill in defining and maintaining the boundaries between the person as volunteer and/or user and the person as committee member.

If the committee includes staff or committee members from other organisations there can be difficult **conflicts of interest** when discussing, for example, whether to apply for a particular type of funding. Similar conflicts of interest can occur if funders are represented on the management committee.

Another difficulty arises from having annual elections and a constant turnover of committee members. Even if the constitution requires annual elections, the organisation can make it clear that it expects committee members to serve for at least two years (assuming they are re-elected the second year).

Better procedures

Regardless of the organisational structure, the following ideas can help people participate effectively on committees:

● committee familiarisation sessions, to encourage people who might be interested in standing for election to learn what it involves, or talking to potential members on an individual basis;

● encouraging new people to participate in small groups which are less threatening than the whole committee;

● an induction pack (see chapter 1) and induction training for all new committee members, and ongoing training available for any interested members;

● encouraging committee members to visit the office and the organisation's sites, so they know what goes on;

● finding out what skills, experience and knowledge people bring to the committee, valuing it and genuinely making use of it;

● sending out agendas and background papers in good time, so people are able to read them and think about the issues;

● providing agendas which are clear about what is being considered, and why (see chapter 5);

● producing short, clear papers which outline the main issues and the options (see chapter 6);

● chairing meetings well, so people stick to the point, listen to each other, respect each other's views and come to clear decisions;

● making opportunities to chat informally before meetings or during a break;

● arranging occasional committee/staff social events or committee/staff/user events;

● creating a sense of partnership between the committee, the manager, staff, volunteers and users, rather than fostering an 'us and them' environment;

● and most importantly, creating an organisational climate in which the committee is seen – and treated – as a positive asset.

Chapter 3:

The good enough manager

Effective management in the voluntary sector requires a combination of common sense, sensitivity, confidence, commitment to the organisation's ethos and values, and good management practice in all areas of work. Some people seem to be naturally good in all of these; others need to acquire skills or sensitivity.

Especially in small organisations, people often move into managerial positions without having had previous management experience or training. From being an advice worker, childcare worker, administrator or campaign organiser they suddenly have to develop proposals for long term organisational or project development, make recommendations to the treasurer or management committee about complex financial issues, manage staff and volunteers, produce a constant stream of reports, agendas and minutes, represent the organisation to the external world – and more.

No one person can be good at all aspects of management. So this chapter looks at how someone can be a **good enough manager,** able to use her or his own strengths, skills and style to best advantage. It covers:

- management concepts such as power, authority and leadership;

- styles of management, and their effects on other people and the organisation as a whole;

- knowledge, skills and qualities which contribute to good management;

- the manager as part of a management team;

- making the most of managerial strengths;

- differences between informal and formal organisations, and what this means for managing them;

- particular issues around managing non-hierarchical or collective organisations.

One of the most difficult problems in voluntary organisations is the unclear boundary between the management committee and the manager(s). The division will depend on the size of the organisation, its management philosophy and its management structure. In larger organisations the responsibilities will be divided between the committee, senior manager and line managers. In a small organisation often no one is identified as 'manager', and staff and volunteers are directly accountable to the committee. Or management responsibility may be shared among all the workers in a non-hierarchical collective structure.

Regardless of how the staff group is structured, a distinction has to be made between decisions about long term goals or direction for the organisation (a management committee responsibility, but always in consultation with staff, volunteers and users) and decisions about how the organisation will carry these out (broadly a staff management responsibility, but within policy and procedural guidelines agreed by the committee).

MANAGEMENT CONCEPTS

Ideas of authority, accountability, leadership, control or power are sometimes seen as antithetical to the spirit of voluntary or community work. If there is antagonism to these concepts, discussions about management may be fraught. But an understanding of these concepts is essential for good management, so some definitions relevant to the voluntary sector are given here.

Management

Management can mean the **process** of managing (making decisions and using resources to achieve desired ends) or it can mean the **people** responsible for the process. In this book 'management' is always used in the former sense; the people responsible for management are referred to as the management committee and/or managers. Managers include senior managers, line managers or workers in a collective with shared management responsibility.

There is also an assumption in this book that everyone involved in working (paid or unpaid) for or managing a voluntary organisation is responsible for their own **self-management.**

The processes of management and self-management are explained in chapter 1.

Authority

Having authority or **being in authority** means having the power or right to do something, or having the right to give orders and make others do it. In an organisation it must be clear where this kind of authority comes from. In most voluntary groups ultimate authority is legally with the management committee or other governing body. Authority for certain activities or functions is delegated to subcommittees or senior staff (or, in a collective, to all staff).

Authority can be **legitimate** (arising, for example, from the law, the organisation's constitution or a job description), **traditional** (arising from the idea that 'we've always done it this way') or **illegitimate** (arising from personal power or from stepping in to fill a vacuum if legitimate authority is not exercised). Confusion arises if there is a conflict between legitimate and traditional authority, or if people are (usually quite justifiably) not willing to accept illegitimate authority.

Being an authority has nothing to do with decision-making or action; it simply means having specialist knowledge. So someone who *is* an authority may not actually *have* any authority. One cause of conflict within organisations is a mismatch between someone who is (or thinks she or he is) *an* authority and someone else who is *in* authority.

A person who exercises authority is **authoritative,** as is a person who is an expert or knowledgeable about something. This is not the same as being an **authoritarian** person: someone who uses her or his authority to force people to do what she or he wants, or who expects complete and unquestioning obedience to her or his authority.

Within an organisation everyone must be clear who has legitimate authority to take decisions or action.

Responsibility

Having responsibility means being obliged or expected to do something. This is not necessarily the same as having authority. For example, a project manager may have **authority** to decide what time to open on Thursday evenings, but the youth leader who runs the Thursday club has **responsibility** for opening up.

Taking responsibility means doing something even without having specific responsibility for it. In many offices no one (or everyone, which amounts to the same thing) *has* responsibility for taking out the milk bottles. But one or two people *take* responsibility for doing it.

Clearly defined responsibility for decision-making, planning and tasks is an essential component of good management.

Accountability

Being **accountable** means being answerable to those who give authority or responsibility. In a voluntary organisation the junior staff are accountable to senior staff; all staff are accountable, perhaps through senior staff, to the committee; the committee is accountable to the members who elected it and to funders; a funder which is a charitable trust is accountable to its trustees, and a funder which is a statutory authority is accountable to the public. If the organisation is a limited company and/or a charity it will be accountable in some ways to the Registrar of Companies and/or the Charity Commission.

Accountability is essential to ensure organisations and individuals do what they are supposed to. At its best, accountability is a smooth process of decisions being made, responsibilities being allocated, and actions being taken and reported back. At its worst it may involve decisions being made without adequate consultation with the people who will have to carry them out, responsibilities not being clearly allocated, and inadequate procedures for monitoring work or reporting it back.

Leadership

Concepts such as management, authority, responsibility and accountability are rooted in the way an organisation is structured and the ways in which decisions and tasks are carried out and reported. Some of these structures and procedures may be formal (explicitly agreed, written down) while others are informal ('this is how we do it'). A manager is given responsibility, within the organisational structures, for ensuring that decisions get made, work gets done and resources are wisely used.

Leadership, however, is a characteristic rooted in **individuals** rather than in organisational structures. It cannot be written into procedures or job descriptions. It refers to an ability to inspire others, to get others to take decisions or carry out work not because they have to but because they want to. Good leaders influence people, but recognise that they too are influenced. Good leaders inspire confidence in themselves, but also have confidence in the people around them and help those people to develop their own confidence.

A **manager without leadership qualities** might get work done efficiently, but the organisation and the individuals within it are likely to become stagnant. A **leader without managerial skills** might inspire a loyal following or lots of new ideas, but may create an organisation going in too many directions at once, or too dependent on the leader to keep everything under control.

A **leader who does not have managerial authority** may build up a following which is in conflict with the manager(s). This can lead to factionalism and in-fighting.

Control

Of all these management words, control is probably the most confusing and most open to misinterpretation.

Legitimate authority used in an authoritarian way is control: 'the coordinator controls staff meetings by never giving others a chance to have their say'. Use of illegitimate authority is also often control.

But control also has positive meanings. **Being in control** of a situation or having a situation **under control** can mean being fully aware of what is happening and being able to make appropriate decisions or take appropriate action. So someone who is legitimately in authority should also be, in this sense, in control.

Unfortunately, control in this positive sense can be a matter of perspective. In a difficult meeting a strong chair might be seen as being too controlling, or being positively in control.

Even when the perspective is relatively clear, the word 'control' can still be open to huge misunderstanding. An organisation must always be in control of its finances; it must know how much money it has and how it is being spent. But if a treasurer says 'I want to be in control of the financial situation' does that mean she or he wants to make every decision about it or simply be aware of the situation?

Control also means setting standards and expecting them to be met (quality control) or restraining something (keeping it under control). Yet more possibilities for confusion.

Power

Power, control, leadership and authority are often used interchangeably, which causes even more misunderstanding. **Power to** act can be defined as the ability or right to do something. **Power over** is the ability or right to make other people do something. Like authority, power can be legitimate or illegitimate; like control, it can be used positively or negatively.

People in management positions often do not like to talk about power or control. They exercise their legitimate authority, they say; they do not exercise power; they do not exercise control. But managers (whether from the committee or staff) who are not aware of the power and the potential for control inherent in their position risk misusing their authority.

Power misused becomes injustice; control misused becomes coercion; leadership misused becomes domination; authority misused becomes authoritarianism. The fact that they can be misused does not mean, however, that such misuse is inevitable. It means people who hold power or authority, are able to exercise control or take on leadership roles have to be aware of what that power, control, authority and leadership mean, and have to use them wisely.

Because people are afraid of being accused of being unjust, coercive, domineering or authoritarian there may be a reluctance to take on or exercise authority in some groups, especially those which seek to work collectively. But in groups in which no one has or takes legitimate authority, decisions are made (if they are made at all) precisely through the misuse of power. The people with the loudest voice, the most authoritarian manner or the most manipulative temperament will take control. Where then is legitimate authority? Where then is accountability?

These issues are complex and sometimes unpleasant, but must be considered by those who manage voluntary organisations.

THE ORGANISATION

The way in which an organisation is managed will be a unique reflection of:

- the **organisational culture**;
- its **organisational development** stage;
- the **organisational structure**;
- the **managerial style** of key individuals in managerial roles.

Organisational culture

An organisation's culture emerges from its history, the type of work it does, its priorities and the sorts of people who are involved (as committee members, workers and users). A culture might be focused on:

- **an individual or small group**: based around a particular individual, often a very charismatic and dynamic founding father or founding mother, or around a small clique;
- **the group and its members**: emphasising self-help, mutual aid and shared empowerment, and involving all members in decisions and tasks;
- **services or activities**: with emphasis on providing services or activities for users/members;

- **tasks**: with emphasis on getting tasks done and achieving objectives.

The culture is also a reflection of the organisation's attitude towards change. This might be, for example:

- **conservative**: resistant to change, new ideas and new approaches; committed to 'carrying on like we've always done';
- **opportunistic**: taking up every new opportunity for funding or change, without necessarily considering how it fits into the organisation's aims and work;
- **entrepreneurial**: constantly developing new services or activities;
- **expansionist**: committed to increasing numbers of users, clients, members etc (but without adding new services).

External factors (such as pressure from funders to move away from being a self-help organisation to providing services) or internal factors (such as a founder or other charismatic leader leaving) can create serious problems. In situations like these, the organisation as a whole and individuals within it may have to act in ways which are incompatible with the established organisational culture. This can lead to confusion, frustration, arguments and organisational splits.

Another aspect of organisational culture is the degree of organisational informality or formality. **Informal organisations** tend to be small, dynamic, based on friendship networks or shared interests, with informal communication channels. Work tends to be defined by the members' interests, on the basis of a subjective assessment of what is or is not appropriate for the organisation. If people do not do what they are supposed to, informal sanctions and peer pressure are applied.

Formal organisations may be large or small. They are much more planned and stable, with targets, job descriptions and formal channels of communication. Decisions about the organisation are based more on 'objective' criteria ('how does it fit in with our strategic plan?'). There are rules, supervision sessions and ultimately disciplinary procedures if people do not do what they are supposed to.

Many people will recognise the transition from informal to formal in their own organisation. This transition can be difficult, especially if strategic plans and disciplinary procedures are imposed on organisations which still operate informally, or if some staff or users want to continue to operate in an informal way even after the organisation is too large for this to work effectively. For managers, it is important to recognise that a management style appropriate for an informal organisation is unlikely to be suitable for a more formal organisation.

Developmental stages

Although every organisation is unique, groups and organisations, like relationships, go through recognisable stages. The early stages have been described as:

- **forming**: coming together as a group, getting to know each other, deciding what the group's concerns and emphases should be;

- **storming**: coming to terms with differences within the group;

- **norming**: agreeing objectives, priorities, procedures, ways of relating to one another;

- **performing**: getting on with the work, without having to spend a lot of time and energy deciding what needs doing and how it should be done.

At times of significant change within a team or organisation, for example when key individuals leave or when the type or volume of work changes significantly, the group may revert to the early stages. This can be confusing for people who are getting on with 'performing', and do not realise why the group is back at the discussing ('forming') or arguing ('storming') stage.

Many problems with annually elected management committees arise from the newly elected group never getting beyond the forming and storming stages. Similar problems arise in organisations with high levels of staff turnover or undergoing rapid expansion.

Structures within organisations

At one extreme a **management structure** may be completely flat, with no one person or group having clear managerial responsibility over anyone else. This is the case in very small groups where the same people are involved in running the organisation and doing its work; it also occurs in some organisations where the management committee and staff see themselves as working jointly and collectively, rather than the committee having managerial responsibility.

At the other extreme are hierarchical organisations with several managerial tiers: perhaps a board of trustees, management committee, several subcommittees and working groups, a director or chief executive, several department heads, line managers and supervisors.

A **staff structure** may also be flat or hierarchical.

If work is divided into separate categories, these may be reflected in the departmental structure. An organisational structure may be based on:

- **geographical areas**: different departments or projects covering different areas;

- **functional responsibilities**: different departments covering, for example, personnel, finance, publicity, service provision;

- **types of services**: different departments or projects covering, for example, individual casework, health education and health campaigning;

- **user groups**: such as different projects for elderly people, teenagers and under-fives.

The overall **organisational structure** is a complex overlay of management structure, staff structure and departmental structure.

The manager within the organisation

The organisational culture, its stage of development and its structures provide the context within which a manager has to work. Into this, each manager brings her or his own levels of managerial experience and competence, and her or his own managerial style. Especially for new or inexperienced managers, many problems arise because of a mismatch between organisational culture and individual approach.

MANAGEMENT STYLES

Management style arises from the interplay between organisational culture and each individual manager's approach to management, and sets the tone for relationships within the organisation. Although there are dozens of ways to classify management styles, voluntary sector management usually falls into six broad categories: authoritarian, authoritative, participative, individualistic, laissez faire and chaotic. These are, of course, stereotypes, and very few groups or individuals consistently follow one pattern.

Authoritative

Authoritative committees and managers make decisions and take actions which are legitimately theirs, but make it clear that workers or others can question those decisions or actions if they have reasonable grounds for doing so.

This style of management only works if the management committee or manager has, and is seen as having, a legitimate right to make decisions or take action in particular areas of responsibility, and is allowed to act accordingly.

Authoritative management is essential when major decisions have already been taken which the manager must implement. It is simply not practical to consult with everyone involved or to involve everyone in a democratic decision-making process every time any decision, no matter how small, must be made.

Participative

Consultative management is similar to authoritative, but the manager or management committee bases decisions or actions on the ideas or opinions of the people who will be affected by the decision, advice from 'experts' or advisers, or consultation with other relevant people. This is usually very effective because it acknowledges and makes use of other people's knowledge and ideas, but positions final responsibility clearly with one person or group.

If the manager knows beforehand what the decision will be and is using consultation as a cosmetic exercise, the management style is authoritarian, not consultative.

Democratic management means everyone concerned in the decision is directly involved in making it. This is a cornerstone of collective management; it may also happen in traditional organisations if certain responsibilities belong to the staff meeting or team meeting rather than to the manager.

Democratic decisions may be made by voting (and should be implemented even if the manager is on the losing side) or by consensus (taking into account everyone's views and ideas and trying to come up with a solution acceptable to everyone, even if they do not fully agree with it). Decision-making is not democratic if workers have the right to make

APPROACHES TO MANAGEMENT

Authoritative

'We have this problem, and it's my responsibility to decide what to do about it. Here's what I've decided; are there any questions or comments?'

Participative

Consultative: 'We have this problem and it's my responsibility to deal with it. Whose ideas or opinions do I need before I decide what to do?'

Democratic: 'We have this problem and the whole group should be involved in finding a solution. What information do they need before the next meeting?'

Representative: 'We have this problem and the representatives from various teams should be involved in finding a solution. What information do they need before the next meeting?'

Authoritarian

Repressive: 'We have this problem, and here's what I've decided you're going to do about it.'

Benevolent dictatorship: 'We have this problem, and I'm sure this is the way you'd like to deal with it.'

Individualistic

Management vacuum: 'We have this problem, and no one seems to be doing anything about it. So I've stepped in and decided ...'

Intrusive: 'I know you're supposed to be dealing with the problem, but you seem to be having difficulties. I'll do it for you.' (Or, even more intrusive: 'I've dealt with it for you.')

Charismatic: 'Isn't it strange, how people always turn to me.'

Laissez faire

Denial: 'We have this problem but I don't think we need to do anything about it. If we leave it alone it will sort itself out.'

False democracy: 'We have this problem and it's my responsibility to do something about it, but I want people to feel involved so I'll mention it at the next staff meeting' (without providing appropriate information or ensuring adequate time for discussion).

Chaotic

'We have this problem and I'm not sure who's supposed to deal with it. I'll mention it to the management committee chair ... no, perhaps it should go to staff meeting first ... I wonder if it's the sort of thing I'm supposed to deal with?'

Authoritative and participative approaches are good. Authoritarian and individualistic might be acceptable in some situations. Laissez faire and chaotic approaches generally lead to poor management.

decisions only so long as they make the 'right' decision (in other words, the one the manager wants them to make).

Major decisions about policy and priorities should always involve people likely to be affected, either by consulting them or involving them directly in the decision-making. But in most organisations it is not practical for everyone to be involved in every decision all the time. It is essential that people be allowed to take individual responsibility for specific aspects of work.

In some situations responsibility for management may rest with **representatives** from groups. For example, a multi-team project may not have an overall project leader or coordinator, but may have central management responsibilities undertaken by a management group made up of represenatives from each team.

This style of management works only if the people involved are willing to take management responsibility, if there are procedures to ensure they actually represent their group's views (rather than just their own) and if their workload is adjusted to ensure they have time for management.

Authoritarian

Authoritarian management is not the same as authoritative.

In **repressive** management, authority and power are used in ways which dominate and negatively control. Complete and unquestioning obedience is expected. The management committee, an officer or manager decides what people will do, and they have no option but to do it.

Because authoritarian/repressive managers expect (and usually get) obedience, this style of management can seem efficient in getting jobs done. But the people who are bossed quickly become alienated, performing tasks not because they want to but because they have no choice. Or they become rebellious, expert at doing the absolute minimum needed to keep the boss quiet and sometimes even more expert at sabotaging what they are doing.

Management committees or managers who are **benevolent dictators** also use authority and power in ways which dominate and control. But they try, or say they are trying, to make decisions and undertake actions on the basis of what they think is best for the workers, the users/clients or the community.

If they make decisions with which workers, users or others agree, this type of management can be reasonably effective. But it depends entirely on the sense and sensitivity of the manager or management committee, with no recognition of the insight or ideas of the workers who will actually be carrying out the tasks or users who will be at the receiving end. If the manager gets it wrong, there can be a great deal of frustration and unwillingness to cooperate.

Individualistic

Authoritative, participative and authoritarian management styles are based on legitimate authority: a right to manage agreed by the organisation. But some managers make decisions or take action without having the authority to do so.

This may occur because of a **management vacuum**: no one is performing specific management tasks and the manager steps in. If this happens the problem should be recognised and steps taken to ensure someone takes responsibility for those tasks.

Or managers may be **intrusive**, usurping or denying someone else's legitimate authority. These managers will not let their workers get on with work or let the management committee make decisions; they constantly interfere or even do the jobs themselves. Intrusive managers should be reminded that they are overstepping the mark; clearer boundaries will need to be set.

A manager who is very **charismatic** or energetic may overshadow everyone else and end up taking (or being given) credit for all the work of the group. This happens where a person is more a leader than a manager.

Laissez faire

Many managers simply abdicate responsibility for management, taking a laissez faire approach: 'If I ignore it, it will go away or will happen anyway.'

Denial is the most common form of abdication: the manager, collective or management committee denies that any decision has to be made, or says that she, he or it does not have responsibility or authority to make it. Denial creates a **management vacuum** in which those with the loudest voices win.

Strange as it seems, abdication can also occur if the people responsible for management try to involve too many people. Managers sometimes create a **false democracy**, saying that they want to involve other people through a consultative or democratic process, but not giving them adequate or appropriate information, time or opportunity to participate. Or managers constantly refer everything back to other people, rather than ever taking a decision themselves.

Chaotic

The last style of management represents a lack of any consistent style. In this chaotic situation, no one knows who is responsible for making decisions or taking action. The goalposts constantly shift, depending on how the management committee, manager or collective feels or who is around at the time. Decisions are made and unmade because no one recognises or respects other people's authority. No one has responsibility for dealing with difficult situations so they fester until they become major crises, or until someone becomes extremely authoritarian.

The right style at the right time

Authoritative and participative styles are generally good. Authoritarian and individualistic approaches may in some situations be considered necessary, but would not be considered appropriate for most voluntary organisations. Laissez faire and chaotic approaches may not do too much damage in the very short term, but soon interfere with the work of individuals and the organisation as a whole.

Good managers know when they can make decisions on their own, when to consult other people, and when to involve all workers in a democratic process. They are not afraid to take decisions or action themselves when necessary, and do not waste people's time by consulting unnecessarily or calling meetings to involve everyone in decision-making on minor points. But they know the importance of involving people appropriately, providing adequate opportunities for staff, volunteers and users to contribute to discussions and decisions about the organisation and their work, and listening to and valuing all ideas.

KNOWLEDGE, SKILLS AND QUALITIES

It is easy to generate a long list of all the knowledge, skills and qualities necessary to be the perfect manager. It may be less daunting to identify one cluster relating to basic knowledge which can be learned through fairly straightforward processes, and another cluster relating to personal and interpersonal skills and qualities which may be innate but can be developed.

Basic knowledge

This cluster can be divided into three:

- knowledge about the **organisation**: what it does, with or for whom it does it, why it does it, how it does it, its ethos and values;

- knowledge about the **field of work**: the political, social and economic context, accepted standards and expectations, what other agencies and organisations are doing and how this organisation fits in;

- knowledge about **managerial functions**: long, medium and short term planning, monitoring and evaluation; financial planning, record-keeping, reporting and control; personnel management; premises management; time management.

As well as this knowledge, a manager must have:

- the capacity to use knowledge or a skill as appropriate.

Personal and interpersonal skills

People start learning these skills from the moment they are born, so someone appointed as a manager should have acquired at least some of them. The others can be developed through awareness and practice. They include:

- **communication skills**: being able to organise and share information (verbal and written);

- **ability and willingness to learn**: listening skills, willingness to be challenged, time and inclination to learn, ability to develop new ways to do things;

- **sensitivity** and **flexibility**: in relation to clients, users and members; to the people who are doing the work; to a wide variety of needs and situations; to changing needs and situations; to one's own needs and situation;

- **leadership**: trusting and having confidence in others; able to inspire confidence in the organisation and its work, in oneself and in others.

MANAGEMENT ROLES

In research over a long period, R Meredith Belbin identified eight roles which need to be filled at management level in any organisation. Each role is equally necessary, and management teams work best if each role is filled. In a voluntary organisation the 'management team' might be the management committee, or the committee plus manager, or a senior manager plus line managers, or all staff members of a collective.

The eight roles are coordinator, shaper, innovator, evaluator, liaison, organiser, team builder and finisher. Sometimes a ninth role, the specialist, is added.

For small organisations it may be more helpful to think in terms of **management strengths** which someone involved in managing has to have. If these strengths are lacking the group may find it difficult to make or follow through on decisions.

- **Coordinator**: chairs discussions, coordinates and makes the best use of each team member's potential and the team's resources to achieve its objectives. A good coordinator is balanced, focused and disciplined, a good listener and judge, but may not be particularly brilliant or creative.

- **Shaper**: a task leader who shapes, through her or his

drive and passion, the way in which the team effort is applied. The shaper gets and keeps things moving but may be oversensitive and irritable, especially if thwarted.

- **Innovator**: generates creative ideas and new strategies for the team, and sees the team's work and problems in unconventional ways. The innovator is intellectually dominant but may be introverted, withdrawn and easily hurt.

- **Evaluator**: provides a critical analysis of problems and situations; evaluates suggestions to help the team make balanced decisions. May be less involved than the others.

- **Liaison**: an outward-looking extrovert who keeps in touch with other teams or organisations and brings in new ideas, contacts and resources from outside.

- **Organiser**: an administrator who turns ideas into tasks, plans, schedules and procedures.

- **Team builder**: emphasises good communication and personal relationships within the team, and supports individuals personally and in their work. Is uncompetitive, likeable and good at listening.

- **Finisher**: maintains a sense of urgency, ensures adequate time is allowed for particularly complex aspects of work, worries about deadlines and completion.

- **Specialist**: an expert with a range of specialist knowledge about the team's work.

Although most people slip into each of these roles from time to time, there will be one or at most two with which each person is most comfortable. If a management team does not have someone filling each role either the team will not operate as effectively as it might, or team members will have to take on uncomfortable roles (which means in turn that they will have less opportunity to contribute in their best role).

For small voluntary organisations, the best use of Belbin's categories is to identify and build on available strengths among committee members and managers, and to identify gaps which need to be filled: either by bringing in new people, or by developing those strengths within the people who are already there.

The not-so-ideal team

Looking at management roles in a rather different way, William Harston (*The Independent*, 2 October 1990) identified seven characters within a management team suffering from 'an all-pervading, initiative-stifling, mind-numbing culture of mediocrity dedicated to preserving inefficiency and indecisiveness'.

- **Sloth**: procrastinates, wastes time, devotes a great deal of effort to evading work, produces endless 'interim reports' but never anything that could mean actually having to do something.

- **Cuckoo**: creates pointless work for other people to do, usually by dreaming up new projects that no one is committed to, with all the work being done by other people (thus keeping the cuckoo free to come up with yet more pointless projects).

Management Team

Steve Simpson

- **Drone**: dull, ponderous, unimaginative, doesn't question the system, doesn't want anything new to happen.

- **Rhino**: afraid of change, and pushy and negative enough to stop it; imposes cumbersome systems with rigid objectives so nothing new can slip in.

- **Hare**: rushes around doing everything at once but nothing very well; a constant source of creative (but nonetheless nearly always bad) ideas.

- **Toad**: sycophantic, vacuous, tries to advance herself or himself by toadying to anyone with any power.

- **Weasel**: undermines everyone else, derides other people's efforts, blames her or his own inadequacies on others.

Obviously this article was not written about voluntary sector management, but it's worth thinking about anyway.

THE GOOD ENOUGH MANAGER

From the morass of information on management functions, styles, roles and skills, on organisational styles and needs, how can individual managers know what is right for them?

The main rules are for managers to trust their instinct, and to aim for consistency. They are unlikely to be trusted as managers if no one knows what sort of person they are or what to expect from them.

There is no point in aiming to be Supermanager; managers who do so will only set impossible targets for themselves and their staff (see chapter 19, on individual stress and the

stress cycle of organisations). Instead, managers should aim to be a **good enough manager**: one who is respected and trusted.

A good enough manager is one who can:

- help individuals and groups identify goals and priorities and develop action plans;

- take responsibility, make decisions and get things done;

- manage her or his own time and energy;

- delegate responsibility;

- trust people to get on with their work, and give them the support they need without being intrusive;

- consult, listen, learn and share;

- be firm without being rigid, and understanding without being soft;

- inspire confidence in herself or himself, in the management process and in the organisation.

It comes down to common sense, sensitivity, and clear awareness of what the organisation and its workers are supposed to be doing.

And what about bad management? Bad managers:

- abdicate responsibility, and are indecisive, unreliable and uninformed;

- undermine other people and stop people from getting on with their work;

- will not consult, listen, learn or share;

- make judgments about people on the basis of stereotypes and prejudices;

- generate lack of confidence in themselves, in management and in the organisation.

ISSUES IN COLLECTIVES

Groups which work collectively or non-hierarchically have to deal with particular issues:

- workers sometimes think that by cutting out managerial and supervisory staff the need for the work undertaken by those staff is also eliminated;

- 'self-management' may be interpreted as meaning individual workers are entitled to do whatever they want whenever they want, so long as they report at some point to the staff or team meeting;

- anyone who takes managerial responsibility may be seen as authoritarian or anti-collective, so no one initiates anything until the situation becomes impossible;

- 'collective management' may be interpreted as meaning all workers have to be involved in all decisions all the time, or even have to agree with all decisions all the time;

- the management committee may be drawn into the anti-management ethos, and may be unable to make effective decisions for the organisation.

Under these circumstances collective working may seem satisfactory in very small informal groups where objectives and philosophy are clearly defined and agreed. But unless the problems are dealt with, collective working is likely to be virtually impossible in larger groups or in groups where there is disagreement about objectives, priorities or standards.

Collectives have the same management responsibilities as other organisations; the only difference is that those responsibilities are **shared among workers** rather than being attached to specific positions in the organisation. In groups which work collectively or non-hierarchically, the responsibilities which managerial and supervisory staff carry out in traditionally structured organisations must be undertaken by the staff or team meeting. The meeting may, in turn, decide to delegate some responsibilities to specific people, either permanently or on a rotating basis.

An excellent analysis of one agency's positive experience in developing collective working practices is *Invitation to Self Management* by Alan Stanton (Dab Hand Press, 1989; 384 pages; ISBN 0 9513862 0 4; £6.95 from Dab Hand Press, 90 Long Drive, Ruislip, Middlesex HA4 0HP).

Management committees in collectives have exactly the same responsibilities as committees in traditionally structured organisations. As in any organisation some committee responsibilities may be delegated to staff but the overall responsibility and legal liability remains with the committee or other governing body.

Chapter 4:

Managing teamwork and involvement

Within the voluntary sector people are very good at talking about cooperation, teamwork and working collectively, but often not so good at doing it. As a result, good management becomes very difficult.

This chapter includes:

- a checklist for identifying some of the blocks to teamwork in individual organisations or groups;

- an explanation of the differences between informing people about decisions, consulting them and directly involving them in decision-making;

- a framework for making decisions or dealing with difficult issues;

- a description of advantages and disadvantages of voting and consensus, and situations where they are or are not appropriate.

Everything in this chapter is relevant for groups which work collectively (non-hierarchically) as well as those which are traditionally (hierarchically) structured, for informal as well as formal decision-making processes, and for meetings of all types including management committee, subcommittee, staff or team meetings.

BLOCKS TO TEAMWORK

This checklist can be used to discover why an organisation, group or team is not as effective as it could be at working together, making decisions together or solving problems together. It is not exhaustive; there are dozens of other reasons. When specific blocks have been identified, action should be taken to improve the situation.

Unclear objectives and responsibilities

- Are the organisation's long, medium and/or short term objectives unclear?

  These need to be clarified, and organisational members, committee members, managers, staff and volunteers should be clear what they are trying to achieve and why.

- Are terms of reference for teams, staff groups, committees, subcommittees or working groups ill defined?

  Terms of reference should be drawn up and agreed by the management committee and appropriate staff.

- Are individuals' roles unclear, with poor or non-existent job descriptions for staff and volunteers, and unclear responsibilities for management committee members?

  Job descriptions should be written or updated for staff and permanent volunteers; a list of committee respon-

sibilities should be drawn up and distributed to all committee members.

Unclear definitions of problems

- Are problems to be resolved or decisions to be made presented in a haphazard way?

  Every issue raised at a meeting should be clearly introduced with a factual statement of the problem or situation, why it is important, what sort of action is required, and how urgent it is. The discussion can then focus first on additional facts about the situation, then opinions, ideas for action, advantages and disadvantages of the various options, and finally a decision. (People who have to make decisions on their own, rather than in a group, will also find this approach helpful.)

- Are problems or decisions defined in a way that alienates some of the people involved, for example by blaming individuals or using provocative terms?

  Care should be taken to present information as factually and straightforwardly as possible, avoiding emotive language, name-calling and other unproductive tactics.

- Are problems or decisions defined so negatively that people find it difficult to put forward constructive ideas?

  Change, even if it is positive, is difficult and can be frightening. People try in all kinds of ways to block effective decision-making and change; it is important to be aware of these blocking mechanisms and challenge them. Chapter 10 looks at issues around the management of change.

Lack of cooperation

- Do some or all of the people involved not know how, or not want, to cooperate?

  It may be necessary to clarify what levels of cooperation are required, or to sort out personal differences or conflicts (see chapter 18).

- Do people seem to be trying to undermine the decision-making process?

  Someone has a vested interest in ensuring a decision is not reached. Better meetings (chapter 5) or supervision processes (chapter 16) may help.

Inappropriate consultative processes

- Do the people responsible for particular areas of work fail to involve others?

  They may not be aware of who should be involved at

each stage. It can be helpful to clarify this before a piece of work is undertaken.

- Do they hoard essential information so other people cannot take part in decision-making?

  People who think they have a right to information may need to ask bluntly for it. Again, it helps to clarify at the beginning who has the right to what kind of information during the decision-making process.

- Do they churn out so much information it is impossible to know what is and is not essential?

  Chapter 6 might help.

- Do they involve people too late?

  A clear timetable right from the beginning may help.

- Do they give the impression the real decision has already been taken and other people are only there to rubber-stamp it?

  People who feel they should have been involved must be assertive and demand an improvement in the decision-making processes.

Inappropriate information

- Do the people who have to deal with problems or decisions fail to get the right information?

  Clearer definitions of the problem and processes will help.

- Do they have too much, too little or out of date information?

  Time must be allowed to sift it, ignore the irrelevancies, determine what is missing and obtain the necessary information.

- Is information presented in a way people cannot understand?

  Simpler language and a standard format for written and verbal reports may make it easier.

- Is there inadequate time to read and digest the information?

  Papers may need to be sent out before a meeting, with a clear indication that they will be discussed at the meeting and people are expected to have read them beforehand. If papers must be distributed at the meeting, time should be allowed for people to read them.

- Is there no opportunity to ask for clarification or additional data?

  Time must be allowed for this.

- Are individuals made to feel stupid if they ask for clarification or more details?

  People need to be more sensitive to the fact that people in organisations are at many different levels of awareness and commitment. Putting people down or making them feel silly or incompetent will alienate them and reflect badly on the organisation as a whole.

Poor time planning

- Is inadequate time allowed for dealing with problems or decisions?

Better planning (chapter 8) and time management (chapter 11) are needed.

- Are matters left until the last minute?

  Again, better planning and time management are essential.

- Are possible consequences (good or bad) not properly considered when a new activity or project is undertaken, so there never seems to be advance warning of potential problems?

  It is never possible to foresee every consequence, but with time and good decision-making processes it is easier to predict and plan for some of them.

Inappropriate decision-making procedures

- Are the people involved unaware of how to cope with differences of opinion or conflict within the group?

  Chapter 18 may help.

- Is the emphasis on finding a 'consensus' solution which everyone totally agrees with, thus making it hard on people who disagree?

  Consensus does not mean everyone has to agree. It takes into account people's differing views but recognises that for the group to proceed, a decision which everyone is willing to accept must be reached.

- Does the group tend to call a vote very quickly, so differences of opinion are resolved by the majority winning and a minority is left dissatisfied?

  More time may be needed for discussion, and the group may need to be more open to the possibility of different solutions emerging from the discussion.

- Are people known to have dissenting views ignored or disregarded?

  Good chairing is needed, to enable people to speak and be heard.

Domination

- Do people who have been involved longest dominate discussions and get their way?

  They probably have too much emotional investment in the group. Somehow they need to stand back and allow others to take full part, even if it leads to the organisation moving in new directions.

- Do staff in the highest-paid positions or with the highest job title or the committee officers dominate discussions and get their way?

  This is one of the most difficult situations to deal with, because no one has the authority (see chapter 3) to challenge them. The best approach is to strengthen those who in this situation are weak, rather than trying to weaken the strong people. If everyone becomes as well informed as possible and takes a strong role in discussions it will reduce the power of those who dominate.

- Do people dominate for other reasons?

  This behaviour often arises from a fear of being challenged, so people who seem quite strong may need

...and finally, let me conclude these brief opening remarks by re-emphasising the need to ensure that black people and women can fully participate...blah...blah!

VERY SLOW CROSSWORD

ZZZZ

better support (chapter 16) to overcome this fear. Or those who feel dominated may need support to challenge the behaviour.

Oppressive behaviour

● Does hidden or overt racism prevent black people or people from ethnic minority groups from participating fully in discussions?

This needs to be challenged in open, constructive ways which enable people to recognise what is happening and their part in it, without becoming defensive and negative.

● Does hidden or overt sexism prevent women from participating fully?

Again, this needs to be challenged constructively.

● Do attitudes or behaviour prevent others, for example people with a disability or people who do not speak English well, from participating fully?

The organisation should make every effort to enable people with special needs to take full part, for example by providing material on tape or in translation, or providing signers or interpreters. It also means asking people what they need, not making assumptions.

● Do the dynamics of the group make it difficult for white people and/or men to participate fully?

This also needs to be dealt with.

Lack of confidence

● Do people who have to deal with problems or decisions lack confidence in the organisation as a whole?

The organisation probably has unclear or unrealistic objectives and unworkable procedures; go back to the beginning of this checklist and deal with those problems first.

● Do people lack confidence in the ability of a particular group (for example staff or management committee) to deal with problems or make decisions?

In the short term, better information will help; in the longer term it may be necessary to strengthen the group through training or co-opting new members.

● Do people lack confidence in each others' ability to deal with problems or make decisions?

Good supervision procedures (chapter 16) can enable this to be discussed and dealt with, although a gap arises if the person doing the supervising is the one in whom there is no confidence. Chapter 22 considers this situation.

● Do individuals lack confidence in their own ability to deal with problems or make decisions?

Support, training and an environment in which mistakes are accepted rather than criticised and condemned can help.

Fear of commitment

- Are people afraid of coming to the 'wrong' conclusion and being seen to fail?

  With good information and discussion it is less likely that a group will make bad decisions, but no one can be right all the time. People will be more willing to take risks if there is an atmosphere of trust and openness and a willingness to learn from mistakes.

- Are they afraid of coming to the 'right' conclusion and being seen to succeed?

  Fear of success may sound paradoxical, but being successful can create a great deal of pressure to get it right next time as well.

- Do people actually want to find a solution or make a decision?

  Often an individual or small group (clique) within an organisation wants to block decisions, even without being aware they are doing it. When a discussion is going round in circles it can help for the chair to ask everyone in turn, 'Do you actually want to see this situation dealt with?' If everyone says yes, the chair can then say, 'Right then, let's concentrate on specific, positive steps we can realistically take, and let's look at them from the point of view of what we are willing to accept rather than what we don't like about them.' If people say they do not want the situation to be dealt with, that has to be resolved before the group can proceed.

Lack of follow-up

- Even when decisions are made, do they never get implemented?

  Every decision should have a name or names attached to it, so everyone knows who is supposed to do what. Better minute-taking and follow-up are essential (see chapter 5).

- Even when a decision is made and implemented, is there no review procedure to see if it was a good decision?

  A review should be built into any major or contentious decision at the time it is made, and the person planning the agenda for future meetings should ensure such reviews are scheduled (see chapter 5).

INFORM, CONSULT OR DECIDE?

Decision-making is often unnecessarily difficult in organisations because no one is certain who has to be involved in the decision-making process, and in what way. A few questions at the beginning of the process can easily clarify this.

- Who needs to be **informed** that a problem is being discussed or a decision is going to be made? Are they being told just for information, or are they expected to participate in the process in some way? (If the latter, they should be included in one of the following questions rather than this one.)

- Who needs to be **consulted?** This means asking people for their ideas or proposals, making it clear (and meaning it) that they will be considered but the final decision will be made by someone else.

- Who needs to be asked for **advice?** This is usually people with specialist knowledge or experience.

- Who has the right to put forward **proposals** based on the necessary research, consultation and advice?

- Who has the right to make a **recommendation** from among the proposals?

- Who makes the final **decision?**

- Who needs to be **informed** that the decision has been made?

- Who will be involved in **implementing** the decision? Will these people have been involved in making the decision, or at least have been consulted? If not, how can they be expected to be committed to implementing the decision?

A FRAMEWORK FOR DECISIONS

This DECIDE framework may make it easier to approach problems or difficult situations.

D: Define

- Define the problem or situation and stick to the definition. Don't keep compounding it or making it more complicated.

- Define clearly who must be involved in the process and in what way (see 'Inform, consult or decide?' above).

- Define a time limit or deadline, at least for a tentative decision.

- Define what information is needed to solve the problem, and who will get it. Information includes opinions as well as facts.

- Make a clear note or minute of everything that has been defined, and ensure all relevant people receive a copy.

E: Explore

- Collect the information without judging anyone's view of the problem or suggested solutions.

C: Clarify

- Make sure everyone involved in making the decision has and understands the necessary information.

I: Ideas

- Think of all the possible solutions: silly as well as serious, ridiculous as well as rational. Use creative problem-solving techniques such as brainstorming and small group discussions instead of simply discussion in the whole group.

● Keep a record of all the suggestions on a wallchart or whiteboard, and in written notes.

● Decide if you need more information to evaluate these ideas. If so, go back to the beginning.

D: Decision

● Accept that no solution or decision will be able to satisfy everyone; any decision will be imperfect and have limitations. Be prepared to compromise.

● Evaluate the suggestions in a clear, calm way, preferably with a chair or facilitator not directly involved in the decision-making.

● Make a decision, by voting if that is your way or if it is necessary, or preferably by coming to an agreement that everyone is willing to accept (see 'Consensus and voting' below).

● Check that everyone directly involved in the decision-making is willing to see the decision implemented, even if they disagree with it. If some are not, decide whether to go ahead anyway (and risk sabotage), or repeat the whole exercise. Do not change the decision at this stage unless everyone involved agrees it should be changed.

● Clarify who will ensure the decision is carried out or the solution put into practice, when and how it should happen, and when it will be reviewed.

● Decide who will ensure the necessary people are informed of the decision, who is taking responsibility for implementing it, and when and how it will be implemented, monitored and reviewed.

E: Enact and evaluate

● Inform the necessary people, and put the solution or decision into practice.

● Assess whether the problem has been completely solved, or if other aspects now need to be considered.

CONSENSUS AND VOTING

When the time comes to make a decision, voting is quick and easy, with a clear result. But this so-called democracy is not necessarily very democratic:

● it can lead to a **tyranny of the majority** in which a strong or powerful clique or interest group always gets its way, thus ensuring powerless or weak people remain so;

● it does not allow for the demands or needs of the minority to be recognised;

● it may leave a dissatisfied minority who are unwilling or unable to go along with the decision, and who therefore sabotage implementation of the decision, leave the organisation or remain within it but become negative and destructive.

Consensus, on the other hand, tries to take into account everyone's views. At its best it is the most democratic way of making decisions or solving problems, because it asks for all participants' ideas then takes the best points from each to come up with something which reflects everyone's input. A consensus solution does not necessarily meet everyone's needs, nor does everyone need to agree it is the best solution. The key is that everyone is willing to go along with it, because they know why this solution has been reached. But it too has its problems:

● consensus is often interpreted as meaning everyone has to agree totally, thus putting a huge pressure on people not to voice their misgivings or doubts and creating a different sort of **tyranny of the majority**;

● even when properly interpreted, a minority can consistently refuse to accept a solution unless it completely meets their needs, thus creating a **tyranny of the minority**;

● consensus decision-making takes a long time and requires commitment from everyone involved;

● it is not appropriate for situations which require an either/or decision.

When decisions are being made, everyone should be clear about how they are being made.

Some decisions, such as election of officers and committee members, accepting the annual accounts and passing formal resolutions, must always be made by voting. The organisation's constitution should list these and indicate the percentage of votes required.

The constitution should also indicate what happens in cases of tie votes. Usually a tie is broken by the chair; this is called a casting vote. It is usually considered good practice for the chair to use this casting vote in a way which maintains the present situation rather than requires the organisation to change.

In organisations without a procedure for deciding tie votes, the status quo (the present situation) should win. If it is a new issue and there is no 'status quo' usually the issue is dropped.

Chapter 5:

Managing meetings

In many organisations there is at least one point on which everyone agrees: meetings are awful. They are a waste of time, do not achieve anything, start late and go on for too long, do not make decisions or make decisions that are unmade at the next meeting ... the list of complaints is endless, and is remarkably consistent from organisation to organisation.

Meetings do not have to be awful. They can be useful, informative, challenging, and even exciting. But good meetings do not magically happen; they need careful planning and managing.

This chapter covers:

- types of meetings;
- cycles of meetings;
- agendas;
- planning;
- chairing;
- participating;
- taking and using minutes.

WHY HAVE MEETINGS?

Good meetings start with a clarification of their purpose. There are broadly six reasons for having meetings:

- **information**: to share information about what has happened or is going to happen;
- **consultation**: to get participants' views or proposals about what should happen, but without the meeting having power to make a decision;
- **business/decision-making**: to discuss what the group should do and how it should be done, and make decisions on the basis of those discussions;
- **legal**: to carry out business which must legally (according to legislation or the organisation's constitution) be transacted;
- **education**: to learn about a topic of relevance to the group, for example by having a speaker, video or discussion;
- **social/support**: to be with friends, share an interest or support each other.

These reasons overlap, but are different. A project meeting in which representatives from several teams report what each team is doing is very different from one in which the team representatives together decide the future direction of the project. An annual general meeting to transact the minimum legal requirements of receiving the annual report and accounts, appointing the auditor and electing the committee has to be planned differently from one which will also include a wide-ranging discussion on the project's future direction (and will this discussion be consultative or decision-making?) and a social event.

The **terms of reference** for a committee, subcommittee or other group will define what issues or topics can be covered at meetings and whether the purpose is informative, consultative, decision-making or a combination. A group with clear terms of reference is less likely to make decisions another group thinks *it* should be making.

Business meetings

Business meetings do not make decisions about everything they discuss. Just as meetings in general are held for different purposes, so individual items are on the agenda for various reasons.

- Items for **information**: straightforward reports about something which has happened or is going to happen. There can be an opportunity for clarification, but information items do not need much discussion. A report presented either verbally or in writing to a management committee meeting or other formal meeting should be formally accepted.
- Items for **discussion**: to be talked about, but without any decision being made.
- Items for **consultation**: to get people's ideas, opinions or proposals, but with the final decision to be made at a later meeting or by another group.
- Items for **decision**: on the basis of proposals or recommendations presented to or made at the meeting.
- Items for **ratification**: to confirm a decision legitimately made elsewhere (for example by the staff meeting, a subcommittee or chair's action) but requiring approval by this meeting.
- Items for **review**: to consider whether a decision already made and put into action was a good one, and whether further action needs to be taken.

Participants become confused and frustrated if they do not know why something is on the agenda: for example, whether they are expected to make a decision or are simply being asked for their views.

Business meetings might be very formal, with motions, proposers, seconders, and addressing all contributions to 'Mister Chair' or 'Madame Chair'. Such rigid formality is usually inappropriate for small groups, and can be very offputting for people who are unaccustomed to meetings or do not know the rules under which the meeting is being governed.

But informal meetings can be just as offputting, in other ways. Issues are not properly introduced, speakers do not stick to the point, there are constant interruptions and no one knows when a decision has been made (or what the decision is).

There is no 'right' level of formality. It will depend on the number of participants, the seriousness of the issues, the level of dissension within the group, and most of all on the organisational culture and the chair's style.

Legal meetings

Some meetings, such as annual general meetings, must be held according to law and/or the constitution and the business they must transact will be similarly defined. Such business includes electing officers and management committee members, accepting the annual report, accepting the annual accounts, appointing the organisation's auditor, and considering motions to change the constitution. It is essential for members to receive proper notification of these meetings and for the business to be strictly transacted and recorded according to the constitution.

Meetings as social events

Secretly, group members often want meetings to be social rather than business occasions. A fortnightly project meeting may be their only chance to meet colleagues from another part of the organisation; a monthly management committee meeting may be their only opportunity to see friends.

Because social gatherings are informal, members try to transfer this informality to the necessary business – as if by conducting the business informally they can somehow gain the social closeness they want from the meeting.

In very small groups this may work. But when a group becomes larger or more complex, the tendency is either to carry on with an informal approach which becomes increasingly inappropriate and ineffective, or to go too far the other way and become rigidly formal.

If people are using meetings as social occasions, it is best to recognise and allow for this. Otherwise participants' social needs may interfere with business or may be met in other ways (such as going to the pub before or afterwards) which exclude some members and give the impression that the group is made up of cliques.

It is not difficult to meet participants' social needs. Groups can, for example:

● provide refreshments beforehand so people want to come early and chat, or afterwards so people want to stay;

● schedule a break during the meeting, which not only allows for informal chat but also gives people a chance to wake up, move around and go to the lavatory;

● at the beginning of the meeting allow five minutes for people to talk informally to the person sitting next to them.

The social and business parts of the meeting must be clearly separated.

THE CYCLES OF MEETINGS

Meetings are often seen as isolated events, happening at a defined time and place. If the agenda and minutes are considered at all, they are seen as part of a linear progression: the agenda leads to the meeting, the meeting leads to the minutes, then the process ends. For the next meeting, it starts over again with the agenda.

One way to manage meetings better is to see them not in a linear way but as part of a cycle (see next page).

The first part of the cycle involves planning and drawing up the agenda and planning the meeting, the second is the meeting itself and the third includes the minutes, implementation of decisions, and following up on decisions or action. The follow-up becomes the first part of the planning for the next cycle.

Each stage in the cycle is essential, and is far easier if the stage before is properly done. As the cycle shows, a good meeting involves far more time beforehand than the meeting itself will take.

Another type of cycle involves listing all the meetings held by an organisation and ensuring they are in a logical relationship to each other. If the development subcommittee wants to take into account the views of project users, it does not make much sense to have the users' meeting the week after the subcommittee has met. If the finance subcommittee has to present a written report to the whole management committee, its meeting should be scheduled early enough for the report to be produced and sent out with the papers for the management committee meeting. An annual (or at least six-monthly) calendar of meetings is a great help, especially if it also includes deadlines for papers, sending out agendas and other essential tasks.

THE AGENDA

An agenda lets everyone know what is going to be covered at a particular meeting. If the agenda is distributed in advance, it gives people a chance to prepare for the meeting. Having an agenda means everyone, not just the person chairing the meeting, has responsibility for getting through all the business.

If an agenda is to be sent out it should be headed with the name of the organisation, the committee or group, the date, time and place of the meeting, and the agreed finishing time if there is one. An agenda for a general meeting, AGM or management committee meeting is the formal notice required under the organisation's constitution. It should, if the organisation is a company and/or charity, include the relevant registration numbers.

If the group has a rotating chair for meetings or a rotating minute-taker their names should be on the agenda. It should also indicate how to get an additional item onto the agenda, and whether there is a deadline for this.

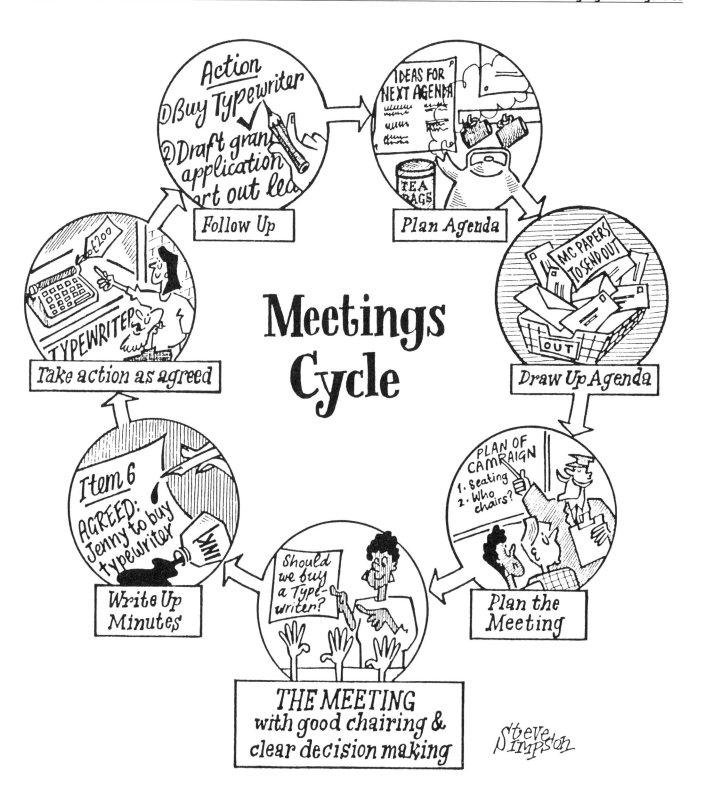

Meetings Cycle

In meetings which are primarily for reports rather than decision-making it may be appropriate to have a standard agenda which lists all the teams or groups which will report to the meeting, or the standard topics to be covered. This does not have to be sent out in advance but should be available beforehand to the person chairing the meeting.

If there is not enough money to send out agendas beforehand or if the group meets so frequently there is not enough time, the agenda should be available at the beginning of the meeting, either photocopied or written on a flipchart.

For staff or team meetings or users' meetings, one idea is to make a grid which can be photocopied onto A3 sheets, with nine or 12 squares labelled with the main types of items discussed at the meeting (for example 'users' activities', 'advice work', 'management committee matters', 'holidays, TOIL and other time off'). This should be pinned up somewhere very accessible, perhaps near the kettle or pigeonholes, and anyone who wants to can enter an item for discussion in the appropriate square. The grid itself can then be used as an agenda or as the basis for drawing up an agenda before the meeting.

A person who calls a meeting and draws up the agenda, but does not necessarily chair the meeting, is sometimes called a **convenor**.

Agenda format

It can be helpful to use a consistent agenda format, for example:

1. Apologies, welcome and agenda review
2. Minutes of last meeting
3. Matters arising not covered elsewhere on the agenda
4. Internal committee matters (new committee members etc)
5. Financial report
6. Funding and fundraising
7. Staff matters
8. Activities or issues specific to this organisation or meeting
9. Training
10. Future meetings (including chair and minute-taker for next meeting, if it rotates)
11. Any other business

An agenda like this tells participants broadly what topics will be covered, but does not give any idea of the specific items for the meeting. Agendas are far more useful if, under each main heading, items to be dealt with are detailed:

After-school and holiday activities

a. After-school club

b. Craft group

c. Swimming club

d. Easter playscheme

This makes it clearer **what** will be on the agenda, but participants still do not know **why** anything is there: for information, discussion, consultation, decision or review. Meetings are far easier to chair and participate in if the **why** is added, and if the agenda also indicates who will introduce the item:

8. After-school and holiday activities

    a. After-school club: report on current and future activities (Sarah).

    b. Craft group: report (Sarah).

    c. Swimming club: report on difficulties with Eastway Pool (Ali). Decision required on response to Eastway.

    d. Easter playscheme: initial proposals from staff (Narinder). Committee is asked to discuss these, make further proposals and decide priorities.

An agenda like this may seem unusual and awkward, but all it does is put onto paper information which already exists in the head of the chair, manager or other key person. With the information given to everyone attending the meeting, more people can understand what is happening and can participate. This is especially important if there are new or unconfident workers or committee members.

A detailed agenda also reduces the frustration caused when someone thinks a decision is going to be made but the meeting only discusses an item, or vice versa.

If a paper relevant to an agenda item has been previously circulated, is enclosed with the agenda or will be available at the meeting, this should be indicated next to the agenda item. It can be helpful to include at the end of the agenda a list of all papers enclosed.

Planning the agenda

An agenda can be drawn up by the person who will be chairing the meeting, the secretary, the manager or anyone who has a clear idea of what the meeting is about. It does not matter who does it, so long as everyone knows whose responsibility it is and how to get items onto the agenda.

Without a clear process for getting items onto the agenda it will be controlled by a particular person or group. Other people will feel they have no right to add items or will have to bring up everything under 'any other business'.

The person drawing up the agenda should go through the minutes of the last meeting, and include any items that need to be carried forward or reviewed. These should not just be left to come up under matters arising.

Staff, officers, chairs or convenors of subcommittees or working groups, and others involved in the group should be asked what they want included.

The **calendar of recurrent business** should be checked. (If the group or organisation does not have one, it should! These are items which come up regularly, for example preliminary plans for the annual general meeting, detailed plans for the AGM, report on the AGM, quarterly accounts, receiving the draft annual accounts, draft budget for next year, final budget for next year, responsibility for the annual report, plans for or reports on recurrent events such as a holiday playscheme.)

Items should be on the agenda in a logical order. There is no point talking about transporting the swimming club to a more distant pool if the group has not yet had the financial report.

Documentation for meetings

Much time in meetings is taken up with reports or background information that could be circulated beforehand, for people to read and consider in their own time. Chapter 6 explains how to prepare such reports; try to do this as much as possible. Clearly indicate on each paper what it is about and which agenda item it refers to, and on the agenda itself put 'Report enclosed' or 'Paper number X enclosed'.

Everyone attending a meeting should read the papers beforehand and make notes of any points they want to raise. People unable to attend should convey their comments in writing or ask an officer, staff person or group member to speak on their behalf.

If a paper cannot be provided until the meeting, **give people time to read it** before discussing the item. No one can concentrate on a discussion while they are reading.

PLANNING THE MEETING

Circulating the agenda

The agenda should be distributed in good time, not so far in advance that people lose it or many new items have to be added at the meeting, but not so late that people do not have time to read the background papers or get other necessary information.

If people need to bring anything with them, this should be clearly indicated. If the meeting is in an unfamiliar venue or there is a new member, instructions on how to get there should be included along with details of creche facilities, access arrangements for people with mobility difficulties and facilities for people with sight, hearing or language difficulties. If refreshments will be available, say so. If people need to indicate in advance that they will need a creche or special arrangements, be sure this is clear.

Timed agendas

Some agendas give an approximate (or even exact) timing for each item. Although this seems rigid it may be the only way to ensure the group can get through a very long or difficult agenda. Knowing why items are on the agenda and planning the time before the meeting means sensible decisions can be made about which items to cut short to allow enough time for the more important ones.

Timings should always be made in consultation with, or agreed by, the person who will chair the meeting. It can be a good idea to include the timings on the agenda itself so everyone shares responsibility for sticking to them, but some groups object to this. (Members may think a timed agenda means the chair or manager has predetermined the meeting.) If there is to be a timed agenda all members must know how to get items included, or a reasonable time must be allowed for matters raised at the meeting.

It is good practice to have a set finishing time or agree one at the beginning of the meeting. No one operates effectively at the end of a four-hour evening meeting.

In drawing up a timed agenda people usually find they need twice as much time as they actually have, especially if they are realistic about when the meeting will start and allow time for last-minute items that come up at the meeting. If there is not enough time for everything that needs to happen at the meeting, the possibilities are:

- shortening the time for some or all items;
- asking for written reports or background information to be distributed before the meeting, rather than having verbal reports at the meeting;
- deciding to carry some items over until the next meeting (but be sure there will be enough time at that meeting!);
- in future, delegating more responsibility to subcommittees or working parties so the meeting does not have to deal with so many issues, or does not have to deal with them in such depth.

'Any other business'

Having an open-ended 'any other business' (AOB) item at the end of the agenda makes it virtually impossible for the chair to ensure the meeting ends on time. It is much better:

- to have a clear procedure for all group members to get items included on the agenda, and allow *only* genuine emergency items (which could not have been predicted at the time the agenda was drawn up, and which need to be discussed at this meeting rather than the next one) to be added to the agenda at the meeting;
- or to require participants to give notice at the beginning of the meeting, during the agenda review, of any items they wish to bring up under AOB. This enables the chair to adjust the timings during the meeting to allow enough time for these additional items.

THE HOST ROLE

Someone must take responsibility for booking and paying for the room, getting it arranged, taking refreshments and necessary equipment to the venue, making or setting out the refreshments, getting all necessary papers and other documentation to the meeting, welcoming people (especially newcomers) as they arrive, and clearing up.

The room arrangement is important. Ideally, everyone should be able to see everyone else; if this is not possible they should at least be able to see the person who is chairing. Sitting around a table makes a meeting more formal which may be an advantage or disadvantage; it also makes it far easier to refer to papers and take notes which is definitely an advantage.

If a creche is provided, the creche workers should know how many children will be coming and what ages, and someone must take responsibility for getting toys and children's refreshments to the venue and being sure there is access to lavatories.

If people have special needs, for example help up the stairs or a position where they can see everyone in order to lip-read, these needs should be met without causing fuss or embarrassment.

Seeing to these practical details is sometimes called the **host** role and is just as important as drawing up the agenda, chairing the meeting or taking minutes.

CHAIRING A MEETING

A chair is responsible for getting the group through its business efficiently and effectively. A chair who genuinely wants to encourage participation will try to ensure everyone present takes responsibility for helping the meeting go smoothly, rather than encouraging dependence on the chair. It is more helpful if obstructive behaviour which disrupts the meeting and upsets people is seen as the responsibility of the perpetrators, rather than the responsibility of the chair. (Obviously if the perpetrators act obstructively, the chair has to intervene. But it is better if people do not act in obstructive ways in the first place.)

The chair has an obligation to know and understand the group's constitution, its aims and objectives, the relevant parts of its history, the basic financial situation, and the main current issues. In well run organisations and in those where the role of chair is rotated, everyone involved in meetings should have this knowledge.

The chair should be sure a proper agenda is drawn up, in consultation with the manager, other staff, officers, chairs or convenors of subcommittees or working groups, and others involved in the group. She or he should make the time to discuss with the secretary or relevant staff person what is on the agenda, why it is there, who will introduce each item and how long each item is likely to take. Without this awareness the chair will not know how to guide or end discussion. The chair must also be fully aware of any background information.

If a group refuses to get an agenda together beforehand, the chair will have to do all the planning in her or his head at the beginning of the meeting. This may work for small groups which do not have to deal with many issues, but in general it is not a satisfactory way to operate.

Openers

The chair, secretary, and person responsible for arranging the room should arrive at least 15 minutes before the meeting is due to start. The chair should ensure:

- there are no last minute major items for inclusion on the agenda, requiring revision of the agreed timings;

- the room is set up so everyone can see each other or at least see the person who is chairing;

- there is a flipchart or whiteboard if required;

- all necessary papers are available;

- someone will welcome people, especially newcomers, as they arrive;

- someone will take minutes.

At the beginning of the meeting the chair should:

- welcome people;

- introduce visitors or newcomers, if appropriate, or ask everyone to introduce themselves;

- ask for apologies for absence;

- briefly explain the agenda, saying which items will need decisions and which are for discussion or consultation;

- if appropriate ask if there are any other items for inclusion, and indicate whether they will be added to the main agenda or be covered under 'any other business';

- say when there will be a break and when the meeting is due to finish.

New items which do not fit under the agreed headings should be included under 'any other business' (AOB) or held over until the next meeting. A chair has the right to refuse to add new items, even under AOB, if the group has a clear procedure for getting items onto the agenda and this has not been followed. (This obviously does not apply to emergency issues which could not have been foreseen.)

The agenda is now a contract for the business which everyone at the meeting has agreed to get through. Any new items which come up should be held over until the next meeting. Allowing people to keep adding items

during a meeting makes it impossible for the chair and the group as a whole to take responsibility for getting through what has been agreed.

Getting through the business

The chair should briefly introduce each item, or introduce the person who will do so. If there is a timed agenda, the chair should indicate how much time has been allowed for the item.

At a meeting where people do not know each other, anyone who speaks should introduce herself or himself.

As far as possible discussion should be kept in the most helpful order: usually facts about the current situation and background first, then opinions and feelings, followed by broad ideas for action, firm proposals, and a decision if one is required. Too often a speaker presents solutions before most of the people at the meeting even know what the problem is!

If the chair (or anyone else) notices points that are unclear, names or initials some people might not understand, misunderstandings or other potential problems, these should be sorted out immediately. The chair should also ensure appropriate time is allowed for language interpretation, signing or other special provision.

The chair should summarise from time to time, especially if the discussion is complex. This is a skill; many people find it easier if they jot down notes of the main points as they are made.

Everyone who wants to should feel able to contribute. One way for the chair to encourage this without embarrassing people is to say 'We've heard a lot from some people, and not much from others. Would any of the rest of you like to add anything?'

A chair must separate her or his role as an individual from that of chair. A chair should spend most of the time listening, keeping the discussion moving, and summarising. If the chair contributes her or his own information or opinions, it should be clear that they are personal views, rather than summaries of the group's position. A chair who feels strongly about an issue or has a lot to say about it should not be chairing the discussion.

If the discussion is complex, the chair can ask someone to serve as a 'scribe' or 'recorder'. At the top of a flipchart or whiteboard the scribe defines the problem or issue, and writes up points as they arise in discussion, perhaps divided under headings like 'facts', 'opinions' and 'possible courses of action', or 'advantages' and 'disadvantages'. Having points written up helps people focus on what is being said, and helps the chair stop people repeating themselves, going over old ground, waffling or going off the point. It is also helpful for people who have difficulty hearing what is being said.

If the chair (or anyone else) refers to a point which is written up it should always be said in full. Never assume everyone can see or read what is there.

A chair must be both firm and sensitive, and not afraid to keep the discussion moving and to the point. This is much easier if everyone knows why the item is on the agenda. Interruptions, personal attacks, irrelevant information or opinions, time-wasting, domineering or aggressive behaviour should not be tolerated. A good chair can handle all of these without offending people, primarily by constantly reminding people what they are supposed to be discussing and working towards.

The chair should watch out for people who are being intimidated into silence or becoming frustrated, angry, fidgety or bored. She or he should not be afraid to defuse the discussion, ask those who have not spoken for their opinions, or call for a break. If absolutely necessary, the chair has the power to adjourn the meeting.

Remember to draw attention to points of agreement rather than disagreement, and encourage group members to build on them.

Using questions in meetings

A good chair can use questions to keep a meeting moving in a focused way. There are several types.

- Question addressed to whole group, to get information: 'Does anyone have experience of this sort of problem?'

- Question addressed to the whole group, to elicit possible courses of action or solutions: 'Does anyone have ideas about how we could deal with this?'

- A question relayed to the whole group, referring to a point made or question asked by a member of the group: 'That's a difficult question [or point]. How would the rest of you deal with it?'

- A question directed at a named individual, to get information or elicit possible solutions, perhaps drawing on expertise or just trying to draw out a quieter member: 'Sajida, how did your group set up its library reference system?' 'Robin, do you have any ideas how we could repair the steps without calling in a builder?' This type of question should always start with the person's name, so she or he actually listens to it.

- For people who are troublesome or keep going on about what is wrong, give the problem back to them. Ask them how they would deal with the situation or how they would answer their question: 'We understand that you're concerned about the late-night noise. What do you think would be the best way for us to deal with it?'

Ending the discussion

One advantage of timed agendas is that the chair can more easily bring discussion to an end, by saying 'We need to move on now, or we won't have time for the rest of the agenda'. If the discussion really does require more time, because people are bringing up new points rather than simply restating what has already been said, the chair can decide (or ask consent from the meeting) to extend the time allowed for this item. A decision will then need to be made about whether to shorten the time allowed for other items, extend the finishing time for the meeting, or carry some items over to the next meeting.

Before ending any discussion the chair must try to ensure that all relevant points have been aired and people understand the issues and implications. The chair must summarise, and explain any action which will be taken to follow up the discussion.

Decision-making

If a decision has to be made about an item, the chair must be sure this happens. Everyone should have the necessary information (see chapter 4), and before asking for a decision the chair or speaker should summarise the main points of the discussion, explain the possible courses of action, and state very clearly what people are being asked to decide.

Proposing and seconding

For legal business, and often for ordinary business as well, a **proposer** puts forward a **proposal** or **motion,** which is then **seconded** by someone else. If no one will second it, the motion is dropped. **Amendments** to the motion may then be proposed and seconded. A vote is taken first on each amendment separately, then on the motion (as amended, if any amendments have been agreed). If the motion is passed it becomes a **resolution.**

In meetings which operate informally there will not usually be motions and seconding. The chair will summarise what appears to be the majority position or a position which incorporates differing views, and will ask for a decision by consensus or voting.

Consensus

If the group operates by consensus the chair should indicate the proposal or a combination of proposals which most people seem to favour and ask if everyone is willing to go along with that option. As indicated in chapter 4, consensus does not necessarily mean everyone agrees with a decision; it means everyone agrees to go along with it. The chair should ask people who do not like that choice for their reasons and what would have to be adapted in order for them to accept it, but should not spend endless time looking for 100 per cent agreement. In any decision where people have strong opinions, some will inevitably be disappointed. (It might help to read chapter 18, 'Managing differences and conflict'.)

Voting

The chair should call for a vote if this is the group's decision-making method. Know beforehand whether the chair can vote. In some organisations the chair does not vote unless there is a tie; in others the chair has a vote, plus a second (casting) vote in case of a tie. (If the constitution is not clear on this point, make a rule and keep it with the constitution.)

The organisation's constitution should indicate whether votes require a majority of **members present** or **members present and voting** to be carried. (Imagine a situation with 25 members present. If 10 vote in favour, eight vote against and seven abstain, the motion is carried if only members present and voting are included, but is not carried if a majority of all members present is required.) If the constitution says nothing to the contrary, a vote is carried if it has a majority of those present and voting.

There are several types of vote.

- **On the nod**: when there appears to be no opposition the chair simply asks 'All in favour?' 'Anyone against?' and assumes the proposal is accepted if no one disagrees. It is important to ask if anyone is opposed. If anyone dissents the chair can call for a vote, or can extend the discussion to try to reach a consensus decision.

- **Acclamation**: asking those in favour to say 'aye' and then those opposed to say 'no'. This only works if there is a clear majority.

- **Show of hands**: asking people to vote by raising their hand, first those in favour, then those opposed, then those abstaining (not voting). In a large group or where the vote is very close or the issue is very controversial, votes should be counted by at least two people.

- **Card vote**: if only some people present are entitled to vote, they might be required to hold up a card in a show of hands vote.

- **Recorded vote**: any member who wishes to be disassociated from a decision (see the section on limiting the liability of committee members in chapter 2) may call for a recorded vote. The name of every member present is called, the member indicates whether voting for or against or abstaining, and each person's vote is recorded and minuted against their name.

- **Poll**: a written vote, either on a printed ballot or a blank paper.

Announcing the decision

For a decision made 'on the nod' or by acclamation, the chair will simply say 'the motion is carried' or 'it has been agreed to ...' If everyone voted in favour, the chair might add 'unanimously'; if no one voted against but there were abstentions the chair might add 'nem con' (*nemo contra:* no one against). For a recorded vote or poll the chair usually announces the number of votes in favour and against and the number of abstentions. For a show of hands or card vote the chair can either simply say the motion has been carried, or can give numbers of votes for and against. When voting for people (for example, electing officers) the numbers are often not announced, in order to avoid embarrassment for the losers.

The minute-taker should record the vote as announced by the chair.

Regardless of how the decision is made, everyone at the meeting should be clear about exactly what has been decided, who will do it, when it will be done, and how it will be reviewed. The chair must ensure all this is clearly stated and minuted.

One of the major causes of unhappiness and frustration in organisations arises from a meeting making a decision without being clear who will do the work. 'We' do not do things; work is done by named individuals acting either on their own or with others. Decisions should never be left that 'we' will do something, or 'it was agreed' to do something. Be explicit about *what* needs to be done, and *who* will do it. If no one is willing or able to take it on, it cannot be done – or it will be done by someone who is likely to feel overworked and martyred. (See chapter 19, on stress and burnout, for what happens in this situation.)

Ending the meeting

At the end of the meeting, the chair should summarise what has happened, major decisions made and actions agreed, and ensure everyone is clear about what they have to do, when and where the next meeting is, how to get items on the agenda, and who will act as chair and minute-taker if those roles rotate. People should be thanked for coming.

PARTICIPATING IN MEETINGS

Much homage is paid in the voluntary sector to participation by users or members, and to the sharing of power and responsibility. But it is very difficult for people to participate in meetings if all information is hogged by the chair, secretary, manager, staff representative or a small clique, and if all power rests with those few individuals.

Elected officers or staff who hold formal power should think seriously about what that power means to them, and whether they are misusing it by trying to control rather than *guide* the organisation.

One key to sharing power is to share information. This does not mean overburdening every member by giving them every bit of paper that comes into the organisation. It does mean individuals with access to information have a responsibility to sift through it and ensure members get what they need in order to be informed participants.

For those who are new to meetings or lack confidence, and for experienced meeting-goers who may not be quite as wonderful in meetings as they think they are, here are a few pointers for good participation.

- **Learn** about the issue being discussed. Read minutes from previous meetings and papers circulated for this meeting. Talk to people.

- **Listen** to other people during the meeting. Pick up on what they are saying, instead of constantly thinking of your rejoinder or barging in with your own ideas or opinions.

- **Think** before you open your mouth. If necessary make notes of what you want to say.

- **Speak** clearly and to the point. Be assertive (clear about what you want to say) without being obnoxious, aggressive or manipulative.

- **Do not be afraid to speak.** The worst that can happen is that you will be made to feel silly or stupid by ignorant, rude people. The best is that others who have less confidence than you will welcome your speaking up and gain confidence and strength from your comments.

- **Be reasonable.** Despite what you think, yours is not the only valid point of view. Do not put people down, try to score points or throw tantrums. Treat other people as you would like to be treated. Let them have their say, even if they are criticising or misunderstanding you, without constantly interrupting. Make notes of the points you want to come back to.

- **Let go.** Even if you are 100 per cent sure the group is making a wrong decision, in the end you may have to let them do it. Everyone makes mistakes, and hopefully the group will learn from theirs. (And refrain from playing the 'Nya nya I told you so' game if it does turn out to be a disastrous decision.)

Frankly, I think the Committee are taking this BRIGHTER MEETINGS thing a bit too far...

TAKING AND USING MINUTES

Minutes are a record of what has happened at a business meeting. This might be a staff meeting, team or project meeting, management committee meeting, users' meeting, annual general meeting, or working group or subcommittee meeting. For meetings which have a legal status (for example AGMs, management committee meetings or meetings of formal subcommittees) the minutes are a legal record of the organisation's business.

Why take minutes?

Minutes are for people who were not at a meeting as well as for those who were present but were not paying attention or need reminding about what happened, and for people who in future need or want to know what the group has done.

Minutes are used to find out:

● what was decided;

● why it was decided;

● what else was reported or discussed;

● what action the reader is supposed to take, and when;

● what action others are supposed to take, and when.

A minute-taker must record information, the main points of the discussion and any decisions accurately and clearly,

and in such a way that everything can be easily located and understood if someone has to refer back to it.

The minute-taker should know the group's purpose, who the members are, who gets the minutes and how they will be used. Discussing the agenda with the chair or other key person before the meeting makes the task of minute-taking much easier.

What to include

Minutes should include:

● the name of the organisation;

● a description of the meeting (for example management committee, staff, equal opportunities working group);

● the date (including the year) of the meeting;

● place of the meeting (if it was held because it had to be under legislation or the organisation's constitution);

● members present;

● other people present and in what capacity (for example as staff, observer, visitor);

● who chaired and took minutes;

● apologies for absence;

● corrections, if any, to minutes of the previous meeting, and the fact that the (corrected, if necessary) minutes were accepted as an accurate record;

- matters arising from the previous minutes, not covered elsewhere;
- a separate minute for each item or topic covered at this meeting;
- date, time and place of the next meeting, and who will chair and minute if this rotates.

A **minute** is a record of what the meeting discussed and decided about a particular topic. It must include:

- any decision reached by the meeting (including a decision not to make a decision);
- action required to implement the decision;
- who will take the action;
- any deadline or time limit for the action.

If it is a formal meeting, for example an AGM, or if legal business is being transacted the minute must also include:

- the full text of any motions and amendments;
- names of proposer and seconder for each motion;
- result of votes, as announced by the person chairing the meeting.

For all items the minute-taker has to decide:

- how much background information to include;
- how much of the discussion should be recorded;
- whether it should be recorded in detail or can be summarised;
- whether to attribute comments to named individuals.

There are no rules about how much or how little to include. The decision depends on who will use the minutes, what they need to know, and what they already know. Each group should, however, aim for consistency in minutes.

The best way to decide how much to include is for the minute-taker to ask herself or himself, 'If I wasn't at this meeting, what would I need to know? What would I also want to know?' It is usually not necessary to record every piece of information reported to the meeting, or every point made in a discussion. But only the minute-taker can decide. In cases of uncertainty, the minute-taker should ask the chair for guidance.

What *is* essential is to record decisions, major factors leading to decisions and what needs to be done.

If a report has been circulated with the agenda or will be attached to the minutes it can simply be referred to and briefly summarised in the minutes: 'The training report (attached) was noted' or 'The admin worker's report (circulated with the agenda) was accepted with appreciation'. It is essential to ensure everyone, including people who were not at the meeting, gets the report.

For complex discussions a good approach is to write something like 'Among the points raised in the discussion were ...' and then to summarise them. If items are on the agenda for consultation the minutes should include a summary of ideas and clearly indicate any which this meeting has agreed should be put forward.

Each minute should be self-contained. It should explicitly

record each decision ('It was agreed ...' or 'It was decided ...') and any action agreed to implement the decision.

Minutes should be impartial and factual. They should not include judgmental words or remark on people's emotions.

Initials, first names only and jargon should not be used unless it is certain everyone who uses the minutes, now and in future, will understand them.

If the situation has changed since the meeting, the minutes should nonetheless reflect what actually happened at the meeting. A note in square brackets can be added to the item to indicate what has happened since ['Since the meeting, James Franklin has been appointed and will start work on 1 June'].

A **report** is a less formal record of what happened at a meeting, covering points relevant to the people for whom the report is intended. A report might, in appropriate circumstances, give the writer's opinions of what happened and might comment on emotions and attitudes.

Identifying separate minutes

If the group or organisation has a consistent agenda format it is easy to develop a linked format for minutes, using the agenda headings as the main headings in the minutes and individual items under each agenda heading as subheadings.

Items in one meeting's minutes can then easily be slotted into the agenda for the next meeting, if they need to be reviewed or if discussion needs to continue.

Numbering the minutes makes it easier to refer back to them, but the system should not be so cumbersome that it is more of a hindrance than a help. There are several easy systems:

- using a standardised numbering system for the agenda and minutes and using the same numbers all the time even if there is nothing to record at a particular number (so number 5, for example, is always financial report, and number 6 is always funding and fundraising);
- numbering from 1 to the end for each meeting;
- numbering from 1 to the end for each meeting, but adding a prefix for each meeting (so for the third meeting in 1993, for example, each minute would have the prefix 93.3);
- numbering from 1 to the end for each year;
- numbering from 1 to the end for each year, but with a prefix for the year (so all minutes in 1993 would have the prefix 93).

Regardless of whether a numbering system is used, each minute should be clearly identified with a brief heading which is underlined, put in bold or put in capital letters. Clearly separate items with a space.

During the meeting

If the minutes are to be written or typed afterwards, the minute-taker takes **notes** during the meeting. But if the minutes are going direct into a minute book, without being written up later, the minute-taker has to be much tidier at this stage and must pay much more attention to layout and presentation.

When taking notes or minutes during the meeting it is essential to understand what is being discussed and try to focus on the main points of the discussion. A minute-taker who does not understand what is going on, cannot hear or is unclear about what has been decided should **ask.** If the minute-taker does not know, other people probably do not know either.

For any decision be sure the notes include what was agreed, what action is required, who will do it, whether there is a deadline, and whether it will be reviewed. A minute-taker who is unsure what has been decided should ask the chair to summarise, or should read out her or his notes and ask the meeting to confirm they are accurate.

When taking notes or minutes during the meeting use headings and subheadings to keep items separate. Leave a few lines between each item, to make it easier to add further points if they come up later in the meeting (and to prevent having to face page after page of unbroken scrawl when the time comes to write up the minutes).

One idea when taking notes is to use a column on the left-hand side of the sheet to star particularly important points and to indicate the initials or name of the person who made each point.

Speedwriting, shorthand or made-up abbreviations can help in note-taking, but notes must be comprehensible and unambiguous. Writing 'Pl bg tv vid conf' may save a lot of time, but there is a big difference between 'Polly will arrange to bring a television and video for the conference' and 'Paulo said we must have a big TV, rather than a small one, if we are going to show the video at the conference'. The minutes themselves must not include speedwriting, shorthand or idiosyncratic abbreviations.

Notes or handwritten minutes must also be as legible as possible. There is a big difference between 'Our financial position means that we can *now* hire an additional clerical worker' and 'Our financial position means that we can *not* hire an additional clerical worker'.

A tape recorder can provide a back-up but should not be used as a replacement for note-taking. The tape recorder will pick up traffic and other background noise, and may not pick up the voices of people who speak softly or are in a corner of the room. It is also quite demoralising to have to listen to a whole meeting again!

Simple minutes

For staff meetings or other small groups where people are in regular contact with each other, but need a record of what was agreed at the meeting, it may be adequate to use a very simple column format with headings 'Topic' 'Main points' 'Decision' 'Who' and 'When'. The columns can be filled in during the meeting.

Confidential items

If an item is considered confidential the chair should state this clearly and indicate what the minute-taker should do. In some cases the chair will keep notes of confidential items; in other cases the minute-taker will be asked to minute the item but give the final version to the chair or someone else rather than including it in the circulated minutes.

Even if an item is confidential, notes or minutes should always be taken. After the meeting they should be kept in an appropriate place. The chair should indicate where, and who should have access to them.

Items considered confidential might include, for example, details of a worker's illness or personal situation, details of rent arrears of an individual resident, difficulties of an individual client or user, or delicate negotiations relating to a lease.

The chair should ensure everyone at the meeting is aware the item is confidential and what this means.

Writing up notes

Immediately after a meeting, the minute-taker should go through the notes with a highlighter pen, marking the most important points to include in the minutes.

Allow enough time for writing up the minutes. Writing up summary minutes can take up to half as long as the meeting; detailed minutes can take as long as the meeting. Verbatim minutes take a minimum of two to three times the length of the meeting if the minute-taker is working from notes or speedwriting, and three to four times if working from tapes.

Minutes should be written up as soon as possible after the meeting. Notes should be kept until after the minutes have been approved at the next meeting, in case there are any queries.

If the notes are not clear, the minute-taker should write down what she or he thinks happened, then ask the chair's opinion. If the chair and minute-taker agree, it is probably accurate. If they disagree, at least two other people should be asked.

Minutes are easier to use if they highlight **who** is supposed to take action:

● underline her or his name in the minutes;

● or have a separate column with the person's name or initials;

● or have an 'action' line or paragraph (set off in some way – indented or in bold or italic) at the end of each item which summarises action and who is to take it;

● or have a separate action sheet at the end of the minutes which lists all the actions and who is to do them. (The advantage of this is that it can be referred to separately from the minutes.)

Number the pages. It is a good idea also to put the date of the meeting at the top of the second and every subsequent page, in case the pages get separated.

It is also a good idea to include at the end of the minutes a list of all papers and reports circulated before or at the meeting. This helps people keep all relevant papers together with the minutes, and enables them to ask for any documents they missed (perhaps because they missed the meeting when the papers were circulated).

Minutes should always indicate who took the minutes (name or initials at the end, or an indication in the list of people present at the beginning of the minutes). This is helpful if there are questions in future about what a particular item means, or if the handwriting is hard to read.

Circulating and using the minutes

Minutes should be circulated as quickly as possible. This helps people who were not at the meeting keep up to date with what is happening, and reminds people of what needs doing. Any documents which were distributed at the meeting should be sent to people who were not there.

The person drawing up the agenda for the next meeting should use these minutes as a starting point. Items which need carrying over for review or for further discussion should have their own place on the agenda, under the appropriate section. It is not good practice to lump them all together under matters arising just because they were all discussed at the previous meeting.

Signing the minutes as a true record

At the next meeting members who were at the previous meeting have to agree the minutes are an accurate record of what was discussed and decided. Only factual points can be changed; this is not the time to reopen discussion. Any corrections are added to the official copy of the minutes (the one which will be signed and kept in the minutes book). The changes should also be noted in the minutes of the present meeting.

When the minutes are corrected and agreed, the chair of the present meeting signs them. This person does not need to have been at the previous meeting, because she or he is signing on behalf of the members who were there.

The signed copies of the minutes should be kept in a safe place in a binder clearly labelled 'Minutes Book'. They are a permanent and legal record of the organisation's business and should be treated in the same way as other legal documents.

All members of a group have the right to see minutes of that group's meetings. So all members of an organisation have the right to see minutes of the AGM and other general meetings; all members of a management committee have the right to see management committee minutes; all members of the finance subcommittee have the right to see minutes of finance subcommittee meetings. An AGM or management committee meeting might insist that its members have the right to see minutes of any subcommittees or working groups which it sets up.

Organisations should have rules about whether other people are also entitled to see minutes. It is good practice to allow all members of an organisation to see minutes of all committees and subcommittees if they ask to. The only exceptions should be minutes relating to individual staff members or users and other confidential items.

Chapter 6:

Managing communication and reports

Communication is an essential part of good management, especially in complex organisations where information must be conveyed among staff, between workers and managers, and between staff and the management committee.

Sometimes a brief conversation or short memo will be adequate; at other times a long and complex document might be required. Regardless of the complexity of the issue or the amount of information involved, the process of presenting it in a usable form is exactly the same.

This chapter looks at:

- ways to ensure effective communication;
- the purpose of various types of reports;
- how to structure and organise a report;
- how to encourage people to read written reports;
- verbal reports;
- annual reports.

EFFECTIVE COMMUNICATION

We communicate all the time: verbally, with gestures and body language, in writing. There are remarkable similarities in the ways people communicate, as well as significant differences rooted in culture, gender, age, education, self-confidence and perception of the environment in which the communication occurs.

Good communication, whether simple or complex, starts with absolute clarity about:

- the purpose of the communication;
- what (if anything) you want people to do as a result of the communication;
- to whom the communication has to go;
- the information you think they need in order to fulfil the purpose of the communication;
- the information they will think they need;
- how much they need to know (anything from a summary of the main points through to full details);
- additional information you would like to give to them, or they might want;
- the most effective medium for the communication;
- possible misunderstandings about the content or nature of the communication.

Effective communication depends on the right people getting the right information, in the right form, at the right time.

Communication also depends on people's willingness to receive the communication: to hear what is said or to read what is written. Many people will absorb information or an idea or opinion only if it reinforces what they already know or believe. Good communication is a two-way process of giving, receiving and responding which can occur only within an organisational culture which encourages listening, openness to new ideas and willingness to change.

PURPOSES OF COMMUNICATION

The form and content of the communication will depend to a large extent on its purpose, so the starting point is always to ask **Why am I communicating?** A single communication may have one purpose, or several:

- **Information**: to tell people what has happened or is going to happen, or to explain an issue. No action is expected.
- **Questioning**: to get information from other people.
- **Persuasion**: to influence the way people think or what they believe. This is usually linked to a desired action or decision.
- **Action**: to ask or tell people to do something. The communication must include enough information so people are aware of whether they are being asked to do something, and therefore have a choice about whether to do it or not, or whether they are required to do it. It must also be clear about what is being requested or required, and why, when and how it is to be done.
- **Background for discussion or consultation**: to enable people to participate fully in a discussion about an issue. The communication must indicate the purpose of the discussion/consultation, and give enough information so people can participate.
- **Background for decision**: to enable people to come to a decision. The communication must indicate the nature of the decision to be made, and give enough information so people can consider the issues fully and then make a decision. It might include proposals or a recommendation, or might leave the options open.
- **Confirmation**: to confirm something already discussed or agreed.
- **Historical record**: to ensure people in future have a record of what happened and why.

Regardless of the purpose, the communicator should always aim to keep the message short, clear, logical and to the point. So the second question is always **What does the reader or listener need to know to fulfil this purpose?** Provide enough information to meet this need, without providing so much that people get overwhelmed or lost in detail.

There is then another question: **Is there anything else they would like to know?** This additional information should be included only if there is a legitimate justification, and only if it does not distract from the primary purpose(s) of the communication.

Choosing the right medium

There is no right way to communicate. The most appropriate medium will depend on what is being communicated and why, how many people are being communicated with, the need for instant response, the complexity of the information and the relationship between the people doing the communicating.

The simplest communications are verbal. These may be face to face, by telephone, in an informal meeting or in a formal meeting. Verbal communications allow instant response, and any misunderstandings can, if they are recognised, be clarified immediately. But there is great potential for later disagreement about what was said, intended or agreed.

With written communications such as memos, letters, short papers or detailed reports there is less scope for later disagreement about what was communicated. And if a number of people need to be contacted, written communication ensures they all get the same information in the same way. There is, however, no guarantee they will actually read it.

Information involving complex numbers, finance or other detail should nearly always be put in writing.

Sometimes it will be most effective to communicate verbally and back it up with written information or a written confirmation of what was said; at other times it will be most effective for the initial communication to be written, with opportunities for discussion and questions.

Graphic communications such as charts, graphs and illustrations can help people understand complex information, but if not sensibly devised may make complicated details even more obscure.

Staff reports

In voluntary organisations it is common for the manager and/or individual staff to make regular reports to a staff meeting or to the committee about what they have been doing. These are often presented with little attention to the questions posed above. What is the purpose of these reports? To keep others informed of the work being done, to monitor progress against agreed objectives, to get advice or decisions on how to proceed, to get personal support for a difficult task? Are such reports best presented verbally, or is it more effective to put them in writing, distribute them beforehand and use the time at the meeting for questions and discussion?

One format for such reports, whether verbal or written, is to have headings for each area of work, with each section containing a brief summary of what the worker expected to do since the last report, what has actually been done, and priorities for the period until the next report. This keeps others aware of what is being done, how the work is developing, and whether backlog is building up. It can make it easier for the worker to say 'no' if new work is being piled on (or to ask the meeting to reset priorities, if there is simply not enough time for existing work and the new work).

Such reports can be made more interesting by starting with 'two things I'm really pleased about since the last report' and 'two things I'm concerned about'. This helps the staff meeting or committee not only to remain informed about the work itself, but also to be aware of underlying issues, which in turn can help colleagues and committee be more supportive.

Reports of this type should be short. In most cases people do not need to know every detail of the work; an overview is adequate.

If specific points in the report need discussion or decision, these should be very clearly indicated (see below).

A long complex report about a variety of topics (covering, for example, premises, personnel issues and service issues) will be easier to absorb and understand if it is divided into a number of short reports, each indicating the decisions which need to be made.

Officers' and subgroup reports

Officers, subcommittees and working groups which meet or take action between meetings of the main committee should also report to the main committee. The basic guidelines are the same as for staff reports.

STRUCTURING A WRITTEN REPORT

The question here is **How can I present the information in a logical way?** A report or other formal communication should have a **beginning** (an explanation of what it is about and why it is being given), **middle** (detailed information in a clear order) and **end** (a summary of the information and a clear indication of what, if anything, the reader or listener is supposed to do with it).

Although reports vary considerably depending on their status and why the information is being presented, a general structure for a written report is:

● **Heading.** This includes heading or title, date and author (individual or group), and may also indicate the individuals or groups for whom the report is intended. If the paper is a draft, indicate the draft number. If it is to be discussed at a meeting, indicate the date of the meeting and whether the paper is for general discussion, consultation or decision. If there are several papers for the meeting give each one a reference number, perhaps linked to the agenda number (see chapter 5).

● **Introduction.** This is a brief statement of what the report is about, why it was written, who wrote it, the main issues and what action, if any, is required.

- **Background.** What led up to the problem or situation.

- **The present situation.** Facts and opinions, clearly separated.

- **Implications for the future.** Again, facts and opinions, clearly separated. The implications might include financial, legal, staffing, premises, time, or the effect on other activities.

- **Summary.** Brief restatement of the main points.

- **Proposal(s) for action.** These should be included only if it is appropriate for the person or group presenting the report to make proposals. Advantages and disadvantages of each proposal should be included. If it is appropriate for the person or group to recommend a specific course of action, this should be included here.

Reports presented to a committee or other group should have a final section headed **Action.** If the report is simply for information, the section can say 'This report is for information only; no action is required.' This is a signal to the chair and members that the report might require some time for questions or clarification, but does not need detailed discussion or any decisions. Or the section can say something like:

1. To decide whether to do anything about ..., or to wait before taking a decision.

2. If a decision is made to take action, to decide what needs to be done to implement it.

3. To decide who should do it, and to whom they are responsible.

4. To set a deadline for the action.

Note that if a decision is required, it is usually appropriate to say the committee or group must decide *whether to do* something. This keeps the authority to make decisions with the committee, rather than with the writer of the report. Saying the committee or group must decide *to do* something implies that the writer has already taken the decision and the group is only rubber-stamping it.

There are, however, some situations in which the 'action required' will be to confirm or ratify a decision legitimately made elsewhere, but needing final approval by the committee. An example is 'to confirm the decision made by the interviewing panel to hire Elana Chowdhury'.

Chapter 5 provides more ideas about how to provide information for effective use at meetings.

Organising the information

An outline helps the writer present information in a logical order. Similarly, subheadings and a numbering system can help readers understand that order, and can also help people refer to specific parts of the report in discussion.

Subheadings should be in bold or capital letters and should be used to separate sections or topics. These might be, for example, 'Background' 'Current situation' 'Options' 'Recommendation' 'Action'; or 'Drop-in sessions' 'Casework' 'Admin' 'Liaison with other organisations' 'Action'. Subheadings break up the text, make it easier for the reader to know what is being written about, and make it more likely that the report will be presented in a logical order.

If numbering systems are used, the most common are alpha-numeric, decimal or sequential.

Alpha-numeric systems use numbers and letters to divide and subdivide sections. A simple system uses only arabic numerals and small letters (1.a,b,c; 2.a,b,c,d,e); more complex systems may use roman numerals, capital letters, arabic numerals, small letters and small roman numerals (I.A.1.a.i). The system might be made even more complex by having some of the characters in brackets.

Alpha-numeric systems can provide several levels of information, but can be confusing in a document with many subsections. They can also be confusing when referring to sections in a discussion; try making sense out loud of III.G.3.g.(iii).

When using an alpha-numeric system it is important to be consistent throughout the document. The best way is to draw up an outline setting out each numbered or lettered section.

A **decimal** system is similar to an alpha-numeric system, but only uses numbers. Theoretically it can be used for any number of subsections, but something numbered 202.3.22.78.6 indicates a certain lack of care in planning the document. In most cases it is best not to go beyond two or three decimal points.

Sequential numbering starts at 1 and numbers every paragraph straight through to the end. This does not give any sense of how various parts of the report fit together, but it does make it very easy to refer to specific paragraphs in discussion. It is therefore usually the best system for draft documents or other papers that are going to be discussed in detail.

If the paper is likely to be very controversial or require very detailed discussion, it can be useful to number every line.

Encouraging people to read reports

There is no point producing a beautifully argued report if no one reads or pays attention to it. So:

- use dry transfer lettering ('letraset'), a headline machine, a word processor, desktop publishing or an enlargement photocopier to create a big, eye-catching heading for written reports;

- create an attractive presentation: margins, space between paragraphs, subheadings, a clear numbering system (if one is being used), a good ribbon on the typewriter or word processor or clear black ink (not ballpoint) for anything handwritten, good quality photocopying or printing on good quality paper;

- make readers feel their views are important and there is a reason for them to pay attention to the report, by stating clearly at the beginning what it is about and stating clearly at the end what readers are expected to do;

- use language people can understand, avoiding (or explaining) jargon, abbreviations and technical terms;

- if appropriate put complicated details in an appendix, so people can choose whether to read them;

- use charts or illustrations if they will make it easier for people to understand and absorb the information;

- use examples if they will not distract from the main issues, but be clear they are examples and not proposals;

- put examples, case studies, quotes or other illustrative material in boxes, to draw attention to them and also to keep them from interfering with the smooth flow of the text;

- send out written reports in good time so people can read them before the meeting;

- if the paper must be distributed at a meeting give people time to read it, or summarise the main points before starting the discussion.

An excellent guide to making written materials look good is *Design for Desktop Publishing: A guide to layout and typography on the personal computer* by John Miles (John Taylor Book Ventures, 1988; 112 pages; ISBN 1 871224 07 1; £12.95 from Spa Books, PO Box 47, Stevenage, Herts SG2 8UH). Although specifically for people moving into desktop publishing, this is one of the best basic guides to designing printed materials such as reports, newsletters and leaflets even on a clapped-out typewriter.

VERBAL REPORTS

Verbal reports should be prepared just as carefully as written reports. An outline is essential, so listeners can follow a logical pattern of information and analysis. As with written reports the beginning should include a clear statement of why the report is being given and what, if anything, listeners are expected to do with the information.

Anecdotes can be amusing but should not distract attention from the purpose of the report.

Complicated information such as financial data should be presented on a handout, flipchart or overhead projector. Remember that people reading a handout cannot simultaneously listen to a speaker.

It can be very helpful to give copies of the report beforehand to the person chairing the meeting and the minute-taker.

A speaker who is unaccustomed to giving verbal reports may find it helpful to practise first in front of a mirror to improve the style of presentation.

ANNUAL REPORTS

An annual report is a review of what the organisation has done in a one-year period, plus a financial report (usually the audited annual accounts) for the period. The annual report usually covers the financial year but might cover a different period, for example a calendar year. The report might also include plans for the next year.

Clarifying the purpose

The procedure for putting together an annual report is the same as for any complex report. Start by looking at the purposes, which might be any or all of the following:

- to inform members, users, funders about what the organisation has done;

- to acknowledge contributions to the organisation (time, money, skills);

- to impress current funders or donors, and encourage them to give more money;

- to impress potential funders or donors, and encourage them to start giving money;

- as a promotional document, to attract more members, users, supporters or volunteers;

- to inform other organisations or agencies what the organisation does;

- to inform the public (people who do not have any direct link with the organisation) what it does;

- to fulfil the legal requirement for companies and charities to produce an annual report on their activities.

The first two purposes are primarily internal. An annual report which only needs to fulfil these purposes can be a simple document with nothing fancy.

The next four purposes (to reach current or potential funders and donors, to get more people involved, or to inform other agencies) seek to create or generate an external or public image for the organisation, with a view towards achieving specific objectives. The content and presentation will have to be tailored to these purposes, with much more background information about the organisation and its objectives. The chatty four-page photocopied annual report which is quite suitable as an internal report is likely to be totally inappropriate as a public relations document.

Informing 'the public' is very difficult as an objective. It is much better to break it down into specific publics and decide what each one needs to know and why.

Although organisations which are registered as companies and charities must produce an annual 'report of the directors' or 'report of the trustees', this does not have to be a detailed report on activities. A short report indicating the broad nature of the organisation's activities is adequate. This is usually in a specified form which the organisation's auditor will know.

How glossy?

As community groups and voluntary organisations become more professional in their work and in the image they seek to present, and as they compete for the attention of funders and donors, there may be pressure to produce glossy, expensive annual reports. But at the same time some funders and donors, as well as the organisation's users or members, may be put off by a report which is inappropriately glossy or which gives the impression of having used vast amounts of the organisation's scarce resources.

Each organisation will need to decide for itself what sort of annual report to produce. The decision will be influenced by:

- whether the primary purposes of the report are internal (for members and users) or external (for funders, donors, potential members or users);

- how many copies will be produced;
- the image the organisation wants to project;
- whether the organisation has easy and inexpensive access to designers, photographers, word processing, desktop publishing or typesetting, good quality photo-copying or printing;
- how much money is available.

It can be helpful to look critically at annual reports from other organisations and think about the kind of image they give, and why such an image would or would not be appropriate for your organisation.

Even an inexpensive annual report can be greatly improved with an attractive cover, big headings, illustrations and simple charts. At the other extreme, even a very expensive report can be ruined by poor design or overly complex charts.

Contents

Just as there is great choice about how the report will look, so there is choice about what to include. The outline given here is standard and can be adapted in dozens of ways:

- guide to contents;
- introduction (usually by the chair) summarising the highlights and main changes during the year;
- what the organisation is, why it exists (its objects), who the members are, who uses it;
- the work of the organisation, divided logically by type of work, type of user, geographical area or chronologically; with each section covering what the organisation wanted to achieve during the year, what it actually achieved, and main plans for the future;
- case studies (real or composite), photos, drawings, charts, graphs, copies of posters or leaflets produced during the year, or other illustrations (note that photographs or drawings of people or case studies of individuals should not be used without their permission);
- liaison and work outside the organisation;
- who manages the organisation (management committee and subgroup structure and members, including members who left during the year);
- who does the work of the organisation (staff and volunteer structure and names, including those who left during the year);
- treasurer's report summarising where the money for the year came from and what it was spent on, with the annual accounts;
- acknowledgement of funders and major donors;
- acknowledgement of major non-financial contributors, for example people who have given time, materials, publicity, use of premises etc;
- and don't forget the organisation's addresses, phone and fax numbers, and its charity and/or company numbers.

The process

Producing an annual report, especially one that will be used as a public relations document, is a big task and should not be left to one person. The usual process is:

- appoint an annual report editor (and small working group, if required);
- editor draws up outline and proposed format;
- working group or management committee decides how many copies should be printed, approves outline and format, decides roughly how long each section should be, suggests ideas for the main points to include in each section, suggests illustrations, sets deadline for text and illustrations, and assigns responsibility for writing, drawing and taking photos;
- editor notifies writers, illustrators and photographers and makes sure they know their deadlines;
- designer is appointed and briefed (this might be someone from within the organisation, or a professional from outside);
- editor gets quotes from printers, chooses a printer and books a time for printing;
- editor chases writers, illustrators, photographers, accountant (for annual accounts) and anyone else contributing to the report;
- editor edits text for spelling, grammar, style and length, writes headings, and writes captions for illustrations or photographs;
- text, headings, captions etc are typed or word-processed and proofread (preferably by at least two people);
- working group or chair approves edited text;
- working group or chair approves design roughs for cover and text;
- get revisions typed or word-processed;
- proofread text again and make corrections;
- get photos and illustrations 'screened', if necessary;
- send text for typesetting, if necessary; proofread and get corrections done;
- paste up, or produce on desktop publishing software;
- final proofread and check for appearance, page numbers etc;
- approve pages for printing;
- get it printed;
- get envelopes, press release, covering letter etc ready for sending out;
- send it out.

Obviously these stages apply to any complex publication, not just annual reports.

Chapter 7:

Developing and implementing policy

Policies define the broad framework within which an organisation operates. This chapter includes:

- reasons for having clear policies;

- a list of typical policy areas for voluntary organisations, with sources of further information on specific issues;

- guidelines for a policy and practice book for an organisation.

WHY HAVE POLICIES?

A policy defines what an organisation does and how it does it. Clear, workable policies are a key to creating a stable organisation which functions smoothly. Examples are stating that the organisation's services and jobs are open to the whole community (an equal opportunities policy), people are admitted to a hostel at any hour of the day or night (a 24-hour policy), the organisation's services are only available to people referred by a statutory or other agency (a referrals policy), or anyone who has been drinking is not allowed on the premises (a policy on alcohol).

A **code of practice** sets out the guidelines or procedures to put a specific policy into practice: how people are recruited for jobs or services, to ensure the organisation offers genuine equality of opportunity; minimum staff cover and security arrangements at night, for the 24-hour opening; which agencies the organisation takes referrals from, and what happens with self-referrals or people who come through other channels; how people who have been drinking should be dealt with.

The constitution is the basic policy document, outlining the organisation's overall objectives, what it can and cannot do, and how its business is transacted. Other policies might be formal or informal, written or unwritten.

Clear policies mean the right to make decisions and take action can be delegated downwards or sideways, because there will be clear guidelines about what is and is not appropriate for the organisation.

With clear policies and procedures there is less likely to be continuous debate or argument about what someone should (or should not) have done in a particular situation. There is more likely to be consistency, which is very important as new people join the organisation, or it gets larger or moves onto split sites. And because there is consistency, it is easier to be, and to be seen to be, fair.

With agreed procedures work becomes more straightforward, thus freeing time for other purposes. Processes do not need to be reinvented every time they need to be implemented, and mistakes are less likely to be made.

While agreed policies and procedures should in general be followed, there must always be scope for flexibility. All policies should be subject to regular review, and procedures should be changed in the light of experience.

In developing policies and procedures it is essential to involve those who will be directly affected, and to ensure that those who will be indirectly affected know what is happening and have an opportunity to contribute if they want to. It should always be clear who will make the final decision about the policy and procedures. Those making the final decision should take into account the views of those who have been consulted, but must recognise they may not be able to please everyone.

The final decision about major policies will nearly always be made by the governing body (which is usually, but not always, the management committee). Responsibility for agreeing less important policies and the procedures for implementing policies may be delegated to a subcommittee, manager(s) or staff.

TYPICAL POLICY AREAS

The policies needed by an organisation will depend on the sort of work it does, its size and its level of formality. A new, small, informal organisation is unlikely to have many formally agreed policies, while one which is larger, older or more complex may have detailed policies and procedures for virtually every aspect of its operation.

This section includes typical policy areas for small and medium sized voluntary organisations. *Voluntary But Not Amateur* may be helpful in developing policies in some of these areas. Information sheets on a wide range of policy-related issues are available from:

- National Council for Voluntary Organisations, Regents Wharf, 8 All Saints Street, London N1 9RL (tel 071 713 6161);

- National Federation of Community Organisations, 8-9 Upper Street, London N1 0PQ (tel 071 226 0189);

- Volunteer Centre UK, 29 Lower King's Road, Berkhamsted, Herts HP4 2AB (tel 0442 873311);

- regional and national umbrella organisations for specific types of work, for example Age Concern England, Pre-School Playgroups Association;

- some local councils for voluntary service, rural community councils and other local development agencies.

Information sheets, model policies or policies from other organisations should never be adopted by an organisation without very careful consideration as to their suitability. What looks good on paper and is absolutely appropriate for one organisation may be quite unsuitable for another. (An example is the funder which tried to force an Asian women's centre to adopt an equal opportunities policy saying it did not discriminate on the basis of race, ethnic origin or gender in providing its services, when the whole reason for the centre's existence was to provide services only for a group defined on the basis of its race, ethnic origin and gender.)

Objectives and priorities

The constitutional aims are the starting point for policies relating to objectives and priorities. These policies are generally agreed by the management committee or other governing body, but may be based on recommendations from workers, volunteers or the organisation's members. If the management committee is not the governing body, there must be absolute clarity about who makes the final decision. Policy areas include:

● what the organisation believes: statements about political, social or economic situations or events;

● what the organisation does: its priorities, what it wants to achieve, with whom it will and will not undertake joint projects, what sorts of things it will and will not do.

Participation and decision-making

The constitution may specify which sorts of decisions must be made by the management committee or by the whole membership, but it will not give details for day to day decision-making. So policies are needed to clarify:

● decision-making methods and procedures: who decides what, when and how, and who is accountable to whom;

● who else is authorised to make decisions, for example if someone is absent from work or if an elected officer cannot be reached;

● what happens when there are disagreements about decisions;

● user involvement: how members or users are consulted or involved in decision-making.

Services, activities and facilities

These policies will be created within the broad framework of the organisation's objectives and priorities. Some must be formally agreed by the management committee or other governing body; others will be decided, formally or informally, by subgroups, managers or workers:

● working methods and procedures: who does what, when and how; job boundaries; who is accountable to whom;

● comments and complaints from users: how users' comments are encouraged, and how complaints are monitored and dealt with;

● opening hours: when the organisation's services are available, whether the organisation can be closed (for example for maintenance or staff training) and who decides to close it, what happens if a worker does not arrive for her or his shift;

● health and safety: requirements for premises, staff, volunteers, users; dealing with breaches of regulations or policy; special policies, for example precautions against infectious diseases;

● confidentiality: who has access to information about users or members, what happens in case of a breach;

● access for people with a disability: how the organisation's services, activities or facilities are to be made available to people with mobility, speech, hearing, sight or other disabilities;

● access for speakers of other languages: policy on translation and interpretation;

● policy on charging for activities, goods, services or facilities;

● equipment: who can use it, safety regulations, responsibility for maintenance and repair;

● stock: who can use it, procedures for keeping track of what is used, responsibility for replacement;

● vehicles: who can use them, responsibility for petrol and other costs, payment of expenses for use of workers' own cars, insurance responsibilities;

● outside contacts: who can negotiate or speak on behalf of the organisation, who can talk to the media.

A national umbrella organisation for your type of work may have policy guidelines on specific aspects of service provision or activities.

At the very least an organisation should have clear policies covering any legal obligations relating to its work. *Voluntary But Not Amateur* chapter 8 covers some of the legal issues relating to public meetings, marches and processions, festivals and street parties, handling or selling food and drink, using minibuses and coaches, looking after children out of school, and looking after other people.

Equal opportunities

The organisation should have not only a statement of intent on equal opportunities, but also a code of practice outlining how it will implement equal opportunities (non-discrimination and positive action) in relation to:

● recruitment and selection of staff;

● recruitment and placement of volunteers;

● conditions of employment, including access to training;

● conditions of volunteering, including access to training;

● recruitment of members;

● recruitment of management committee;

● promoting and publicising the organisation.

It should cover non-discrimination, positive action, and where appropriate provision to meet special needs in relation to:

● recruitment of users;

● provision of activities or services.

It should also cover:

● dealing with racist, sexist or other personally abusive

actions by staff, volunteers, users, members, committee members and visitors.

Many umbrella organisations, national bodies and established local organisations now have comprehensive equal opportunities policies and codes of practice. It may be possible to get some of these and adapt them.

It is important to ensure an equal opportunities policy takes full advantage of the provisions within the Race Relations and Sex Discrimination Acts for positive action and meeting special needs, but without going beyond what is legally permitted.

Major sources of information on equal opportunities in employment and service delivery include:

- Commission for Racial Equality, Elliot House, 10-12 Allington Street, London SW1E 5EH (tel 071 828 7022);

- Equal Opportunities Commission, Overseas House, Quay Street, Manchester M3 3HN (tel 061 833 9244);

- Employment Service, Rockingham House, 123 West Street, Sheffield S1 4ER (their *Code of Practice on the Employment of Disabled People* is very good and includes an outline policy);

- National Aids Trust, Room 1403, Euston Tower, 286 Euston Road, London NW1 3DN (tel 071 383 4246);

- *HIV and Aids: Policy guidelines for voluntary organisations and small employers* plus policy guidelines on equal opportunities for lesbians and gay men, from Lesbian and Gay Employment Rights (LAGER), St Margaret's House, 21 Old Ford Road, London E2 9PL (tel 081 983 0696);

- information on job sharing and other flexible working patterns from New Ways to Work, 309 Upper Street, London N1 2TY (071 226 4026);

- *Voluntary But Not Amateur* chapters 1, 2 and 8.

Financial control

Financial policies are made by the treasurer, finance sub-committee and/or management committee or other governing body, in consultation with workers responsible for financial matters. They include:

- financial decision-making: who makes which decisions;

- budgets: how they are drawn up, budgetary controls, how variances (expenditure or income above or below budget) are dealt with;

- expenditure: who can authorise expenditure;

- cheques: who can sign;

- cash: petty cash procedures, security of cash on the premises or in transit;

- financial record-keeping: documentation required, who has access to financial records;

- gifts and payment for services: who keeps gifts or payments made to workers carrying out work duties (for example, payment for appearing on a radio programme or a gift given to a care worker by a client).

See chapter 20 and *Voluntary But Not Amateur* chapter 7 for more details about financial policies and procedures.

Premises

A starting point for policies relating to rented premises is the lease or other agreement setting out the terms on which premises can be used. Policies for rented premises or for premises owned by an incorporated organisation will be agreed by a premises subcommittee and/or the management committee or other governing body. If the organisation is unincorporated and owns its premises, the holding trustees with responsibility for the premises will have to make major decisions, usually based on recommendations from the management committee or other governing body. Policies might include:

● how premises are used;

● who can and cannot use premises;

● security: access to keys, burglar alarm codes etc;

● responsibility for cleaning;

● health and safety requirements relating to premises;

● procedures for bookings, deposits, security.

Sources of information include:

● Health and Safety Executive, Baynards House, 1 Chepstow Place, London W2 4TP (tel 071 229 3456);

● London Hazards Centre, 308 Grays Inn Road, London WC1X 8DS (tel 071 837 5605);

● *Managing your Community Building* by Peter Hudson (National Federation of Community Organisations, 1992; ISBN 0 900787 15 5; £13.95 from NFCO, 8-9 Upper Street, London N1 0PQ);

● *Voluntary But Not Amateur* chapter 4.

Personnel issues

Employment and personnel policies will be developed by the management committee or other governing body or a personnel subcommittee in consultation with workers and/or the union. If developed by a subcommittee, they may need to be approved by the management committee or other governing body.

The details of many personnel policies and procedures will be included in the written terms and conditions of employment (employment contract), equal opportunities policy, disciplinary and grievance procedures and training policy. There is more information about these in chapters 15 to 17. Personnel policies include:

● recruitment and selection procedures for employees, trainees and volunteers, and ensuring these procedures meet the requirements of the organisation's equal opportunities policy;

● induction programmes;

● probationary period: probationary reviews, what happens if work is unsatisfactory;

● pay: salary scales and increments, salary reviews, when salaries are paid, whether advances are allowed and how they are authorised, overtime payments, whether payment is by cash, cheque or direct credit into the workers' accounts;

● eligibility for pension schemes;

● expenses for staff, trainees and volunteers: what can be claimed, how to claim, documentation required;

● timekeeping: hours of work, whether mealtimes are included, flexitime procedures, whether flexitime is completely flexible or includes core hours which must be worked, absence, overtime, time off in lieu;

● sickness: arrangements for sick pay, notification required for sick leave, what happens in the case of long term illness or if a worker becomes disabled;

● holidays and leave: whether all staff must take public holidays or other set leave periods, period of notice required for leave, time off for religious or cultural holidays;

● maternity, paternity, adoption and dependants leave: how much, who decides, how much notice is required;

● compassionate or discretionary leave: how much, who decides;

● arrangements for supervision, support, formal reviews or appraisals;

● access to training and other staff development opportunities;

● promotion;

● disciplinary procedures: what they cover, verbal and written warnings, appeals;

● grievance procedures;

● retirement and redundancy policies and procedures;

● confidentiality of information relating to staff, trainees and volunteers;

● relationships between management committee, managers and the union or unions.

Information on a very wide range of personnel issues is available from:

● Institute of Personnel Management, 35 Camp Road, London SW19 4UX (tel 081 946 9100);

● ACAS, 27 Wilton Street, London SW1X 7AZ (tel 071 210 3000), especially their *Employment Policies* booklet;

● Volunteer Centre UK, 29 Lower King's Road, Berkhamsted, Herts HP4 2AB (tel 0442 873311);

● *Voluntary But Not Amateur* chapters 2 and 3;

● the addresses under equal opportunities, above.

Difficult situations

One common difficulty is the lack of clear policies on serious situations which occur infrequently. It is far easier if the organisation has guidelines so they do not need to be reinvented each time a problem occurs:

● use of alcohol or illegal drugs on premises;

● action in case of violence or threatened violence;

● action in case of racist, sexist or other personally abusive or offensive behaviour;

● action in case of suspected theft by someone connected with the organisation;

● action in case of break-in or burglary.

THE POLICY AND PRACTICE BOOK

There is no point in developing policies if no one knows where they are or what they say. Every organisation should have a policy and practice book. A named person (manager, administrator, chair, or someone else) should have explicit responsibility for putting into it all relevant documents, and for ensuring that other people get the documents they need. Everything in the policy book should be dated. If a document is still in draft form it should be clearly labelled 'Draft'; when it is approved the final version should indicate 'Accepted by Management Committee 24/1/93' or whatever.

While a ring binder may be sufficient to start, the policy and practice book may soon expand into a lever arch file ... or two ... or three. It should be kept up to date and old material should be thrown away.

A policy and practice book may seem unnecessarily bureaucratic but it can save endless time when 'I know we talked about that sometime a couple of years ago but I can't quite remember what we decided'. It is also useful when new staff join the organisation. When the organisation wants to improve its practice, it knows what it is currently doing and can start at square two instead of always going back to square one.

The policy book should include:

- formal policy documents such as constitution, equal opportunities policy, health and safety policy, confidentiality policy, contracts of employment, disciplinary and grievance procedures;

- copies of any minutes from general meetings, management committee meetings etc which have policy implications (be sure each minute clearly indicates which meeting it was, and the date);

- procedural guidelines, for example booking procedures for a community room or a minibus;

- any document which relates to policy or procedure. This might be as simple as a one-line memo saying 'Please note: all petty cash vouchers must be accompanied by a receipt and must be signed when you receive the money from petty cash', or might be very detailed.

It should be clearly divided into sections and if necessary subsections, to make it as easy as possible to find documents. New materials should be put in at the back of each section (so each section is in date order, with the most recent at the back).

Possible section headings are:

- Administration procedures

- Constitution

- Confidentiality

- Development plans and priorities

- Equal opportunities

- Financial procedures

- Health and safety

- Meetings: procedures and guidelines (including terms of reference for subcommittees)

- Outside bodies (media, police etc)

- Personnel policies

- Premises and security

- Service provision (for a multi-purpose organisation, there might need to be a section for each area of work)

- Staff recruitment and selection

- Volunteer policies.

In a multi-site organisation it may be appropriate to have a policy book at each site. It may also be appropriate for the manager to have her or his own copy, with another copy accessible to other staff, trainees, volunteers and committee members. All new workers and committee members should be made aware, at an early stage in their induction, of the existence of the policy book and what it contains. It may be appropriate to give them their own copy, or to go through relevant sections with them.

When a policy or formal procedure is agreed it can be helpful to indicate in the top corner where it should be filed in the policy book. This makes it more likely it will get to the right place. Some organisations indicate in their minutes when a particular minute will be included in the policy book.

Yes, it all takes time ... but in the long term it saves time, and helps the organisation function more effectively.

Chapter 8:

Managing the planning process

Planning is one of the keys to success in most activities, but voluntary organisations and the individuals who manage them find all sorts of reasons not to do it. And because they are unwilling to plan even what they are doing from day to day or month to month, it is virtually impossible to think coherently about **development** (adapting existing policies, activities or services or creating new ones to meet new or different needs) or about long term **strategic planning.**

Without clear aims and policies any organisation will find it difficult or even impossible to set priorities, sensibly monitor its work, evaluate its effectiveness, and put together development proposals that make sense in terms of what the organisation is doing and still needs to do.

With the move towards longer term (three year or longer) grant funding, service agreements or contracts, funders are requiring evidence that the organisation can commit itself to providing the agreed services or organising the agreed activities over an extended period. This is leading to a new emphasis on long term planning.

This chapter includes:

- definitions of types of planning and terms commonly used in planning;

- an 'action spiral' model for development and planning;

- sample terms of reference for a development sub-committee;

- guidelines for drawing up a development plan, strategic plan or business plan.

The next chapter covers monitoring and evaluation, and chapter 10 looks at how organisational change can be effectively managed.

TYPES OF PLANNING

Planning can be divided in several ways:

- **strategic** planning: long term, with a broad overview of policies, current activities and new activities;

- **tactical** planning: steps to implement a strategic plan or reach long term goals;

- **recurrent** or **cyclical** planning: for events or activities which occur regularly or must be regularly undertaken, for example quarterly reports, annual accounts, monthly supervision sessions with staff;

- **project** planning: for a specific, time-limited piece of work;

- **operational** planning: to keep the organisation or team

functioning smoothly and able to carry out the work it has to do;

- **day to day** planning: specific actions needing to be done immediately;

- **contingency** planning: allowing for the unforeseen.

Crisis management involves dealing with one crisis after another, rather than planning for them and trying to minimise the risk of them occuring. Even if the crises are adequately handled, it is not good management. The reality is that most crises are not unpredictable; they can be anticipated and planned for.

Strategic planning nearly always refers to long term planning. Tactical, operational and project planning may be medium term or short term. It is not easy to define long, medium and short because they are different for every organisation and for different activities within the organisation.

THE LANGUAGE OF PLANNING

Aims and objectives

The words 'aims', 'objectives', 'objects', 'goals' and 'targets' are often used interchangeably. They all mean 'what we want to do or achieve'. What is important is not what they are called, but the **time scale** involved.

An **aim** is an overall objective or goal: what the organisation would achieve if it was 100 per cent successful. It defines why the organisation exists, its purpose, its reason for being. This is sometimes called the organisation's **mission,** as expressed in a **mission statement** or **statement of core purpose.**

Objectives are what the organisation wants to achieve within certain time periods. All of the organisation's objectives, whether long, medium or short term, and all its activities should be in line with its core purpose.

The time periods for strategic objectives in a fairly well established small or medium sized organisation might be three to five years for long term, two to three years for medium term, and 12 to 18 months for short term. For a larger organisation long term might be as long as 10 or 20 years, while for a new organisation long term might be as short as one year.

Short term or immediate objectives (for this year, this month, this week) might be called objectives, goals or targets.

Strategy

A strategy is a plan to reach goals or objectives. In an organisational context it usually refers to long term planning.

- A **development plan** or development strategy sets out what the organisation wants to do and achieve over a fixed period. It involves new activities, changes to existing activities, or new users.

- A **strategic plan** looks at how all the developments slot together, and the resource implications (people, money, time, equipment, premises).

- A **business plan** sets out projected costs for the organisation's activities, anticipated income, cashflow projections (when the income will come in, set against when payments have to be made) and financial requirements to cover costs.

These terms are often used interchangeably.

Policies

Policies define the framework within which an organisation makes choices to achieve its aims (see chapter 7). These choices might relate to priorities, activities or procedures. Clear policies and procedures make planning, prioritising and decision-making far easier for everyone within the organisation: staff, management committee, volunteers and users.

Activities

Activities are what an organisation actually does.

In a campaign these activities might be called **tactics** (steps in a campaign) and could include research, publications, lobbying, petitions or demonstrations.

In a community group they might be **services**: welfare rights advice, running a playgroup, providing education or training. For an arts group activities might include putting on plays or running a poetry group.

Sometimes activities include the provision of **facilities**, for example a housing association provides houses and flats; a community group might have rooms for hire or photographic equipment which people can use.

Sometimes activities involve the **production of goods** for sale or free distribution.

Running the organisation (infrastructure) includes activities such as fundraising, financial management, decision-making, publicity, correspondence and cleaning.

Activities do not actually fall into these neat categories! But whatever kind of activities an organisation provides, they will need to be planned.

Priorities

When an organisation decides certain activities are most important or most necessary to achieve its objectives, it has defined its priorities.

Setting priorities always means saying 'no' to the activities for which there is not enough time, energy or money. That is not easy, so many voluntary organisations do not want to do it. They end up trying to do *everything* because they are unwilling to concentrate on specific activ-

ities. While organisations are still quite small this can work, but as they grow and face pressures (for example from funders or users) they collapse if they remain unwilling to set priorities.

Having clear objectives and policies can help an organisation set priorities and change them as circumstances change.

Systems and procedures

Procedures define the way an organisation carries out its activities: the people, paperwork and actions needed to get something done. A set of procedures is sometimes called a system.

THE ACTION SPIRAL

One way to think of development or planned change is as a spiral which starts with pressure to change and includes:

- an assessment of needs, pressures, demands and the context in which development will take place;

- clarifying or confirming the organisation's core purpose and broad objectives;

- collecting information;

- setting objectives;

- planning;

- implementation;

- monitoring achievements against short term targets;

- monitoring achievements against longer term objectives;

- review;

- evaluation;

- which becomes part of the assessment of needs, pressures and demands for future development.

This spiral is appropriate regardless of whether development is based on **expansion** (deliberately taking on new activities or expanding existing ones), **evolution** (letting new activities emerge from existing ones), or **contraction** (because of cuts in staff or funding). It is also appropriate for objectives such as involving users in decision-making, computerisation or restructuring the management committee.

This process is sometimes called **management by objectives** (MBO). MBO rigidly applied can restrict rather than enhance organisational and individual development. But sensibly used it can provide a clear and shared framework for setting priorities, focusing people's energies and the organisation's resources, and achieving real results which can give everyone a sense of pride in their work and in the organisation.

The context for development

Development usually arises from some kind of pressure on the organisation. This might come from:

- existing or potential users or members, funders, the committee, staff or volunteers;

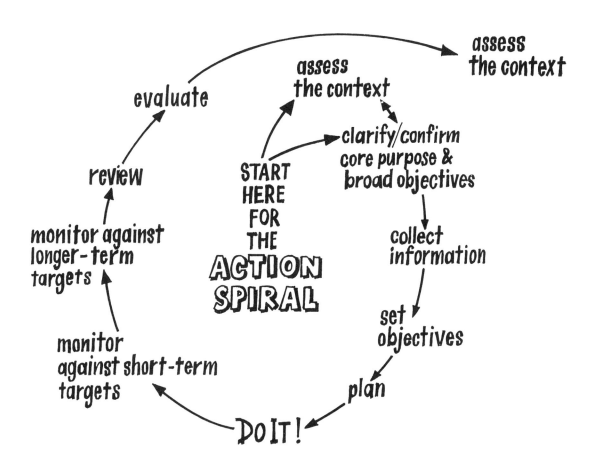

- pressure on resources (time, money, premises, equipment);
- social, economic, demographic, political or legislative changes external to the organisation;
- awareness of new or unmet needs.

In many organisations the reaction is to respond immediately to any new demand or pressure. This leads to haphazard development, internal conflicts if there are inadequate resources to do everything taken on, and wasted energy. Development proceeds much more smoothly if it is planned.

Confirming core purpose and broad objectives

The development process must take place within the context of the organisation's overall aims, mission or core purpose: why the organisation exists and its main purpose.

In many organisations the people involved have very different ideas about the organisation's core purpose. This needs to be clarified at an early stage in the development process. A community centre whose core purpose is to become a focus for activities involving the whole community is likely to go down a different development path from a community centre whose focus is on people who, because of discrimination or oppression, have traditionally been denied access to activities and services.

Core purpose should be extended into broad objectives such as 'develop work which directly involves a very wide range of local organisations and individuals' or 'develop activities for the increasing number of refugees who are

moving into the local area'. If the organisation has vast resources, it might be able to achieve both purposes. But at a time of increased need and diminishing resources, there must be clarity about what is most important for the organisation to try to achieve.

If the organisation's core purpose and broad objectives are clear, they need only be confirmed at this stage.

Activities will then be developed within the framework of these broad objectives. The first community centre might develop drop-in advice sessions run by volunteers and might involve dozens of small local groups in organising an annual community festival; the second might put its energies into developing English classes, advice sessions with interpreters, in-depth casework, and activities which bring together local and refugee children.

Every new activity should be assessed against the core purpose. If the organisation seems to be heading in new directions which do not fit in, it may be time to reassess the core purpose.

Exercises for clarifying core purpose and objectives are included in *Planning Together: The art of effective teamwork* by George Gawlinski and Lois Graessle (Bedford Square Press, 1988; 88 pages; ISBN 0 7199 1202 4; £11.95 + £1.50 p&p from Plymbridge Distributors, Estover Road, Plymouth PL6 7PZ).

Collecting information

The next stage in the spiral is to assess the need or situation and the organisation's ability and suitability to do something about it. This involves doing research or collecting and assessing information about, for example, the extent of a particular problem, what has already been done about it and similar situations both locally and in other areas.

The initial information might cover demands or pressures from users, funders, management committee or workers; potential changes in users (planned or unplanned); or actual or potential changes in legislation, society as a whole or the community served by the organisation.

The information might come from statistics (numerical information) about the present situation, projections or forecasts about the future, personal observations, or historical data (statistics or observations about the past). Statistics are sometimes called objective data, and observations and opinions subjective data. But the way statistics are presented and used can be very subjective.

Sources of information include statistics collected by the organisation, statistics from sources such as government or local authority departments or the census, other records, written questionnaires, personal interviews, and written documents such as reports, books or minutes.

The next step is to collect and assess information about resources, services or activities external to the organisation available to meet the need or deal with the situation. It may be there is no need for the organisation to undertake something new; it can simply refer people to other organisations.

If the need cannot be met elsewhere, the organisation's position must be assessed. This starts with determining whether it has clear policies about undertaking this sort of work, and how it should do it.

Next comes an examination of the organisation's resources:

● **money**: available now and in the future, likely economic changes (including inflation) and how they might affect the organisation, possible changes in funding patterns and priorities, donations, sales;

● **time**: available now and in the future, increased time needed for a new activity (not only for the activity itself, but also for extra administration, communication, fundraising, bookkeeping and other essential support);

● **workers**: current and future, staff and volunteer skills and abilities, training or retraining needs versus available time and money, scope for redeployment within the organisation;

● **premises**: current and future use of space, pressure on space, conflicting demands (room A may be available at 10.00 Saturday morning, but there is no point agreeing to run a meditation class in room A if there is a band practising in room B), health and safety considerations.

Other factors which need to be considered at this stage include:

● **commitment** and **energy**: even if there is enough time and money, the will may not exist to take on a new activity;

● **resistance to change**: from workers, users, funders, management committee, others affected by what might happen;

● **external factors**: political changes, legal constraints, possible changes in other organisations.

Setting objectives

The next stage is to decide whether to undertake an activity, clarify what kind, and set objectives. Or if the organisation is contracting, this is the time to decide what can be cut back, combined or streamlined.

At this point consultation is essential, to ensure as many people as possible have a say in what the organisation should do and how.

● Analyse the information collected at the research stage. What does it mean in terms of this particular organisation, its users or members?

● Develop or clarify the organisation's policies about meeting this need.

● Decide whether the organisation has the commitment and resources to undertake an activity to meet this need, and if so what is most appropriate. Or decide how activities can be adapted or cut to meet new constraints.

● Set clear, time-limited objectives. These should be as specific as possible: not just 'set up volunteer-run advice sessions' but 'recruit and train at least 10 new volunteers by 31 October, set up the first advice session by 1 November, have at least 18 trained volunteers and three three-hour sessions each week by 31 March'.

● Set a time to review progress, assess objectives to be sure they are realistic and make any necessary changes.

Planning

Now is the time to turn objectives into specific targets and plans. What needs to happen to achieve the objectives? Who will do it?

● Think about what needs to happen each quarter, month and week. Be sure things are in a logical order, with enough time allowed for consultation and decision-making. (You can't advertise for a new worker until the job description and person specification have been drawn up and approved.)

● Ensure the necessary resources (especially time) are available to enable it to happen.

● Be sure everyone involved in the work knows what they are supposed to do, when, and how it is to be reported back.

Implementation

It is only at this stage, after considerable time and energy have gone into thinking, analysing information and planning, that the organisation should actually start (or stop, in a contracting phase) doing the activity.

Monitoring against short term targets

During the implementation stage the person or people involved must continuously review and adapt the plans. Timetables and targets should be seen as jackets, not strait-jackets: they need to fit the organisation and its workers, but should not restrict movement. If deadlines and targets are not being met, assess *why*.

● Were they unrealistic to start with? It might be necessary to revise the objectives and timetable.

● Is other work preventing us from meeting the deadlines? It might be necessary to confirm priorities and improve time management (see chapter 11).

● Do we lack the information, skills or equipment to get on with the work? It's obvious what needs to be done to remedy this.

● Has the situation changed? Perhaps these objectives are no longer appropriate, and need to be reconsidered.

Monitoring against longer term objectives, review, evaluation

These stages are covered in detail in the next chapter.

Monitoring means collecting information about something while it is happening; **review** means putting the information into a usable form; **evaluation** means analysing the information.

Evaluation will show whether the activity succeeded, what went well and what failed, and whether there are needs which remain unmet or problems which remain unsolved. And those needs or problems become, in turn, the starting point for the next round of the action spiral.

In most organisations, of course, several spirals are going on simultaneously, related to various aspects of the organisation's work.

TERMS OF REFERENCE FOR A DEVELOPMENT SUBCOMMITTEE

A development (or policy and development) subcommittee can do preliminary research and planning in order to cut down the amount of information the whole management committee has to sift through. Another possibility is to have subcommittees with responsibility for specific aspects of the organisation's activities.

A development subcommittee might include the manager, another staff member directly involved in providing the organisation's services, activities or facilities, and two management committee members with specific interest or expertise in the organisation's work.

Its terms of reference might include some or all of the following:

● to assess needs for expanded, revised or new activities, services or facilities;

● to consult with staff, volunteers and current users about ways to meet those needs;

● to set priorities for meeting specific needs;

● to draw up proposals for expanded, revised or new activities, services or facilities, and to present them to

the management committee or other governing body for approval;

● to determine the financial implications of the organisation's activities, services or facilities, draw up draft budgets (in consultation with the treasurer and/or finance subcommittee), explore funding possibilities, and present relevant financial proposals to the management committee for approval;

● to determine the staffing implications and draw up proposals for staffing (in consultation with the personnel/staffing subcommittee, if there is one), and present relevant staffing proposals to the management committee for approval;

● to set clear, time-limited, written objectives;

● to draw up timetables and targets for achieving objectives (in consultation with the people who will be doing the work);

● to decide appropriate procedures for monitoring provision and use of activities, services or facilities;

● to decide appropriate procedures to review and evaluate provision and use of activities, services or facilities;

● to ensure staff, volunteers and users receive necessary training and support;

● to ensure the development subcommittee, management committee and other relevant bodies receive regular reports on the progress of the work.

STRATEGIC PLANNING

The development plan

A strategic plan starts by looking at how the organisation will develop over an agreed time period. This will include:

● **Programme development**: mainstream or ongoing services and activities for users/customers/members, ongoing campaigns etc. This includes current activities as well as new ones.

● **Project development**: one-off or time-limited activities, campaigns etc. A successful project might in due course become part of the organisation's ongoing programme, or might lead to the creation of an independent organisation.

● **Product development**: if the organisation produces goods or sells its services, it may think in terms of product development.

● **Organisational development**: building and sustaining the organisation, for example membership, publicity, fundraising, lobbying for funding, developing new sources of income, networking, partnership with other organisations, staff development.

● **Operational development**: keeping the organisation going, for example administration, finance, filing, computerisation, moving premises.

For each area of development, the plan will ultimately describe:

- what the organisation does now;
- what will stay the same;
- what the organisation will do more of;
- what the organisation will do less of;
- what will be dropped completely;
- what will be done differently;
- what new activities will be taken on.

The process

A development or strategic plan might be drawn up by one or two people and imposed on the organisation, but this is not good practice.

It is important to find time to involve committee members, staff, volunteers and the organisation's users/clients/members in discussions about how they would like to see the organisation and its activities change and develop. Before this happens it is important to be clear about:

- who will make the final decision about what is and is not included in the plan;
- how they will get the information they need to make these decisions;
- how they will get any necessary professional advice, for example on legal issues, fundraising strategies, costs of development;
- who should be consulted (asked for their ideas or advice, even though they will not be involved in the final decision);
- who needs to be informed beforehand that a long term plan is being drawn up, even if they are not going to be directly consulted or involved in the decision-making;
- who needs to see the plan afterwards.

Consultation may be most effective if it happens *before* anything is committed to paper. As soon as ideas or proposals are on paper they become, in some people's minds, fixed and immutable. The best process is one which involves:

- consultation sessions with relevant people;
- discussion of their ideas within a working group or development subcommittee;
- discussion of the financial, personnel and premises aspects of development proposals, with the working group or development subcommittee or with other relevant people or subcommittees;
- access to professional advice if needed;
- one or two people drawing up a draft;
- consultation at various levels within the organisation;
- drawing up a revised version based on the consultations;
- final approval by the management committee or whichever body has the authority to make the final decision.

All this takes a lot of time.

Differences and conflict

Strategic planning reaches the core of an organisation, the most fundamental commitments and values of the people involved, and their sometimes rather narrow self-interest. The process of deciding what the organisation should concentrate on, what it should prioritise and how it should change can never be painless. What is positive for some users or staff might well be perceived as negative by others. It is important that time is allowed for discussing these differences and for coming to an agreed way forward.

Chapter 10 looks in more detail at the process of managing change and resistance to change.

The strategic plan

A strategic plan intended for management use within the organisation will be considerably different from a plan intended primarily to impress potential funders or backers. Strategic plans do not all follow the same format but the following outline will provide a starting point. A plan does not have to include all these sections.

Introduction

This is an overview of what the organisation is, what it does now and what is proposed in the strategic plan. It includes:

- what the organisation is and its aims or core purpose ('mission statement');
- summary of the organisation's main activities, users/clients/members, and sources of funding;
- period covered by the strategic plan;
- who was involved in the process of drawing up the plan;
- brief summary of main changes anticipated in the period covered.

Organisational assessment

This should be based on an assessment of the organisation's strengths and weaknesses in relation to its programme, projects, products, organisational factors and management/administration. It will include:

- what the organisation is good at;
- gaps in provision and other weaknesses.

The context for change

For the strategic plan to make sense, people will need to understand why certain choices have been made. This section might be quite long or very brief, depending on the organisation's situation. It might include:

- factors external to the organisation, such as local or national political factors; new legislation; unmet needs in the community; economic, social or demographic changes; changes in funders' priorities; changes in other organisations (for example pressure on one organisation because another has closed);
- needs, demands or pressures from current users, clients or members;

- needs or demands of potential users;

- factors within the organisation such as use of premises, facilities or equipment; time pressures; pressures on or from staff, volunteers or committee members; the need to diversify sources of income.

Programme development

For each area of **current** and **new** activity or service:

- purpose of the activity or service (why the organisation does it or should do it);

- what the organisation is now doing, and for or with whom;

- what needs to be done, and why;

- factors to be taken into account when planning for the period;

- objectives for the period for each activity or service;

- implications for time, staffing, premises, equipment, management and administration;

- effects on other activities or services;

- how much it will cost, and where the money will come from;

- assessment of the level of risk involved in undertaking the development;

- plans and timetable for implementation;

- how progress will be monitored;

- how the activity or service itself will be monitored and evaluated, and against what criteria (these might be called performance indicators, and are covered in more detail in chapter 13).

Project development

As above, for each current and new project. Because projects are time-specific there should be a clear indication of what will happen when they end, or how the decision will be made about what will happen.

Product development

As above, for each current and new product. Special attention will be given to known or potential markets for each product.

Organisational development

As above, for each aspect of organisational development. This might include, for example, a membership drive, a publicity campaign, developing a new source of income, developing networks with other organisations, or proposals to involve users in the organisation.

Operational development

As above, for each aspect of operational development. This might include, for example, computerisation, creating new

policies (see chapter 7), consolidating the filing system, undertaking a fundraising drive, or developing staff or management training.

Personnel implications

What the development proposals will mean in terms of staffing, volunteers, recruitment and induction, staff and volunteer training, supervision.

Implications for premises

What the development proposals will mean in terms of premises.

Implications for equipment or other facilities

How the proposed developments will affect use of equipment and other facilities; new equipment required.

Management and administration

How management and administration will be affected by the development proposals.

Costs and funding

In a development or strategic plan this section might be fairly short; in a **business plan** it will be very detailed. It will include:

- proposed costs, with assumptions about inflation, for each area of the organisation's work (in business plan jargon, each area of work is called a **cost centre**);

- assured income for each cost centre;

- possible sources of other income for each cost centre;

- projected surplus or deficit for each cost centre, and how deficits will be covered;

- cashflow: when money will come in, when it has to go out, how any cashflow shortfalls will be covered.

Budgets will usually be projected using a variety of assumptions, for example 5, $7^1/_2$ and 10 per cent inflation; grant funding increasing and/or decreasing at various rates; or different rates of fees charged for membership subscriptions or services.

Timetable

For each main area of work there should be a timetable showing objectives and targets, and indicating when progress will be reviewed. The timetable might be in three-month blocks for the first year, six-month blocks for years two and three, and annual blocks thereafter.

The timetable will also indicate when the strategic plan as a whole will be reviewed and updated. This should usually be 12 to 18 months after it is implemented, but it may need a major review earlier if there are significant funding changes.

Chapter 9:

Managing monitoring and evaluation

Effective monitoring and evaluation are impossible if the organisation does not know how to make decisions about its work, does not have clear objectives, and does not know how to plan sensibly. So it is important to read chapter 8 before moving on to this chapter. This chapter looks at:

- why monitoring and evaluation are undertaken, and how they may be influenced by vested interests;

- what monitoring is, and how to do it;

- how to put the information into usable form;

- what evaluation is, and how to do it.

Sources of more detailed information about monitoring and evaluation are:

- *Evaluation in the Voluntary Sector* by Mog Ball (Forbes Trust, 1988; 72 pages; ISBN 0 9513352 0 0; £4.95 from Forbes Trust, 9 Artillery Lane, London E1 7LP);

- *Quality of Service: Measuring performance for voluntary organisations* by Alan Lawrie (Directory of Social Change, 1992; 94 pages; ISBN 0 907164 82 X; £8.95 from DSC, Radius Works, Back Lane, London NW3 1HL);

- *Measuring Success: A guide to evaluation for voluntary and community groups* by Rodney Hedley (Advance, 1985; 52 pages; ISBN 0 901171 50 6; £3 from Advance, 444 Brixton Road, London SE9 8EJ);

- *Working Effectively: A guide to evaluation techniques* by Warren Feek (Bedford Square Press, 1987; 45 pages; ISBN 0 7199 1177 X; £4.95 + 62p p&p from Plymbridge Distributors, Estover Road, Plymouth PL6 7PZ);

- Charities Evaluation Services (1 Motley Avenue, Christina Street, London EC2A 4SU, tel 071 613 1202);

- Thamesdown Evaluation Project (Thamesdown Voluntary Service Centre, 1 John Street, Swindon SN1 1RT).

This chapter focuses on **programme evaluation**. This covers evaluation of the organisation's programme work and its projects, as well as organisational and operational development (see chapter 8). Increasingly voluntary organisations are being expected to monitor specific services provided under service agreements or contracts; this kind of evaluation, using **performance indicators**, is covered in chapter 13.

Sometimes the organisation itself, rather than its work, is evaluated. This might involve looking at how the organisation is structured, how decisions are made or how people relate to each other. This is sometimes called **organisational** or **process evaluation** and is considered in chapter 22.

DIFFERENT INTERESTS

There are several reasons for assessing and evaluating the work of voluntary organisations:

- **funders** want to ensure the organisation is doing what it is supposed to with their money, is providing a good service, and is giving good value for money;

- the **voluntary organisation** wants to prove to itself and to the external world, especially funders, that it is providing a good and necessary service, is meeting genuine needs and is capable of doing what it said it would do;

- the organisation may also want to emphasise unmet needs which need further funding;

- the organisation needs to ensure it is accountable to users of its services;

- **workers**, both paid and volunteer, need the satisfaction of being able to identify progress and results;

- **members** and **users**, who often have a heavy emotional investment in the organisation, need to feel they are part of a successful group;

- the **management committee** and **managers** need evaluation as an internal management tool, to assess the shortcomings of the organisation and its workers and what was not done, as well as strengths and what was done.

If the organisation has set clear and realistic objectives, planned effectively and met its objectives, there will be no conflict between these purposes. If the organisation has not done what it set out to do there may need to be a 'public' version of the evaluation which emphasises the positive aspects of what was achieved, and an internal evaluation which looks more critically at what was not achieved and why not. There is nothing wrong with this, so long as the public evaluation is not dishonest in any way.

Evaluation as a management tool

As part of the action spiral (see chapter 8) monitoring and evaluation can help an organisation increase its effectiveness by identifying strengths and gaps, achievements and unmet needs. For evaluation to be useful in this way it is essential for it to be as honest and comprehensive as possible. But it should never be done in a way that undermines the confidence of staff, volunteers or users in themselves or in the organisation; the emphasis must always be on what has been achieved. This is why it is so important to have clear and realistic goals right from the start.

Evaluation for or by funders

Funders will want to be sure the organisation has done what it was supposed to with the money, and has done it effectively. The organisation needs to be sure it can show this.

An evaluation undertaken *by* funders is likely to have a hidden purpose: either to prove the organisation is excellent (because the funder is committed to continuing its support) or to show the organisation is not doing what it is supposed to (as a justification for cuts). If an organisation has done an evaluation based on its own criteria it is more likely to be able to challenge a negative evaluation by a funder.

Funders may collect information from voluntary organisations by visiting them or by requiring specified information to be sent in or forms to be completed. The funders' liaison officers or grants officers then prepare a report analysing the information and making recommendations to the funding body. Sometimes the funding body also plays a developmental role, for example by assisting with identifying and implementing changes suggested by the monitoring and evaluation.

For a variety of reasons voluntary organisations view these exercises with caution:

● funders often focus more on quantitative (statistical) than qualitative measures;

● funders may use evaluation criteria with which the organisation disagrees or which are not appropriate to its activities or philosophy;

● if problems are identified through the monitoring and evaluation process, funders may try to impose inappropriate changes;

● the results of monitoring and evaluation may be used to justify cuts in grant aid.

A monitoring and evaluation approach led by funders may produce a distorted picture of how the organisation is operating, and may not be the most effective way of ensuring either accountability for use of public funds or high quality services or activities.

The best prevention against the risks of distortion is for the organisation to undertake its own monitoring and evaluation. This is often called **self-evaluation**.

MONITORING

Too often in the voluntary sector monitoring simply means keeping statistics: how many tickets are sold, how many people use the organisation's activities or services, how many people from various ethnic groups apply for jobs. This type of monitoring is important, but on their own such numbers are meaningless.

Even worse, monitoring can sometimes mean inventing numbers. This is not only meaningless, but also dishonest and incompetent.

Effective monitoring is part of a much broader process that includes:

● determining needs or problems;

● assessing available resources;

● establishing clear and realistic goals or objectives;

● developing activities or services to meet those goals;

● collecting information about what the organisation is doing while it is doing it;

● putting the data together to review what has been done;

● evaluating whether the objectives have been achieved, needs have been met or problems solved;

● learning from the experience and applying what has been learned to future work.

Monitoring is pointless unless the organisation has objectives against which to measure its achievements. And objectives, in turn, are meaningless if they are not based on a clear assessment of needs and what the organisation can realistically hope to do to meet those needs.

Good research is the key to this process. It occurs before objectives are set (in the assessment of needs, problems and resources) and continues as information is collected about the activities and services being provided and who is using them.

Research about **what is happening while it is happening** is monitoring.

What can be monitored

To ensure the organisation is collecting the information it actually needs in a form it can use, careful thought must be given beforehand to what is being monitored, and why.

Monitoring will cover the most relevant or important topics from among the following:

● the organisation's **programme and projects**: what it provides (activities, services and facilities), who provides them (staff, volunteers, users), what they are used for, how they are used, how people find out about them, what users think about them;

● **users, clients** or **members**: who uses the activities, services or facilities, and who does not use them;

- use of **resources**: how, when and why staff or volunteers' time is used; how, when and why money is spent; how, when, why and by whom the premises are used; how, when, why and by whom equipment is used;

- **what the organisation is doing**: how much time is spent on various types of work, how individual pieces of work fit together and what they contribute to the organisation's activities or services; what needs are being met; what needs are not being met;

- **decision-making processes**: how decisions get made, who is involved in decisions, who is not involved.

This list is far from exhaustive; each organisation will have its own priorities for monitoring.

Further information about performance indicators (criteria for monitoring specific services) is in chapter 13.

Getting started

When there is some clarity about *what* needs to be monitored, it becomes easier to think about *how* to collect the information. Think about questions such as:

- Who needs this information? Why?

- What sort of information is needed?

- How can it be obtained?

- Who are the most appropriate people to collect it?

- What is the most appropriate time to collect it?

- What is the most appropriate way to collect it?

- Who will collate it (bring it all together, count it up, make sense of it)? How will the information get to this person or group?

- How will the collated information be presented to workers, management committee members or others who need to see it?

Who does the monitoring?

Advice on what to monitor can come from the committee, workers, users, funders or people with professional evaluation skills from outside the organisation. The final decision about what should be monitored will depend on the purpose(s) of the monitoring exercise.

The decision about what is being monitored will lead to decisions about how best to do it: by collecting statistics, keeping workplans or diaries, observing what is happening and/or interviewing people.

The organisation may be able to draw up appropriate forms for statistics, logs or diaries, or may want to get outside help from a council for voluntary service, relevant umbrella organisation, voluntary sector evaluation service or statistics department at a local college. Once the forms are drafted, tested for suitability and agreed, the organisation's workers should be able to use them to collect the necessary information.

Similarly, interview questions or written questionnaires can be drafted and tested by the organisation's committee members or workers, or by someone from outside the organisation. If questions are drawn up by people who are not experienced in survey techniques, try to have them

checked by someone with relevant experience. This can help ensure the interviews or questionnaires are phrased in ways which elicit the necessary information. (If you ask 'What did you like or not like about the service?' on a written questionnaire and the response is 'quality of advice', you have no way of knowing whether the respondent was satisfied or dissatisfied with the quality.)

Interviews might be carried out by workers or others closely involved with the organisation; this has the advantage that the interviewer is known and trusted. Disadvantages are that respondents may be unwilling to say anything negative to someone they know (especially someone who is responsible for providing services to or for them) and inexperienced interviewers may allow their own biases to creep into the interview questions and responses.

Interviewers from outside the organisation may be more or less likely to get open and honest responses from the people being interviewed. Much will depend on the kind of impression the interviewer makes, the extent to which the respondent understands the purpose of the interview, and how good the interview questions are.

Questionnaires can be distributed or administered by anyone. Even more than with interviews it is important to ensure the questions elicit appropriate answers, because it can be difficult (or impossible, with questionnaires filled in anonymously) to get clarification of an obscure response.

When to monitor

For some activities it may be appropriate to monitor every day. For others, sample days, weeks or months are used. Clearly any periods used as a sample must be typical of the whole period they are meant to represent; if they are not, significant variations should be noted. (For example, if attendance is always monitored during the first full week of every month, it will be worth noting that attendance was unusually low because of bad weather or unusually high because the local newspaper had just run a long article about the project.)

COLLECTING DATA

Statistics

The simplest form of monitoring is quantitative: based on quantities or numbers. It is not difficult to devise record-keeping forms and procedures to collect this sort of information, if the questions about what is being monitored and why are considered.

But even when these questions have been answered, procedural guidelines are essential. For example, it may seem quite straightforward to collect information about numbers of users. But if a user comes in for a while in the morning, goes away then comes back in the afternoon, is she or he counted once or twice? There are no rules; each organisation must decide for itself. If it is important to monitor the number of different people who use the project **each week**, they should only be counted once in the week. If **daily** use needs to be monitored, users should be counted once for the day. If it is important to monitor the number of people who attend **each session**, they should be counted for each session. Guidelines such as these must be established before monitoring starts or as soon as anyone becomes aware that there is confusion or a discrepancy in the way information is being collected.

Statistical monitoring seeks to be objective. If two people monitor the same work, they should come up with the same results. The basic question when collecting statistical information is **how much?** or **how many?**

Factual information

Non-quantitative information can also be collected. This might include, for example, the topics covered in training courses, the type of advice given by an advice worker, or the training and other support provided to volunteers.

In compiling factual information the basic questions are **what did we do?** and **what effects did it have?**

Workplans and diaries

Workplans and diaries can provide a useful record of how time has been spent and what individual workers have done. However they can only be useful if there is an agreed procedure for keeping the information, if all workers cooperate, and if people are honest about what they have and have not done. The underlying questions here are **who did what?** and **when?**

Observation

Monitoring can be based on observations by the person or people undertaking an activity, or by someone not directly involved in the activity. Unless observations are carried out by trained observers working with agreed criteria, observations tend to be **subjective** (based on a person's interpretation of what is going on) rather than **objective** (based on information which can be proved in some way). For example, if a trainer says 15 people attended a course and they covered certain topics, that is objective information; if the trainer says people participated 'a lot' and 'seemed to enjoy themselves' that is subjective.

Subjective observations can be very useful but beware of hidden bias and prejudices which influence how information is interpreted.

An observer will ask **what am I seeing or hearing?**

Interviews and questionnaires

Good monitoring directly and systematically seeks information from the organisation's users, participants, members or clients. Ideally this should be done **formally**, by asking them specific questions on a written questionnaire or in an interview. Interviews may be done individually or in a group setting.

Questions can be **open** or **closed**. With closed questions the range of possible answers is defined by the questioner. They might be simple yes/no questions or multiple choice. 'Did you feel the service was useful to you?' is a closed question, as is 'Which of the following aspects of the service were most useful to you? Tick one or more.'

Open questions allow people being questioned to frame the answer in their own words. 'How was the service useful to you?' and 'How could it have been more useful?' are open questions.

Open questions usually bring out more information and feelings but it is difficult to analyse the information, because everyone uses different language and talks or writes about things in different ways. Closed questions elicit less information but it is more easily used.

Good monitoring usually requires a combination of open and closed questions. It should of course involve a wide range of people broadly representative of the organisation's users or members.

Informal monitoring involves simply chatting to people or eavesdropping on conversations. This is not usually very satisfactory. A statement that 'people said it was great' might be based simply on overhearing one or two people say they really liked whatever it was; it is not necessarily a representative view.

Questionnaires or interviews to follow up people who have used the organisation's services or activities, or to find out why people have dropped out, can be a useful form of monitoring. An interview when someone leaves an organisation or stops using its services is called an **exit interview.**

REVIEW

Monitoring on its own achieves nothing; it simply means the collection of information. The next step is review: putting the monitoring data in a usable form, and looking back at a specific project or activity or at a defined time period.

A review is a statement of what happened based on the available information. A review might indicate, for example, what activities and services were provided during a certain period, and how and by whom they were used. This will mean collecting together the monitoring data, sifting through it and compiling it in some way. This is easiest if careful thought was given *beforehand* to what information needed to be collected and how it could most effectively be collected and stored.

As with monitoring, a review should be as objective and comprehensive as possible. The easiest way to conduct a review is to have done careful monitoring during the work.

Reviews often include people's observations or their interpretations of events. These can differ from person to person, so a representative selection should be included.

Who does the review?

A review might take place through discussions at a committee meeting, joint committee/workers/users meeting or a special **awayday**. An outside facilitator (see chapter 22) might be brought in to help the group remain focused on the issues and to ensure everyone can participate, without one person from within the group having to chair the discussion. An awayday will usually involve evaluation (see below) as well as review.

Or a review might be purely in written form, as a presentation of statistics and other information about what the organisation has done and achieved. This might be written by someone from within the organisation or an external researcher or evaluator.

EVALUATION

Monitoring is the process of collecting information; the review is a straightforward statement of 'this is what we did'. Evaluation involves putting a **value** on the work. It is an assessment of:

● whether the organisation met its objectives and if not, why not;

● whether the work was worth doing;

● whether it was done well;

● what else the organisation did;

● whether resources were well used;

● what remains to be done.

Effective evaluation involves three essentials:

● the objectives must be clear right from the beginning, and must be written down;

● there must be adequate information about what happened, so monitoring must have taken place throughout the project and the information collected must have been carefully collated and reviewed;

● the people doing the evaluating must be willing to be critical of their organisation, themselves, and their activities. There is no point evaluating something if people will not be able to bear admitting they did not really achieve what they set out to do.

Evaluation can only be really useful if there is also a fourth factor:

● after the evaluation people must be willing to change or allow the organisation to change.

Change might mean agreeing that the original objectives have been met and setting new ones (for existing or new activities). Or the organisation might have to adapt, change, or completely scrap what it is doing, in order to try to meet the original objectives. Alternatively it might decide to adapt, change or completely scrap the original objectives and start again.

Who does the evaluation?

If the organisation has used external people to help with monitoring or review, they might well be involved in the evaluation. Someone could be brought in from a voluntary evaluation service, polytechnic or college, council for voluntary service or relevant umbrella organisation, or an independent consultant might be used. It is essential to be absolutely clear about whether the outside person is expected to be a **facilitator** (helping the group to do the evaluation itself) or a **consultant evaluator** (actually doing the evaluation). The distinction between a facilitator and consultant is explained in more detail in chapter 22.

An external evaluator can help the group look clearly at itself, its work and its achievements, but external evaluators can also use inappropriate or irrelevant criteria or carry out the evaluation in ways which are inappropriate to the organisation. These risks can be minimised by having a clear brief for the evaluator about what is being evaluated and the purpose of the evaluation.

Presenting evaluation data

When writing up the results of evaluation, the format for writing a report (chapter 6) may provide a starting framework. The evaluation report should include:

● what the organisation wanted to achieve (its objectives);

● background information about the organisation and why these objectives were prioritised;

● what information was collected, and how it was collected and analysed;

● what the information shows;

● how the evaluation was undertaken, and who was involved;

● whether the original objectives were met;

● what else was achieved;

● new needs which have become apparent, and what the organisation proposes to do about them.

It is dishonest to lie, but it is not dishonest to present information in the most positive way. Stress the good points: what the organisation achieved, what needs it met, the variety of users or activities. If objectives were not reached indicate why, and mention what steps are being taken to

Chapter 10:
Managing change

Many problems and tensions in voluntary organisations arise because managers, workers and management committees have not thought through the processes and possibilities of change, and are not prepared for it when it happens. But regardless of whether change is expected or unexpected, minor or major, positive or negative, there are ways groups can equip themselves to cope.

The action spiral (chapter 8) outlines a process for planning for change; this section offers some guidelines for implementing the process, and for coping effectively with changes which cannot be predicted.

It covers:

● creating an environment for change;

● dimensions of change;

● attitudes to change;

● dealing with the unexpected;

● taking control;

● responses to change;

● managing worst-case situations such as having to sack a worker, redundancy, closure.

AN ENVIRONMENT FOR CHANGE

Introducing and dealing with change can never be painless, but with foresight and good management the process can be much smoother.

This involves:

● having good decision-making procedures, so decisions can be made quickly when necessary, and so people know how decisions about difficult situations will be made;

● developing an organisational culture in which change is seen as positive;

● developing an organisational culture in which people are comfortable expressing their feelings, both positive and negative, about change;

● developing an organisational culture in which situations are dealt with calmly and rationally, rather than in a panic;

● developing an organisational culture which focuses on creating options and taking action to deal with changing situations, rather than one dominated by anger, blame or a sense of being a powerless victim of external circumstance;

● having clear objectives, priorities and policies (see chapters 7 and 8) so decisions about change, even those that have to be made quickly, are made within an agreed framework;

● developing good systems (see chapter 21) and ensuring more than one person knows how to operate them, so the organisation is not desperate if a worker gets ill or leaves unexpectedly.

DIMENSIONS OF CHANGE

The key factors in managing change are:

● maintaining as much control as possible over the situation, by anticipating change and developing a range of responses;

● involving, insofar as possible, people who will be affected by the change in any decisions about it;

● accepting that some aspects of change will be negative, and trying to minimise the negative effects on individuals and the organisation.

The managerial skills and processes involved in managing change will depend on the source and nature of the change. In general it is harder to manage changes which are unexpected, originate from outside the organisation or have long term implications; and easier to manage changes which can be predicted and planned for, originate from within the organisation or are fairly short term in their effects. The chart on the next page illustrates some of these factors.

ATTITUDES TO CHANGE

Every individual and every organisation should be constantly changing: doing new things, or doing old things in better ways. A fossilised individual or organisation which expects everything always to be done in exactly the same way is unlikely to satisfy anyone for very long.

On the other hand too many changes, especially if they are imposed without enough consideration and without letting people know what is happening, will probably lead to a chaotic organisation where nothing gets done because no one knows what they are supposed to be doing. In this situation people's fear of change and the unknown will lead to resistance, antagonism and possibly sabotage.

An environment of constant change can be very exciting for ambitious, dynamic people but unsettling for those who are more conservative and who like routines. (There is more about this in chapter 19, on managing stress.) While

MANAGING CHANGE

	Harder to cope with	Easier to cope with
Source	External	Internal
Need for change	Imposed/no choice	Our choice
Anticipation	Unexpected	Predictable
Lead time	None	Months
Pace of change	Rapid	Slow
Scale of change	Big	Small
Impact on individuals & organisation	Major	Minor
Time scale of impact	Long term	Temporary
Perception of change	Negative	Positive
Management of change	Unplanned	Planned
Organisational culture	Resistant to change or constantly changing	Stable but willing to change

it is important to create an organisational culture in which changes, adaptations and improvements are welcomed rather than feared, there must also be a commitment to an underlying stability and predictability.

DEALING WITH THE UNEXPECTED

Two workers out of four on the team hand in their notice within a week of each other ... a worker is diagnosed with cancer and will be off for six months ... the organisation gets a legacy for £44,000 ... the office window is left open, the office is burgled and ransacked and there are torrential rains that night and everything gets soaked (fortunately not the cheque for £44,000) ... the Guardian publishes the organisation's address at the end of an article and the phone doesn't stop ringing for three days ...

These are real situations; they all mean major change of some sort for the organisation. Current work, priorities and timetables are disrupted, major decisions have to be made about short term and long term work, and workers and users need emotional and/or practical support.

Personal responses to the unexpected

When the unexpected happens the first responses are often disbelief and denial. This may be very short term (opening the envelope with the cheque and shrieking 'I don't believe it!') or may last for several weeks or months. During the denial period people need to be kept informed of what is happening, but should not be rushed into making decisions unless this is essential.

The next response to unexpected positive events may be jubilation and excitement, followed by a sense of anxiety since even happy events are often surprisingly stressful. For negative events, disbelief and denial are usually followed by anger, then by fear and anxiety.

During the phases of strong emotion (jubilation, anger) and uncertainty (fear, anxiety) people may find it hard to think sensibly about the future. Everything is totally rosy or totally bleak. They need opportunities to talk about what is happening, and their fears. The best way to do this will depend on the situation, the organisation, and how people relate to each other in the organisation.

For negative events there may be a stage of blaming or scapegoating, or of feeling betrayed: 'How could they apply for other jobs without telling us?' 'Why did she keep smoking?' 'Who left the window open?' It is very important that these feelings be dealt with and not be allowed to fester and undermine personal relationships or the organisation's work.

Long term situations

In due course people pass through these stages into some sort of acceptance, and can start to look at options for the future. The clearer the organisation and the people in it are about priorities, the easier it will be to deal with unexpected events which have long term consequences.

In addition to sensitivity about what people may be feeling, these sorts of events require:

● good **communication channels** to tell people what is happening and how decisions will be made about how to proceed;

● **time** to develop and assess the options;

● **support** for the people most affected by any changes.

Situations needing immediate response

The more confident a manager is, and the more she or he is respected, the easier it will be to make quick decisions when these are called for, as in the case of the burglary and flood, or when staff need to be quickly redeployed to cope with the phones and requests for information. In this situation there is no time to develop and assess options; quick action is needed. These situations require:

● decisiveness on the part of the manager;

● clarity about the **limits of the manager's authority**, and what needs to be approved by the chair or someone else (can the manager on her or his own initiative hire a temporary worker for a week to deal with the phone?);

● clarity about **essential services or activities** which *must* go on, no matter what else is happening;

● excellent **communication channels** within the organisation, so everyone knows what is happening and what is expected of them.

The negative effects of the unexpected can be reduced by a general culture of good management, and by generating a sense that things are under control. Panic, on the other hand, is likely to lead to a sense of powerlessness, lack of control, individual and organisational stress and bad decisions.

TAKING CONTROL

Most changes are not unexpected. To a greater or lesser extent they can be anticipated and planned for, and there will be time to develop and consider a range of possible responses.

One of the advantages of strategic or long term planning, especially if it is rooted in a careful analysis of the political, social and economic context, is that organisations can to a large extent take control over their future. They may not get all the funding or support they need, but at least they

will pursue what they want rather than waiting to see what turns up.

Even if strategic objectives cannot be met, people at least have a starting point from which to adapt: 'We're clear about what we want to achieve. If we can't do it the way we want, what's the next best way to work towards those ends?'

The same holds true for shorter term or minor changes. Planning for change forces individuals to take a careful look at the organisation and their role within it. For some this may be exciting and challenging, for others terrifying. It opens the possibility of significant or obvious success or significant and perhaps even more obvious failure. Successful implementation of planned change requires genuine sensitivity to the concerns of workers, users, committee members and others; time to listen and explain, time to help people overcome their fears or perhaps temper their enthusiasms.

Planned change is more likely to be successfully implemented if there is clarity about processes of consultation and decision-making, with opportunities for everyone directly affected by the changes to participate in some way.

Unless people have been involved in the planning process and understand what is being proposed and why, the initial response to new ideas is likely to be resistance. This can be pre-empted by involving them, but if that is not possible resistance may be overcome by:

● explaining the proposals, and ensuring people know the background and why key decisions were made;

● explaining the decision-making process, and why some people were not involved in it;

● listening carefully to people's comments;

● not becoming defensive;

● asking for suggestions about how the proposals can best be implemented;

● genuinely considering the suggestions, and negotiating new options;

● keeping people informed about what is happening.

Anticipating the need for change

Some changes which should probably be predictable seem to sneak up: suddenly realising that rising unemployment means many more men are home during the day so more men are coming to a training centre's courses; suddenly realising the pre-school children who came to the nursery are now school age and no one is providing after-school activities for them; suddenly realising the membership drive has brought in so many new members the part-time administrative worker cannot cope with the increased workload.

Some changes are less predictable, such as a war somewhere leading to many more refugees moving into your area or a key staff member leaving. Even these, however, can sometimes be anticipated.

For many organisations the first response to such pressures is hastily to develop new activities or hire new staff. In periods of easy funding this may be appropriate but in the current economic and political climate it is increasingly important to assess the relative importance of

any move in terms of the organisation's core purpose, agreed objectives and current activities.

It may be that one way of ensuring the organisation's survival is to develop new activities in response to changing needs, new sources of funding or other external factors. There is no problem with this, so long as people are aware of the possible effects, both positive and negative, on existing activities and on the people involved (both workers and users). The whole purpose of anticipating the need for possible change is to give people opportunities to consider and assess these effects.

Risk management

For voluntary organisations dependent on external funding, the most significant source of major change is likely to be a change in funding: a new grant, a reduction, a total cut, a change in funding relationship from grant to service agreement or contract.

Other sources of external change might include a landlord raising rent so much the organisation has no choice but to leave, or a funder requiring a merger of two organisations.

To some extent the possibility of these changes, if not the actuality, can usually be predicted. This is where it is important to have good contacts, to be part of networks where information can be shared, and to read publications which monitor political changes.

Voluntary organisations are increasingly faced with the need for **risk management**: having to decide whether to take major financial risks, for example whether to proceed with a project even though the funding is not guaranteed. For complex decisions involving finance and possible personal liability, managers and the management committee or other governing body may need access to professional legal or financial advice. These contacts should be developed and briefed long before a final decision has to be made.

If this sort of external change is likely, the organisation may need to develop two (or more) scenarios: 'If we get the contract we will develop in this way, which involves significant expansion; if we don't get it we will develop in this way, which involves significant reduction in what we do'. While this is in itself time-consuming and probably demoralising, it reduces the risk of organisational collapse if the worst does happen. (And in this case, 'the worst' might be either scenario.)

Personal responses to change

When a change perceived as negative is necessary, even if it has been anticipated for a long time, the first response is usually despair and a sense of powerlessness, followed by anger and possibly fantasies of revenge. A major positive change is likely to be greeted ecstatically, followed by a rapid let-down and fear of what the organisation has let itself in for.

These strong emotions should not be denied, but good managers will help people move beyond them into the stage of implementing the agreed plan (if one has been agreed beforehand) or developing a plan of action. A previously agreed plan will need to be reconsidered in the light of reality: is it still relevant? If a new plan has to be developed the process should be gentle, giving people opportunities to explore possible alternatives before committing themselves or the organisation.

Through this period committee members may need to make very difficult decisions, and may rely on the manager for accurate information and perhaps for recommendations about action. Staff, volunteers and users may express their sense of powerlessness, despair, anger or fear in unproductive ways, and may need a great deal of support.

This may leave the manager in an isolated position, having to support everyone else but with no sources of support for herself or himself. While there are no easy answers to this situation it is helpful if the manager has built up professional support networks (with colleagues from other organisations) as well as personal support networks (family, friends). Obvious advice (get enough sleep, eat properly, take breaks during the day, let go of work in the evening and at weekends, get enough exercise) is all very relevant during this period.

Whether the situation is objectively awful or wonderful, the manager needs to be able to look at it rationally, and without getting too emotionally entangled in what is happening. Ultimately people will be helped through a period of major change by:

● having opportunities to express what they are feeling, either in a group or in one to one settings;

● having opportunities to suggest ways to deal with the situation, and knowing their suggestions are being seriously considered;

● knowing why decisions, even unpopular ones, have been made, and respecting the authority of the person or group who made the decision;

● having a sense that something is being done about the situation;

● participating in doing something about the situation;

● feeling that they can rely on the committee, the manager, colleagues and the organisation as a whole not to go to pieces.

THE WORST

There are no easy rules for dealing with ordinary change, and it is even harder to deal with worst-case situations: having to sack a worker, redundancy, closure, a serious accident caused by a worker, a violent incident involving a user, discovering the finance officer has embezzled vast sums.

The range of emotions will be the same as for any unexpected event. The most important guidelines for managing these situations are:

● stay calm, and as rational as humanly possible;

● be clear about who has to make decisions and take action, and ensure others are aware of this;

● avoid making unnecessarily hasty decisions, or pressuring others into hasty decisions, especially when they are still responding very emotionally to the situation;

● be aware of the likely emotional effects of serious situations, and try to ensure workers get the support they need (see the section on support in chapter 16);

● give people opportunities to talk about the situation, but try to keep it from dominating the organisation and interfering with essential work;

● don't keep things secret unnecessarily; doing so will only contribute to the spread of rumours and gossip;

● but be aware of issues of confidentiality, especially in situations involving staff disciplinary matters or users;

● be absolutely clear, and be sure everyone else is clear, about who can talk to the media or police, and under what circumstances;

● if situations involve a dispute, try to keep them from becoming confrontational (see chapter 18, on managing differences and conflict);

● before taking any action, try to assess the options and implications, and if possible talk it through with someone not directly connected with the organisation or the situation;

● eat properly and get enough sleep. The situation may be horrendous, but it will seem even worse (and you might well actually make it worse) if you are exhausted and are living on caffeine, doughnuts and alcohol.

Chapter 11:

Managing time

Good management means not only being clear about what needs doing, but also ensuring the organisation as a whole and individual workers are able to do it. This requires careful management of one of our most precious and most mistreated resources: time.

Within the voluntary sector people are often totally unrealistic about what can be achieved. Impossible goals are set, tasks pile up, frustration and stress result. People become so overwhelmed they are unable to use time effectively. Tempers flare; more time is wasted in arguments and conflicts. This is why stress management (see chapter 19) and time management are so often linked.

There are only three important points to make about time management.

- **Time is finite.** Extra time cannot be manufactured – but people can learn to make the most effective use of the time they do have.

- **Time lost or wasted cannot be replaced.** But what sometimes seems like wasted time (taking a lunch break, going for a walk, staring into space, watching rubbish on TV) is often a good use of time; and what sometimes seems like a good use of time (rushing about being terribly busy) is often wasted.

- **You must say no** to people or pressures if other matters (including looking after yourself) must take priority. The keys to time management lie in being able to identify priorities and being able to say no to non-priority demands which will not fit into the available time.

No matter how worthy the cause or organisation, no matter how necessary the service, no matter how committed the workers or volunteers, there are still only 24 hours in a day, 168 hours in a week. And of those hours, only a fixed number can be devoted to work. The number will vary depending on people's non-work commitments, but it is worth remembering that trade unionists and others fought for centuries for workers' rights. Self-exploitation or exploitation by a 'good cause' is no less wicked than exploitation by capitalist bosses.

This chapter covers:

- attitudes to time management;
- steps in time management;
- the importance of the work environment;
- prioritising, and being clear about how long tasks take;
- forward planning;
- weekly and daily planning;
- how to use time well each day;
- valuing other people's time;
- delegation.

ATTITUDES TO TIME MANAGEMENT

In British and American culture the manager who works 60 hours a week is often seen as a good manager. In other cultures, such as Sweden, the opposite is true: it is the bad managers, who cannot effectively organise and plan their own work and the work of the organisation, who stay at their desks night after night with endless piles of paper around them.

If a 'good' manager is culturally defined as one who is constantly rushing about, has heaps of paper on the desk and works 12 to 15 hours a day, there may be little incentive to slow down, clear the paperwork and go home at a reasonable time. This may be fine for some people, but this pressure has equal opportunities implications for people with different cultural expectations, or people whose home commitments make it impossible for them to spend so much time at work. And a manager who consistently works long hours can make other staff, who go home at a reasonable time, feel inadequate; this can lead to resentments and an organisational 'stress cycle' (see chapter 19).

Quite apart from cultural definitions, some people are workaholic and *need* to be busy and pressured all the time. It makes them feel important to have so much to do and to be so much in demand.

At the other extreme are managers who can't see what all the fuss is about. If the work gets done it gets done; if not, tomorrow is another day. With this attitude colleagues become demotivated; they may lack the energy and sense of challenge needed to perform at their best.

Most voluntary organisations have a commitment to carry out specific activities or provide specific services within an agreed time period. The effective performance of those activities or services involves additional commitments such as planning, communication and administration, all of which require time. A laid-back attitude may jeopardise effective performance, but so too might a constantly hassled and pressured attitude. The ideal is somewhere between: a sense of busy-ness and commitment, without either devaluing or over-emphasising the importance of getting tasks done when they are supposed to be.

STEPS IN MANAGING TIME

The essential steps in good time management are:

- **wanting** to use time more effectively;
- **clarifying** what needs to be done, and its level of priority;
- **planning** what needs to be done;

- **organising** what needs to be done;
- **doing it**;
- **monitoring** what is being done, and revising plans accordingly.

Although people complain about not having enough time, they often have very little desire or motivation to change the situation. After all, change is difficult. Some people thrive on pressure and can only get work done if they are up against a tight deadline, while others can never see what the fuss over deadlines is about; for all of them, learning to manage time might mean rethinking their whole attitude towards work and the clock.

THE WORK ENVIRONMENT

The physical environment can contribute significantly to better use of time:

- a blackboard or whiteboard indicating where people are and when they will be available;
- a place for everything and everything in its place (it may be trite, but it's nonetheless valid);
- labelled cupboards, desk drawers, filing drawers, boxes, bookshelves, magazine racks;
- keeping everything needed for specific tasks in one place;
- tidy desks with papers sorted logically, so they are easy to find (some time management books recommend clearing the desk of everything except what is being worked on at the moment and clearing the desk completely before leaving, but this may be an impossible ideal);
- storing items which are used regularly where they can be easily reached, and moving items which are hardly ever (or never) used out of the way;
- throwing away rubbish and clutter;
- arranging desks so they are not on the well trodden paths to the photocopier, kettle or lavatory, or other places where people regularly pass or congregate;
- creating a quiet room, or at least a quiet corner, for undisturbed work or discussions;
- using filing cabinets, bookshelves or screens to divide open plan offices;
- making (and using) 'do not disturb' signs.

The intention is not to create an institutional environment, but to cut down on time lost through unnecessary interruptions and endless searches for items 'I saw somewhere but can't remember where' or 'I'm sure were here yesterday'.

PRIORITISING

Time management depends on clarity about priorities: for the organisation, the team or project, and the individual. If the organisation or team does not plan effectively (see chapter 8) it is virtually impossible for individuals to manage their own time well.

The starting point for prioritising an individual workload lies in asking:

- What are we as an organisation trying to achieve?
- What are we as a workgroup, team or department trying to achieve?
- How does my work in general fit into what the organisation and team are doing?
- How does this particular task or demand fit into it?
- In relation to my current work, my overall work or the work of the team or organisation, is the task or demand **essential**, **important**, or relatively **unimportant**?
- In relation to when it must be done is the task or demand **urgent** (absolutely must be dealt with now), **demanding** (someone demanding attention now, but not for an urgent matter); **necessary** (should be dealt with now to keep up with work and avoid getting behind, but can wait if necessary), or relatively **unpressured**?
- Do I personally find this kind of task or demand **very satisfying**, **moderately satisfying**, or a **total drudge**?

Priority order would be:

1. **Essential** and **urgent**
2. **Important** and **urgent**
3. **Essential** and **demanding**
4. **Important** and **demanding**
5. **Essential** and **necessary**
6. **Important** and **necessary**
7. **Essential** and **unpressured**
8. **Important** and **unpressured**
9. **Unimportant**

If people are constantly dealing with categories 1 and 2, organisational priorities need to be examined; it is trying to do too much, or too much is being demanded of individual workers.

People who are constantly dealing with categories 3 and 4 (or even something unimportant but demanding) are probably too available; they need to learn to prioritise demands and say no to those which are minor or can wait. (Just because someone is at the door now or has rung now does not mean you have to be instantly available.)

People who deal primarily with categories 5 and 6 may have their work well under control, getting tasks done before they become urgent and keeping up with routine work. However, they need to be sure they are not avoiding more pressing tasks or demands which need to be dealt with first.

People who are constantly dealing with categories 7 to 9 are procrastinating, putting off dealing with higher priority work either because they do not realise it is high priority, or because they get a buzz from leaving high priority work till the last minute and doing it under pressure.

Anything from 3 to 9 can go one step up the list if it is also very satisfying. Unfortunately, it can't go down the list if it's a total drudge.

Most work, of course, does not fit into these tidy categories, but it is a useful discipline to think of tasks or demands in terms of their relative importance to the work overall, the level of time pressure, and degree of personal satisfaction.

HOW LONG DOES IT TAKE?

Many people do not have a clue how long anything takes, and will underestimate wildly. Effective time management requires a basic awareness of:

- how many hours are spent working each week (this is not necessarily the same as how many hours people are *at work*, if much time is spent chatting and gossiping or if much time is spent working at home or on the train);

- the average time spent on individual tasks (clipping and filing the newspaper cuttings, doing the PAYE, writing the management committee minutes, dealing with the paperwork for each client);

- the proportion of time spent on broad areas of work which are more or less predictable (visiting tenants, organising and running creche sessions, servicing the management committee, producing and sending out a quarterly newsletter);

- the proportion of time spent on broad areas of work which are variable (depending on how many people come to the advice session and how much follow-up each case requires, the number of requests etc).

To get this information it may be necessary to do a **time monitoring exercise** for a week, month or even quarter (depending on the pattern of work). This in itself is time-consuming but people can be astonished at the results. Some monitoring systems ask workers to record what they do in every 15-minute period. A simpler system is based on a grid, with work categories (perhaps based on the job description) across the top, and the days of the week, divided into morning, afternoon and evening, down the side. After each morning, afternoon and evening the worker writes in the total hours worked in that session, and divides the time across the various work categories. At the

end of each week the categories are totalled, and the worker can indicate whether this was a typical week.

People often say they cannot plan their work because there are too many unpredictable demands: clients walking in the door needing immediate attention, people ringing for information, or whatever. While it may not be possible to predict exactly how much time these demands will need in any one day, it is nearly always possible to predict, with considerable accuracy, how much time they will take over a week or month. With this information it is then possible to allow an average time per day or week for this type of work.

FORWARD PLANNING

For people who do want to manage their time better, the key is planning, and this starts with **thinking**. The guilt that usually accompanies thinking (rather than 'doing') must be overcome, and time must be found to define clearly what has to be done.

A good diary, with plenty of room for entering tasks as well as appointments, is essential. Everything that needs doing should be written down, and tasks which can be planned ahead should be scheduled. If it turns out not to be possible to do them at the planned time, they can be rescheduled.

There is a tendency in many voluntary organisations to say 'We can't plan ahead, because we never know what's going to happen from one day to the next.' But even in the most user-centred or member-centred organisation it is possible to plan large chunks of work.

Long term planning

Steps required to achieve the objectives outlined in the development plan or strategic plan (see chapter 8) should be entered in the **forward plan**. This includes consulting people, writing papers or reports and getting them approved as well as all the other stages in changing an activity or introducing something new.

Cyclical planning

Management committee meetings and other recurrent meetings should be scheduled several months in advance, and the people who service them should enter all the necessary steps (see chapter 5) in the forward plan and their diaries. As well as helping in time management, this kind of preparation also has positive psychological effects. People feel comfortable when events occur in predictable cycles; this sense of regularity can be enhanced by ensuring people are not constantly surprised by events which are in fact cyclical and predictable.

Monthly accounts and financial reports, annual accounts, audits, annual reports, annual general meetings, staff reports to the management committee, holiday activities, grant applications: all of these are predictable and the time needed for them can be planned and scheduled.

One way to plan for cyclical events is to use a cyclical workplan. Divide a long sheet of paper into 13 columns. In the left-hand column list the main areas of cyclical work, for example internal meetings (committees, general meetings, AGM), external meetings, regular events, finance, fundraising, regular publications. Label the other 12 columns with the months, either calendar year or financial year. In each square put what needs to happen in that month every year.

If the AGM is in October, for example, the cyclical tasks might be:

- June: booking speakers and the room, drawing up the draft agenda;

- July: getting the agenda approved by the management committee, chasing the accountant for final accounts which will have to be sent out with the agenda;

- August: get notice of meeting, agenda and accounts printed; arrange catering, creche and interpreters;

- September: send out papers, confirm room bookings, confirm speaker arrangements.

Cyclical workplans help to ensure tasks which are entirely predictable do not become crises because no one thinks of them until the last minute.

The cyclical workplan should be used in conjunction with the forward plan.

Desk time

Other tasks recur daily or weekly. One way to ensure time is available for them is to allow for a fixed block of **desk time** every day for dealing with the post and making phone calls, and a longer block every week for correspondence, filing, preparation for meetings, and other necessary tasks. And having made the commitment to have this block of time, **stick to it**. It should be entered in the forward plan and the worker's diary and treated the same as a meeting or other fixed appointment.

If a scheduled block has to be cancelled, it should be rescheduled. If it cannot be rescheduled, it is a signal that the individual worker, the team and/or organisation as a whole must reconsider their commitments and priorities. Additional time cannot be manufactured simply because there is not enough of it.

One-off tasks

The forward plan should also, of course, include one-off meetings, appointments or tasks, along with time for preparation and/or follow-up.

WEEKLY AND DAILY PLANNING

The forward plan covers a period of anything from a month to a year or more. Workplans and to-do lists cover shorter periods, ranging from a day to a month.

Workplans

One type of workplan is based on blocks of time: half hours, hours or half days, depending on the type of tasks. A basic grid, covering a day, week, fortnight or month, can be drawn up on A4 or A3 paper and photocopied to make a workplan. Or flipchart paper and felt pens can be used.

Meetings, other events that must be attended and other commitments (for example reception duty) should be filled in, as should blocks of desk time and lunch breaks. (A lunch break is a legal right and obligation, and also makes good sense in terms of reducing stress at work. It is a warning signal if workers are too busy to have lunch.)

The rest of the workplan will be for specific tasks: those which are recurrent, those which are one-off but can be planned in advance (such as preparing for a speech or an appointment), and those which are immediate.

A general guideline is to allow **20 per cent more time** for each task than you think it will take. There are three reasons for this:

- until people are very experienced at time management, they tend to underestimate, often wildly, the time required for any task;

- even the busiest, most workaholic people need time to go to the lavatory, chat, make a cup of tea, or relax;

- the telephone will ring, someone will need attention, something will conspire to ensure the task does not get done in the allotted time.

If a job involves a great deal of reacting to other people's needs and demands, an appropriate percentage of time should be allowed for this. There is no point filling 80 per cent of the workplan time with defined tasks if 30 per cent of the worker's time is typically spent dealing with 'unpredictable' demands.

Tasks in the forward plan and cyclical workplan should be entered on the workplan, either within the desk time or in a specifically allocated block (don't forget the 20 per cent margin). This step is important to ensure these tasks get done, without falling to the bottom of the list as too often happens.

To-do lists

A to-do list is a more detailed itemisation of specific, very detailed tasks to achieve what is included in the workplan. To make it:

- list all the tasks that need to be done in the time period (usually a day or week);

- divide them by type, for example all phone calls together, all tasks involving going out of the office, all correspondence;

- prioritise the items in each batch (see 'Prioritising', above);

- put them in priority order onto the to-do list.

As tasks are completed they should be crossed off the to-do list and new tasks added, so the list is always up to date and priorities can be accurately assessed. The list will need to be regularly reviewed and rearranged, as 'necessary' tasks move into the 'urgent' category.

Workplans and to-do lists allow for two realities (the amount of work that needs doing and the amount of time available) to be matched. They show how much can be fitted in, and if unexpected demands or events intervene, they can help workers make realistic decisions about which tasks must be done and which can be held over.

If there's not enough time ...

While they can help workers use the available time in the most effective way, workplans and to-do lists cannot create additional time.

If there is not enough space in the workplan and to-do list even for the highest priority commitments and tasks, there are only three immediate possibilities:

- delegate some tasks to another person who has time to do them;

- reassess priorities and demote some tasks to a lower category;

- spend less time on the tasks that need doing. This might mean accepting a lower standard than usual.

If in doubt about which tasks can be deprioritised, ask: 'What is the absolutely worst possible thing that can happen if I don't do this task today?' This sometimes makes it easier to identify highest priorities.

Working a few hours overtime for a week or two may be another possibility, if it is feasible to take time off in lieu later. But **working overtime week after week is not an appropriate way to manage time**. If people are consistently working overtime and never feel able to take time off in lieu, the organisation is being unrealistic about its objectives and resources (see chapter 8) and workers are on the path to burnout (see chapter 19). The team or organisation will need to reassess its overall priorities.

USING TIME WELL EACH DAY

Time management means **using the workplan and to-do list each day** and sticking to it. If something else has to be done instead, the new task must be higher priority than those in the to-do list. Just because something is happening *now* does not necessarily mean it is top priority. It is possible (though difficult) to ask someone to come back or ring back later.

Tasks should be kept manageable, by dividing them into **time-limited steps**: not 'I want to get the annual report

written this week' but 'I want to get the section on last year's educational programme finished before lunch, and the one on last year's welfare and advice work done between lunch and the staff meeting.'

Before a task is started, everything needed for it should be in one place. **Good filing and other systems** are essential for good time management (see chapter 21). It is far more efficient to spend 10 minutes filing each day than the same time looking for something which has not yet been filed (and has probably fallen behind the filing cabinet and won't be found till you move offices in three years).

Routines also help. Repetitive tasks should be broken into steps. If the steps are complex or hard to remember (for example, all the forms that need to be filled in when a new client is referred) devise a checklist.

Time management means **avoiding or minimising interruptions**. It is possible to close the door, tell people you cannot chat, unplug the phone or put on the answerphone. If it is essential and urgent (higher priority than the tasks on the to-do list) to chat or take phone calls, conversations should be kept short. If that is not possible, the workplan must be revised.

If there is no receptionist, institute a **rota** for answering the phone and dealing with visitors. Without a rota, everyone in the room looks up whenever the phone rings and waits for someone else to answer it, so everyone's work is disrupted. With a rota, one person's time may be totally disrupted for the morning but at least everyone else can get on with other work.

Before going home, the following day's workplan and to-do list should be revised on the basis of what has and has not been done today.

Quality time

Some people are morning people, ready to start working the moment they reach their desk; others don't wake up until mid-afternoon. Some are useless at evening meetings; others are at their peak. Quality time, when energy is at its highest, should be devoted to work requiring concentration or imagination. Low energy time should be kept for routine and straightforward work.

PREPARATION

Good time management involves being prepared for meetings, appointments or other work. This means:

- doing any necessary background reading;

- having the right papers available, with key points highlighted;

- thinking through beforehand points that need to be made;

- providing background information or papers in time for them to be read and absorbed if people will be expected to make a decision.

Many busy people find it helpful to have a set of folders labelled for each day of the week. Once a week, they put into the folders all the papers they will need for meetings or appointments each day.

Some people have a similar system for a whole month, but this can make it difficult to locate papers if they are needed beforehand and no one can quite remember where they are or the date of the meeting. Papers that 'go missing' are frequently in a monthly system such as this.

FINISHING WHAT IS STARTED

Even if it means revising the workplan, tasks should be finished. If this is consistently not possible, the tasks should be divided into smaller segments and time allocated for them individually. It boosts morale to finish something, even a small part of a larger task, and cross it off a list; it saps morale continually to transfer an unfinished task from one day's to-do list to the next.

VALUING OTHER PEOPLE'S TIME

People are often blissfully unaware of how much they waste other people's time. This kind of time-wasting is bad for the organisation and bad for morale.

Meetings should start punctually. A person who keeps 11 people waiting five minutes is wasting an hour of productive time. A person who keeps 11 people waiting 15 minutes wastes half a day. (How many people could your welfare rights centre have seen in that time? How much of the filing that you 'never have time to do' could have been done?)

Similarly, appointments should start on time. People who are delayed or have to be absent should let someone know, so time is not wasted waiting in vain.

Listening is also a key to good time management. Much time is wasted by not listening to what people are saying, not trying to understand what is being said, not asking for clarification, talking at the same time as others, interrupting, jumping to conclusions, putting people down, rejecting what people are saying and in general being rude. This wastes time in several ways: points have to be repeated, things are not clear so are done wrong, people feel devalued and put down so the organisation becomes bogged down in conflict and stress.

Finally, it is important **not to wreck other people's priorities and workplans**. If colleagues say they are busy they must be allowed to get on with what they are doing, even if their priorities seem misguided. (If a worker does consistently prioritise inappropriately, that is a matter for managerial action; see chapter 16.)

DELEGATION

Delegation is not one worker simply telling or asking someone else to do something the first worker cannot or will not do; it is giving people the right to make decisions about how the work will be done. For delegation to be effective, it must involve:

- trusting people;
- giving them the necessary background, skills and confidence to do the task;
- supporting them;
- letting them make their own mistakes;
- helping them learn from their mistakes;
- giving them praise and credit for what they have done.

Delegation is time-consuming, but it is a better investment in time than doing everything oneself.

People to whom tasks are delegated must be clear about exactly what is expected of them, to whom they are responsible, and what to do if they need help or advice.

People who delegate tasks must be able and willing to clarify what needs doing, share information and skills, and stand back. A good manager is pleased, not threatened, when another worker learns how to do a job as well as the manager.

Chapter 12:

Managing in the contract culture

Within the funded voluntary sector the major change of the 1990s is likely to be the shift from grant funding to service agreements and contracts. Even if organisations do not themselves enter into these new funding relationships, the development of the **contract culture** will have a significant impact on the voluntary sector as a whole.

This chapter looks at:

- differences between grants, service agreements and contracts;

- reasons for the change from grants to service agreements and contracts;

- possible financial and legal implications;

- possible implications for services;

- the role of the management committee or other governing body;

- what a contract or service agreement includes.

Chapter 13 covers the service delivery aspects of contracts.

The main voluntary sector publishers are committed to producing regular factsheets, booklets, books and/or training packs on issues relating to contracts. Starting points are:

- *Beginner's Guide to Contracts* by Jo Woolf (London Voluntary Service Council, 1992; 80 pages; ISBN 1 872582 55 9; £7.95 from LVSC, 68 Chalton Street, London NW1 1JR);

- *Getting Ready for Contracts: A guide for voluntary organisations* by Sandy Adirondack and Richard Macfarlane (Directory of Social Change, 1990; 139 pages; ISBN 0 907164 64 1; £7.95 from DSC, Radius Works, Back Lane, London NW3 1HL);

- *The Implications of Service Contracts for Small Voluntary Organisations: Training pack* by Peter Bird (London Voluntary Service Council, 1992; 100 pages; ISBN 1 872582 85 0; £12 from LVSC, address above);

- *Getting Ready for the Contract Culture: Training pack* by Sandy Adirondack (Directory of Social Change and National Council for Voluntary Organisations, 1992; £10 from DSC, address above);

- *Contracts for Social Care: The local authority view* (Association of Metropolitan Authorities, 1990; 50 pages; ISBN 0 902052 85 3; £10 from Directory of Social Change, address above).

The National Council for Voluntary Organisations (Regents Wharf, 8 All Saints Street, London N1 9RL, tel 071 713 6161) has a range of publications on contracts. Many national umbrella organisations and local councils for voluntary service also have relevant materials.

THE LANGUAGE OF CONTRACTS

Grants

A grant is given to a voluntary organisation by a statutory authority, charitable trust or other body, either for general purposes or for a specific purpose. In law it is generally considered to be a one-sided donation or gift, rather than a payment in exchange for goods or services.

Most grants from statutory authorities, and some from other bodies, include management or financial conditions (for example, that the group which receives the grant will provide quarterly financial reports to the funder, or will follow equal opportunities employment practices). Grants with these sorts of conditions may simply be called grants or grant aid, or may be called grants with conditions, **grant aid agreements** or **grant aid contracts**.

Service agreements

Some funders use the term **service level agreement** to mean a grant aid agreement which specifies a defined level, amount or quantity of service, for example 'eight three-hour advice sessions per week' or 'day care for 60 clients per day'.

Many funders are using the term **memorandum of agreement** or **service agreement** for a funding arrangement similar to a grant aid agreement or service level agreement, but with a more detailed specification of the service being funded, how the service will be provided, required standards or quality, what the funder will provide, and any management and financial conditions required of the service provider (the voluntary organisation).

The terms grant aid agreement, grant aid contract, memorandum of agreement, service agreement and service level agreement are often used interchangeably or are used to mean different things by different funders. It is always important to clarify what people mean by the terms they are using.

Contracts

Contract is a legal concept and refers to a legally binding and legally enforceable agreement. For a contract to exist in law there must be:

● an **exchange of consideration**, which means an exchange of anything of material value: goods, services, money, or the promise of any of those;

● **unconditional offer and acceptance** by both (or all) parties to the contract, so every side both offers something and accepts something;

● the **intention** to create a legally binding relationship.

Except in a very few circumstances which are not relevant here, a contract can exist only if all three conditions are met. So if these three conditions are met the agreement is a contract and is legally binding, even if it is called a grant aid agreement, service agreement or something else. If the three conditions are not met the agreement is not a contract, even if it is called a grant aid contract, service contract or something similar.

The question of whether an agreement between a local authority or other funder/purchaser of services and a voluntary organisation is or is not a contract will probably depend on intention. **It is essential to clarify during negotiations whether the intention is for the agreement to be legally binding.** The general presumption of the courts is that business arrangements, such as payments for provision of a service, *are* intended to be legally binding, regardless of what they are called.

Contracts are usually written, but do not have to be; there are many examples of verbal contracts (though not in relation to voluntary sector funding!). Contracts do not have to be long or complex, and do not have to be in legal language. They do not have to be drawn up by a lawyer, but any voluntary organisation should *always* take legal advice before entering into *any* agreement which is or might be held to be legally binding.

Service specification and conditions

Usually in a service agreement or contract, the type and quantity of service to be provided, and the expected standards or quality, are specified in more detail than in a grant or grant aid agreement. But they do not have to be; some grants are very specific about what is to be provided, and in some service agreements or contracts the nature of the service is left undefined.

Management and financial conditions

A service agreement or contract will generally have a range of conditions relating to issues such as financial reporting, levels of staffing, insurance etc. These may or may not be more detailed than the conditions which are part of a grant aid agreement.

Purchasers and providers

With service agreements and contracts, local authorities and health authorities will no longer be funders of the voluntary sector; they will be **purchasers** of services, and voluntary organisations will be **providers**.

In the language of contracts, the voluntary organisation will be the **contractor** and the purchasing authority will be the **client**. This is a complete shift in the use of the word client, which until now has referred to the user of services.

Forms of payment

Under grants, service agreements or legally binding contracts, payment may be made in various ways.

● **Block payment**: a lump sum for a service, activity or facility. The number of users is usually not specified. Most grants involve this type of payment.

● **Price by case**: the purchaser and voluntary organisation agree a price for each type of case or each unit of provision, and the purchaser pays for services as required. One form of this is a **per capita** fee paid to the organisation for each person it works with. Another is a **spot** payment where a purchaser pays for a single person or single unit of provision, in a one-off transaction unrelated to any other arrangement.

● **Cost and volume**: a lump sum for an agreed volume or amount of service, with payment on a price by case basis if additional service is required or if the number of users exceeds the agreed level.

LEGAL STATUS

Because a grant is assumed to be one-sided there is no exchange, so it probably cannot be a contract, even if both parties say they intended it to be legally binding. However, legal opinion differs about this.

When two parties agree that one will provide goods or services and the other will pay for them, an **agreement** exists. If both sides intend the agreement to be legally binding, a **contract** exists. So a grant aid agreement or grant aid contract, service level agreement, service agreement or memorandum of agreement can be a contract, regardless of what it is actually called, if the intention is to create a legally binding relationship.

The difference between an agreement and a contract is that a contract can be enforced in the courts. If one side does not fill its side of the bargain, the other side can sue for **non-performance** of the contract or for **breach** (breaking) of contract. The court can require the first side to do what it was supposed to and can also require it to pay **damages** to the second side to compensate for any financial loss.

Who intended what?

Often the intention of the parties to an agreement is not clear. If things go wrong, one side might say it intended the arrangement to be legally binding, and the other side might say it did not. If such a case went to court it would be decided on the basis of what a 'reasonable person' would have intended in such a situation. Courts usually assume that business arrangements are intended to be legally binding.

Because the legal status of grant aid agreements, service agreements and similar agreements is not clear, it is possible that cases will eventually go to court: for example, if a funder/purchaser wants to sue for return of funds that were not used according to the terms of a grant aid agreement or service agreement. It is not at all clear whether such funding agreements would be considered to be legally binding.

Some funders/purchasers are including in service agreements a clause saying there is no intention to create a legally binding relationship. If both parties (the purchaser and the voluntary organisation) accept this, it is unlikely a court would ever rule that the agreement is legally binding, but it could conceivably happen.

Because of the uncertainty over the legal status of grant aid agreements and service agreements, **it is good practice to treat all funding arrangements as if they are legally binding, even if they are not**. Except in strict legal terms it does not really matter what the piece of paper is called, and whether it would or would not be considered legally binding by a court. The important thing is that an organisation should not enter into any agreement unless the committee and managers understand all of it and are very confident they will be able to meet all the conditions set out in the agreement.

REASONS FOR THE CHANGE

Increased accountability

Public bodies at all local, regional and national levels are becoming more concerned about accountability and about the quality of the services being provided by them and by the groups they fund. The expectation of the public bodies is that service agreements or contracts will make the relationship between the funder/purchaser and the voluntary sector clearer and more stable. Everyone will know what the voluntary organisation is expected to provide and what type of support (and funding) the public body will give.

Market economy

Recession, economic pressures and political ideologies have combined to create an environment in which cost-cutting is one of the main incentives for changes in public services or in the way the services are provided. There is a view that the 'free market', with open competition among potential suppliers, leads not only to cheaper services but also to better services and more choice for consumers (service users).

Compulsory competitive tendering

This commitment to competition and the market economy is enshrined in the Local Government Act 1988, which says certain types of local government services can no longer automatically be provided by the local authority; the services *must* be put out to competitive tender. This is called **compulsory competitive tendering** (CCT). CCT contracts might be won by the private (commercial) sector, by the local authority's own workforce (direct services organisation) putting in a bid, by a not-for-profit organisation, or by a voluntary organisation or consortium of voluntary organisations.

Local authorities as 'enablers'

There is also pressure towards service agreements and contracts from other central government legislation. The NHS and Community Care Act 1990, for example, says local authorities should shift away from providing services and move towards 'enabling' other agencies and organisations to provide them. If the local authority does this, it will need to ensure the providers are actually providing good quality services. One method is through a service agreement which describes the services in detail or a contract which not only describes the services but is also legally binding.

Other pressures towards competition

Because of the pressure towards economy, value for money and accountability, many local authorities will put out to competitive tender even those services they do not have to. A social services department, for example, might invite competitive bids for running its residential services for elderly people. This is called **voluntary competitive tendering**. As with CCT, the contract might be won by the private sector, a direct services organisation, a not-for-profit organisation, a voluntary organisation or a voluntary sector consortium.

Competitive tendering can be through **open tendering**, with public advertisements inviting potential providers to **express an interest**, followed by a shortlisting process with detailed bids invited from among those who have expressed an interest. Or it can be through **select list tendering**, where the purchaser invites bids from potential providers who are already on an approved list.

Other pressures towards contracts

Even where there is no competitive tendering at all (where there is **direct negotiation** between the purchaser and the organisation it wants to undertake the work) the outcome might be a contract, so the purchaser can be sure it will get the services it wants. However, a negotiated arrangement might lead to a service agreement or even a grant aid agreement rather than a contract.

FINANCIAL IMPLICATIONS

It is still too early to know how the grant-funded voluntary sector will be affected by the widespread introduction of service agreements and contracts. This section and the following sections outline some of the main issues and possible implications.

Security of funding?

Many funders are moving towards a three-year or five-year funding period, even for grants, but there are difficulties because of financial restrictions.

A three-year or five-year grant or service agreement will usually be reviewed every year. The voluntary organisation could lose the money if the services it is providing do not meet the agreed standards, or if the organisation does not fulfil the conditions of the agreement (for example, providing financial reports or monitoring information). If the funder/purchaser withdraws funding without good reason, the voluntary organisation could try to say it is in breach of contract, but if the agreement is not legally binding there is not much the organisation can do about it.

With a legally binding contract, the funding is more secure

(provided, of course, that the organisation meets the conditions). But some funders/purchasers are writing into contracts that they have the right to terminate the contract if their funding priorities change, or if they do not have adequate funds. **Do not accept any such condition without taking legal advice**. A **break clause**, giving either party the right to terminate the agreement at defined times, may seem like a good idea but it can easily be used to the detriment of the voluntary organisation.

For some services it may be possible to negotiate a **rolling contract** which is rolled over (extended for a year) after each annual review of the organisation's services. With a rolling contract the organisation always has a three-year contract in place. Obviously a purchaser will only agree to a rolling contract if it has a long term commitment to purchasing the services (for example, running residential care services for elderly people) and if it is convinced the organisation can provide services over a long period.

The end of grants?

While some funders have said they will continue grant aid to the voluntary sector, others are changing all grants, or all grants of more than a certain amount, into service agreements or contracts. Groups which do not want to make this commitment will lose their funding. Other funders are retaining grants for new or innovative work, or for work which does not lend itself to being defined within a specification.

It is important for voluntary organisations to campaign for a continuation of grant aid, especially for work which is not suitable for contracts and for small or new groups which cannot, or do not wish to, commit themselves to contractual obligations.

It is also important for individual organisations not to get panicked into accepting funding with conditions they may not be able to meet. For some groups it may be more appropriate to seek other forms of funding.

No funding for core costs?

Many voluntary organisations have received grant funding to cover **core costs**: rent, office costs and other overheads, and salaries for administrators, managers, caretakers and other workers who may not, especially in larger organisations, provide direct services.

Voluntary organisations which run several activities or services will have to become more proficient at working out the full cost of a project or service: not just the direct costs but also all the indirect costs such as share of administration and managerial time, phone, share of the rent, heating etc. Those central or core costs will have to be shared out (**allocated**) between the different services or projects, and will have to be included in the funding application or tender bid.

Organisations which run only one service probably already include all these costs in their application.

Organisations which receive funding *only* for core costs are in a different situation. This will need careful negotiation with the funder/purchaser. The funder may decide to pay only for a specific definable purpose, rather than making a contribution towards core costs or general costs. Or the funder may decide to continue these as grants, or

come up with a way of wording such funding within a service agreement.

Practical guidance on costing is given in *Costing for Contracts* by John Callaghan (Directory of Social Change, 1992; ISBN 0 907164 81 1; £8.95 from DSC, Radius Works, Back Lane, London NW3 1HL).

Problems with partial funding?

As with a grant, an organisation may not get all the money it asks for under a service agreement or contract. In this case it will need to make the same sorts of decisions as if it had applied for a grant and not been awarded all of it:

- Can we realistically do what we are supposed to do with the money available?
- Can we top up the money from other sources?
- Can we provide the services or activities more cheaply than originally budgeted?

It is not prudent to agree to do something without reasonable confidence that the necessary money, people and other resources will be available, but there may well be alternatives to the original plans.

IMPLICATIONS FOR SERVICES

Loss of autonomy?

With cuts in local authority funding it is possible that only those organisations which provide direct services will continue to get funding. This may put pressure on other organisations, especially those involved in advocacy or campaigning, to move into service provision.

No organisation should make this sort of decision without carefully considering all the implications. It may (or may not) be more appropriate to go back to being a skint, volunteer-based campaign. Or it may be possible to use some funds from service provision to subsidise advocacy work. These are complex decisions, possibly involving deeply held values about the organisation's integrity and equally deep commitments to flexibility and survival in changing times.

Tighter specification of service?

One of the reasons for the shift towards more tightly defined funding arrangements is to make voluntary organisations think through what they are doing, who they are doing it with or for, what the objectives are, and how the organisation can assess whether it is providing a quality service with worthwhile results. Without this information a local authority or health authority could legitimately be asked why it is providing funding.

Organisations which have never defined their services in this way may find it strange and difficult at first, but most find it helpful and worthwhile. By being able to define what it is doing and why, the organisation is in a much stronger position: not only for getting grants or service agreements from current funders, but for getting funding from other sources as well.

Marginalisation of small groups?

Small groups or new groups may find themselves at a disadvantage. Without time or expertise to develop the necessary planning processes, financial systems and service monitoring procedures, they may be unable to compete with larger, more established voluntary organisations. They may not be, yet, in a position to commit themselves to providing defined services. If grant funding is phased out, there may be few alternative sources of income.

This is especially likely to affect groups which are already marginalised in many areas: black and ethnic minority groups, women's groups, groups in rural areas, groups dealing with unpopular issues.

Less flexibility?

One fear is that with service agreements or contracts, voluntary organisations will not be able to respond flexibly to new or changing community needs.

Every service agreement or contract should have a variation clause setting out the procedures if either side wants to change the agreement. The service agreement or contract can usually be changed at any time but both sides will have to follow the procedures and will have to agree the change in writing. In some situations it may be possible to use the variation clause to change the nature of the service being provided, or to extend it to new users.

One way to reduce the risk of needs changing is to think through very carefully how needs might change in the next three or five years (see the section in chapter 8 on strategic planning).

More pressure to deliver?

An organisation which finds it cannot deliver what it is supposed to (even under a grant or service agreement, but especially under a contract) must look seriously at *why*:

● Were we unrealistic about how much time, energy and/or money a service or activity would require?

● Has there been an unexpectedly large demand?

● Have we had problems with staff shortages, premises, or whatever?

As soon as there is some clarity about why the difficulties are happening, the situation should be discussed with a representative of the funder/purchaser, with a request that the service agreement or contract be reviewed. But **under a legally binding agreement the organisation is legally obliged to provide the services it agreed to, even if they turn out to cost more than anticipated.** The funder/purchaser does not have to negotiate a variation.

A changing role for volunteers?

People work voluntarily because they want to, not because they have to. There may be a serious conflict between reliance on volunteers and a legal commitment to provide a specified level of service. This conflict may become especially acute if the organisation's volunteers themselves have special needs.

Or volunteers may be used as a way of reducing the costs of a service and thus making it more likely that the voluntary organisation will put in the cheapest bid and win the contract. This has moral and possibly legal implications.

These and related issues are explored in *The Impact of Contracts on Volunteers* by Giles Darvill (25 pages; £2 from Volunteer Centre UK, 29 Lower King's Road, Berkhamsted, Herts HP4 2AB).

More paperwork?

For an organisation which has been keeping proper financial records, statistics, feedback questionnaires and other information, the change to service agreements or contracts should not make too much difference. But organisations which have been rather casual about such things will have to tighten up their financial and administration procedures and will have to keep much better records about finances, users and the services being provided (see chapters 9, 20 and 21).

It is important to be clear from the start how services and clients will be monitored, to avoid collecting unnecessary information. This is covered in more detail in chapter 13.

LEGAL IMPLICATIONS

Risk of legal proceedings?

With a legally binding contract, either party can take legal action against the other. In reality, however, most such situations are dealt with informally, without ever getting to court.

The legal status of grant aid agreements and service agreements is less clear, but this lack of clarity does not mean it is safe to sit back and say 'We can do anything we want, because they can't take us to court.' Apart from anything else, this attitude may jeopardise future funding.

More security for the organisation?

If a funder/purchaser does not fulfil its side of a contract, the voluntary organisation could take (or threaten to take) legal action. However, legal action is expensive and time-consuming, and the voluntary organisation would have to be quite certain the ends justified the means.

If the voluntary organisation takes legal action under a grant aid agreement or service agreement, a court might rule that the agreement is legally binding on both parties; this would almost certainly be a long and expensive process.

Greater risk for committee members?

Whether the organisation has grants, service agreements

or contracts, the individual members of the governing body (usually the management committee) could be held personally liable if the organisation does not do what it is supposed to with the money or does not provide everything it committed itself to (see chapter 2 for more about committee members' liability).

If an organisation is unincorporated it cannot enter into legal agreements in its own name, so a contract will be with individuals acting on behalf of the organisation. They retain personal legal responsibility for ensuring the organisation fulfils its side of the contract.

When an organisation incorporates (becomes a company or an industrial and provident society) any legal agreement is with the organisation itself, rather than with individuals acting on behalf of the organisation. And in most situations, the personal liability of individual committee members is limited to £1 or £5. They would only be liable for more than this if they individually, the committee or the organisation acted fraudulently (dishonestly) or negligently (irresponsibly), or if the organisation carried on operating when it did not have enough money to meet its financial obligations when they came due. This is explained in chapter 2 of this book, in *Voluntary But Not Amateur* chapter 1, and in *A Practical Guide to Company Law for Voluntary Organisations* by Bev Cross (Directory of Social Change, 1992; 48 pages; ISBN 0 907164 73 0; £5.95 from DSC, Radius Works, Back Lane, London NW3 1HL).

Any unincorporated organisation with substantial income, whether from grants, service agreements, contracts or other sources, should seek legal advice about whether to incorporate.

Issues around charity trading?

Charities are in general prohibited from trading, and most charity constitutions specifically prohibit permanent trading. 'Trading' in this context means charging for goods or services, or being paid for them.

Grants are not considered as trading by the Charity Commission or Inland Revenue. It is not clear whether providing services under a service agreement would be classed as trading. Providing services under a contract would almost certainly be classed as trading.

However, even if the organisation is a charity, and even if the constitution prohibits permanent trading, and even if providing services under a service agreement or contract is classed as trading – the charity can probably still do it. **The prohibition on charities undertaking permanent trading does not apply to primary purpose trading**, which is any trading in direct furtherance of the charity's primary objects.

The primary objects will be defined in the governing instrument (constitution, memorandum and articles of association, trust deed etc). If what the charity is being paid to do falls directly within those purposes, there is no problem. If it does not fall within the primary purpose or if the primary purpose is unclear, it is important to check with the Charity Commission. If a charity enters into a service agreement or contract which is not primary purpose there is a possibility of tax or legal problems later.

If the organisation is not a charity these restrictions do not apply.

If a charity wants to undertake trading which is not primary purpose there are three possibilities.

● It can seek Charity Commission approval for changing its objects. In general the Commission is reluctant to allow charities to change their objects unless a very convincing justfication can be given.

● If what it wants to do is charitable under charity law, it can set up a separate charity to take on the contract.

● If what it wants to do is not charitable, it can set up a non-charitable organisation. The non-charity can covenant or GiftAid most or all of its profits back to the charity, thus legally avoiding tax on any profits.

If a new organisation is set up it would probably be incorporated, so in the first case it would be a charitable company and in the second an ordinary (non-charitable) company. A non-charitable company set up to undertake trading which is not primary purpose is sometimes called a **trading company** or **trading subsidiary**.

Some legal advisers who are not specialists in charity law do not seem to know about primary purpose trading, and tell charities they *must* set up a non-charitable company if they enter into a contract to provide services. Even with covenanting or GiftAiding of profits, there are still significant tax and other advantages to carrying out work within a charity rather than within a non-charity. So do not be pushed into setting up a non-charity if it is not necessary.

For more information, see the chapter on incorporation in *Getting Ready for Contracts*.

Needing to register for VAT?

Grants are not subject to value added tax. Contracts are almost certainly **business activities** under VAT law, and are therefore potentially subject to VAT. If HM Customs & Excise (which administers VAT) decides service agreements are business activities they too become potentially subject to VAT.

Even if the services or activities being provided are acceptable under charity and tax law, **they could still be subject to VAT**. VAT is a *very* complicated issue. In general, personal social services or welfare services for people who are elderly, ill, disabled, in need etc are exempt from VAT if they are provided by charities and if the charges (what the charity is paid for providing the services) only cover the costs. Childcare and vocational training are also usually exempt from VAT. **Other services may be subject to VAT even if they are provided by charities**. Many (but not all) activities carried out by non-charities are subject to VAT.

If a business activity is subject to VAT, and the organisation's income from VATable activities is more than the threshold (£36,600 in 1992-93), the organisation will have to register for VAT and charge VAT on all its VATable activities. So instead of 'charging' a local authority £40,000 to run a service the organisation would have to charge £40,000 plus £7000 VAT, then pay the VAT over to HM Customs & Excise. If the organisation also charges its users, it would have to add 17.5 per cent VAT to the fees.

This does not actually cost the local authority extra because it is registered for VAT and can reclaim the £7000 VAT paid to the voluntary organisation. But the users, not being registered for VAT, cannot reclaim the extra 17.5 per cent they have to pay.

Registering for VAT is not necessarily a bad thing, because it means the organisation can reclaim the VAT it pays on equipment, stationery or other expenditure. But VAT involves additional bookkeeping and paperwork.

Each local VAT office makes its own decisions and there is no clarity about how they will define service agreements. In the meantime there is a chapter on VAT in *Getting Ready for Contracts*, and leaflets on VAT for charities and for other voluntary organisations are available from any local office of HM Customs & Excise.

If the services being provided under a service agreement or contract might be subject to VAT, **get financial advice immediately**. If an organisation does not register for VAT when it should, the organisation and its committee members could become liable for a large fine and all the back VAT which should have been collected.

THE ROLE OF THE COMMITTEE

The management committee or other governing body will have to make major decisions about whether to enter into a service agreement or contract, budgets, service specifications and other complex issues. If the organisation has paid staff the committee will probably rely on them for information and recommendations, but the final decision should be made by the members of the governing body. This is because they, rather than the staff, are legally responsible for ensuring all the terms of the service agreement or contract are carried out.

It is essential for the committee to know about the shift from grant funding to a service agreement or contract and to understand the implications of more tightly specified services and conditions. It may be necessary for the committee to get specialist legal, financial or management advice, and this will need to be budgeted for.

The committee may want to consider co-opting people with specialist legal or financial expertise. The Action Resource Centre (102 Park Village East, London NW1 3SP; tel 071 383 2200) runs **Lawyers in the Community** and **Accountants in the Community** schemes in some areas. These match volunteer lawyers and accountants with community organisations.

With the move to service agreements and contracts the need for a genuine partnership between the committee, the manager and other staff and volunteers, and the organisation's members and users becomes even more important. With crucial decisions about the organisation's future to be made, people need to be able to communicate openly and honestly with each other and to work together within a changing external environment and possibly a changing organisation.

DRAWING UP A CONTRACT

There is no set format for a contract; indeed, a contract can be written on the back of an envelope or can even be verbal. But service agreements or contracts between a funder/purchaser and a voluntary organisation are likely to include some or all of the items listed in this section. More detailed information on what to include in a contract is given in *Getting Ready for Contracts*.

A contract or service agreement is two way. It sets out what the organisation must do, and also what the purchaser must do. It protects the organisation from the goalposts suddenly being changed, but it also commits the organisation to the existing goalposts. Even if the agreement is not in the form of a legally binding contract, the organisation should think very carefully about the implications of committing itself to anything.

Most contracts go through several drafts before they are finally signed. Each draft should be:

● dated on the top of every page, including page 1, so it is easy to see which is the most recent version;

● clearly marked 'Draft' on every page, so it cannot be taken as the final version.

Always look carefully at the most recent version; even an apparently minor change in wording or a typing mistake (such as leaving out the word 'not') may have significant implications.

If anything is not clear ask for an explanation *in writing*. This is especially important if the contract or service agreement is written in incomprehensible legal language. 'We didn't know what it meant' is no defence if the organisation is subsequently unable to meet its side of the agreement.

WHAT A CONTRACT INCLUDES

Not all of these items will be relevant for all organisations or types of service. But it is worth thinking about *whether* each one should be included.

Introduction

This section defines the parties to the agreement. It includes:

● Parties to the contract

● Powers under which they are acting

● Representatives for each side

● Start date and duration

Service specification

The service specification defines the service(s) to be provided and the required quantity and quality.

Description of service

● The organisation's aims

● Type of services, activities or facilities to be provided

● Service objectives

● Where the services will be provided or located

● When the services will be provided

● Whether fees are to be charged for services, and how they will be determined

● How the services relate to overall provision by the purchaser

● Support (if any) to be provided by the purchaser, for example access to vehicle maintenance, local authority training courses or architects

● Possibility of provider subcontracting to other providers.

Service standards

● Required standards of service

● Performance indicators to assess quantity and quality of service

● Involvement of users and others in decisions about services

● Procedures for dealing with complaints by users.

Users/clients

● Eligibility criteria

● Target groups

● Referral or admission procedures

● Maximum/minimum limits or targets for numbers

● Assessment/review of users while using the service

● Discharge procedures

● Involvement of users in decisions about the service

● Complaints procedures for users.

Equality of opportunity

● Compliance with equal opportunities legislation and policies

● Procedures for ensuring fair access to services

● Requirements for translation, interpretation, special facilities etc

● Equal opportunities monitoring.

Management responsibilities

● Which decisions require consultation with the purchaser

● Procedures for such consultation and for resolving disputes

● Involvement of the purchaser's representative(s) on the provider's management committee or other governing body, and a statement that such representative(s) shall not have voting rights on any matter relating to the contract

● Confidentiality of information

● Statement that the voluntary organisation has the right to make all decisions, other than those covered in the agreement, about eligibility for services, method of provision and management of the service.

Monitoring and evaluation

One issue which needs to be absolutely clear is whether the purchaser is monitoring only the services provided under the contract or service agreement, or is monitoring all the organisation's services. The contract might include:

- Arrangements, if any, for a liaison group or other body to oversee or advise on services

- How services will be assessed, and by whom

- Monitoring reports to the purchaser or liaison group: content, frequency

- Other monitoring procedures, for example periodic inspections, surveys of users, meetings with users, independent (external) assessment

- Access by purchaser to premises or services

- Provision for annual or other formal reviews

- Procedures for negotiating changes in services due to changing needs or demand.

Financial conditions

This section sets out how much the service will cost and how payments will be made.

Costs

- Basis for payment (block, per capita, cost plus volume)

- Cost of services in the first year

- Management costs

- Portion of costs to be covered by purchaser/funder

- Provision for inflation increases

- Provision for other increases during the year (for example if new salary scales are negotiated or if per capita costs increase unexpectedly).

Payment

- When the purchaser will pay (quarterly, half-yearly, annually), when the services will be paid for (in advance, midway through the period, in arrears), and deadlines for payments

- Whether payment is contingent on the purchaser receiving financial reports or other information

- What happens if the provider can provide the service for less than it has been paid.

Financial monitoring and review

- Financial reports from provider to purchaser: how often, how much information, how they will be monitored

- Procedures for verification of financial reports

- When annual accounts have to be submitted

- When budgets for the following year have to be submitted

- Procedures and timetables for negotiating agreed budgets for future years

- Procedures for reviewing and varying unforeseen financial costs.

Other conditions

Other conditions might cover staffing, premises, equipment, and insurance.

Personnel issues

- Staff numbers and/or ratios

- Staff structure

- Provisions relating to recruitment and selection of staff

- Involvement by purchaser in staff recruitment and selection

- Procedures for police checks on staff

- Requirements for staff qualifications and/or experience

- Provisions relating to terms and conditions of employment

- Holiday, sickness and maternity cover

- Detailed provisions if the provider is taking over staff from the purchasing authority or other employer (this is a very complex area involving continuity of service, pensions, trade union arrangements and much more)

- Use of part-time staff, agency staff or trainees

- Use of volunteers within the contract

- Staff and volunteer training and development.

Premises or accommodation

If the purchaser is providing accommodation, the contract might include information about this. However, it is nearly always better to have premises matters in a separate lease or licence. If these are in the contract they might cover:

- Terms and conditions for occupying premises

- Responsibility for insuring premises

- Responsibility for maintenance and repair of premises

- Support from the purchaser, for example access to local authority architects

- Health and safety requirements.

Equipment and vehicles

- Use of vehicles or equipment provided by the purchaser

- Responsibility for insuring contents, special equipment, vehicles, drivers

- Responsibility for maintenance, cleaning, repair and replacement

- Ownership of existing and replacement equipment, vehicles etc

- Support from the purchaser, for example access to vehicle servicing.

Indemnity and insurance

- Responsibility for public liability insurance and any insurance specific to the provision of the services
- Responsibility for underwriting damages not covered by insurances
- Evidence of insurances.

Variation, renewal, termination

This section will include provision for changing or ending the contract, and for dealing with disputes.

Review and variation

- Scheduled reviews (how often, who is involved, process)
- Procedures for altering or varying the contract (for example, due to unforeseen changes in need or costs)
- Procedures for complaints by either party
- Procedures for resolving disputes between the parties.

Renewal

- Procedures and timetable for negotiating extension or renewal.

Breach

- Procedures and timetable for dealing with breach of contract by either party
- Procedures and timetable for dealing with disputes about breach.

Termination

- Procedures and timetable for negotiating termination not involving breach (non-renewal)
- Procedures and timetable in case of termination because of breach
- Procedures for dealing with disputes about termination.

Notice

- Where reports, correspondence etc have to be delivered.

Signatures and dates

Note that anyone signing on behalf of any organisation *must* be authorised to do so, and *must* specify that they are **signing on behalf of the organisation**. The signatory should nearly always be the chair, secretary or treasurer, rather than a member of staff.

Chapter 13:

Managing performance indicators

As the voluntary sector moves into the contract culture it increasingly has to come to terms with the language of commerce and industry: performance indicators, inputs and outputs, outcomes, quality assurance. No longer is it enough simply to run a service or organise an activity; the organisation must be able to define and assess what it does, in order to include these definitions and procedures for assessment in a service agreement or contract.

There are six broad categories of indicators to assess what a voluntary organisation does:

- **quantitative**, based on numbers or statistics related to **input** (what goes into the provision of a service or activity), **activity or service outputs** (what the organisation provides or produces with the inputs) and **user outputs** (how many people use an activity or service);

- **financial**, based on cost;

- **qualitative**, based on how good the service or activity is;

- **process**, based on how decisions are made and how people are involved in the service or activity;

- **outcomes**, based on what happens as a result of the service or activity;

- **comparative**, based on comparing what this organisation does with what others do, or with doing nothing at all.

These indicators overlap and may be used separately or together.

This chapter covers:

- performance jargon;

- the six types of indicators;

- implications of introducing performance indicators.

These issues are explored in detail in:

- *Quality of Service: Measuring performance for voluntary organisations* by Alan Lawrie (Directory of Social Change, 1992; 94 pages; ISBN 0 907164 82 X; £8.95 from DSC, Radius Works, Back Lane, London NW3 1HL);

- *Quality and Contracts in the Personal Social Services* (Association of Metropolitan Authorities, 1991; 95 pages; ISBN 1 85677 009 5; £12.75 from AMA, 35 Great Smith Street, London SW1P 3BJ or from DSC, address above).

Most workers already use some sort of indicators to assess whether a service or activity is working well. But in the changing voluntary sector environment:

- these indicators need to be agreed before the service or activity is provided;

- indicators may be defined not only by the workers who provide a service and the people who use it, but also by funders or by others outside the organisation;

- indicators may be formalised in contracts or service agreements;

- these indicators will be used to assess the work of the organisation, and funding could be at risk if work does not meet the agreed standards.

MONITORING AND EVALUATION

There is considerable overlap between performance, monitoring and evaluation, and chapters 8 and 9 provide a good starting point for thinking about performance indicators.

However, monitoring and evaluation tend to refer to what the organisation wants to achieve and actually achieves within a fixed period, either in relation to the whole organisation or to some services, activities or projects within it. Performance indicators are about defining, in a way that can be written into a contract or service agreement, how the organisation or the purchaser will assess whether a specific service is being adequately provided.

Performance indicators form part of the organisation's monitoring and evaluation procedures.

PERFORMANCE INDICATORS

Performance relates to what the organisation does: the services it provides, the activities it organises, the goods or services it produces.

- **Performance indicators** are ways to measure or assess specific aspects of what the organisation is doing, for example how many children come to the creche and how much time is spent on different activities.

- **Performance expectations** or **performance standards** define an agreed minimum level of performance, for example the minimum (or maximum) number of children who should be coming for each session, and what proportion of time should be spent on different activities.

- A **performance target** is a commitment to improve the standard of performance within a certain period, for example to increase average numbers from 12 to 15 per session by 31 March, or to take the children to the library at least once a fortnight starting next month. Targets can only be used if existing standards are clear.

Performance might relate to quantity, quality, outcomes, cost or involvement.

Approaching performance indicators

When thinking about performance indicators the best starting points are to ask:

● What services or activities do we provide?

● Who uses each service or activity?

● What are we trying to achieve for each user group?

● What standards or expectations do we already have about the quantity or quality of services to be provided, number or type of users, or the results we are working towards?

● How do we already assess whether we are achieving those standards or expectations? Are these methods working well?

● Are there other ways to assess how well we are doing?

This approach is rooted in the organisation's own values, objectives, priorities and ways of working. Some of the indicators already used, perhaps very informally, within the organisation can form the basis for the more formal performance indicators required by funders/purchasers.

QUANTITATIVE INDICATORS

Indicators based on quantity – of services, users, time or whatever – are the easiest and therefore the most common. Numbers or statistics are collected and at the end of the period are collated and assessed against any targets which have been set. Quantitative indicators are often called **performance measures**, because they measure what is going into or coming out of the organisation.

Three types of quantitative indicators are:

● **inputs**;

● **activity or service outputs**;

● **user or customer outputs**.

These can be compared with each other to give **averages** or **linked measures**.

To use quantitative measures there must be appropriate and workable procedures for monitoring numbers (of people, visits, time, bookings, whatever). This is covered in chapter 9.

Inputs

Inputs are what goes into a service. Input measures might include the number of workers involved in a service, the amount of time spent on it, how premises are used, equipment, the financial costs, and the number of enquiries or potential users.

Activity or service outputs

In manufacturing, output refers to the amount of goods produced. In the voluntary sector, it is more likely to refer to the type and amount of services or activities provided by the organisation. Output measures might include, for example, the number of sessions run by the organisation, number of home visits, number of bookings for premises, number or percentage of voids (empty units), or number of training packs produced.

User, client or customer outputs

But what if no one comes to the sessions or buys the training packs? User, client or customer outputs relate to the **numbers of people** who use a service, take part in an activity or buy a product. Measures might include total number of users, clients or members, number of new users, number or percentage of referrals from certain types of agencies, number or percentage from specific groups (such as ethnic, age, gender), number or percentage of cases closed or number of training packs sold.

Making sense of the numbers

In themselves, most of the numbers relating to inputs or outputs are meaningless. They gain meaning only by:

- being linked to each other, so inputs are directly related to outputs, or activity or service outputs are directly linked to user outputs;

- *or* being averaged to give, for example, average number of clients per session, average number of sales per week, average time to respond to complaints;

- *and* being put into some sort of context where change can be assessed: either compared to figures from a previous period, or being set against agreed targets for this period.

For example we might use the following measures:

- the **inputs** are one advice worker (staff) using the counselling room and most of the reception area (premises) for 46 weeks of the year for three hours a week (time), plus using her office for approximately seven hours a week for necessary administration and follow-up;

- to run 46 weekly drop-in advice sessions (**service output**);

- at which 225 different people are seen over the year, of whom 62 per cent come once, 23 per cent come twice, and 15 per cent come three or more times (**user outputs**).

These statistics are interesting but do not reveal very much about whether the organisation is doing what it set out to do, or whether the work is being done well.

Averages

Another type of quantitative indicator is based on averages rather than straight numbers, for example average number of visits or amount of time per client, average length of stay, average number of new users per month, average response time to deal with a new referral or a complaint. Many averages are derived by setting inputs against outputs (for example average number of clients per session, average time spent with each client).

Quantitative measures in value-based organisations

Because quantitative indicators look at what the organisation does in terms of how many, how much, how quickly or how cheaply, they are often considered inappropriate for value-based voluntary organisations.

One way to make quantitative indicators more relevant is to include within them **organisational aims**, **method** and **values**: what the organisation is trying to achieve, how it provides its services and why it does it that way. For example:

- if the **aim** for a local community centre's advice work is to ensure local people know about and have access to welfare and housing benefits and public services

- the inputs might be one advice worker using the premises for the time described above

- to run 46 weekly drop-in advice sessions (service outputs)

- based on self-referrals and on referrals from other local community organisations (**method**), and committed to encouraging people to follow through on their queries themselves rather than rely on advice workers or other professionals to do it for them (**values**)

- which sees the 225 people described above (user outputs).

But even within a value-based framework, indicators based on inputs and outputs are limiting and often irrelevant. It is more appropriate for most voluntary organisations to move beyond inputs and outputs to **outcomes**: what happens as a result of people using the service. For example:

- of the 225 people seen, 26 per cent got new or increased benefits and 8 per cent learned about and joined adult education courses as a result of contact with the centre (**outcomes: immediate or short term results**)

- and all those who joined adult education stayed with the courses for at least six months, and at the end of that period had improved their literacy, numeracy and/or basic job skills (**outcomes: longer term impact**).

There is a real risk that if voluntary organisations do not develop appropriate qualitative indicators, funders/purchasers will focus solely on quantitative measures, without taking into account quality of service or outcomes.

FINANCIAL INDICATORS

For financial assessment the organisation must be aware of the **total cost** of providing a service: not just the **direct costs** (such as the cost of an advice worker and the extra telephone needed for the advice work) but also **indirect costs** such as share of rent, gas and electricity, administration time and management time.

The most common financial indicator is **unit cost**: how much it costs per client, visit, hour, day or whatever. This is found by dividing the total cost by the number of clients, visits, hours etc.

In a time of financial constraints and increasing emphasis on value for money, there is a risk that funders/purchasers will force voluntary organisations to cut costs in order to meet unreasonable financial targets.

QUALITATIVE INDICATORS

Qualitative indicators assess not how much is provided or how much it costs, but **how well** it is provided or how good it is.

Qualitative indicators are often divided into those which are considered to be **objective** (for example, assessment against externally agreed standards, or by an external assessor) and those which are seen to be **subjective** (such as user satisfaction, or self-assessment). But even so-called objective indicators are based on subjective assumptions about what does and does not constitute a 'good' service. These assumptions may or may not be valid for a particular voluntary organisation.

Qualitative indicators should include not only the service itself, but also the way it is managed.

Quality assurance refers to the process of agreeing quality standards and targets, implementing procedures to reach the targets, and regularly monitoring results against the standards and targets.

Externally agreed quality standards

For some types of work, such as residential homes, agreed standards exist and the organisation's work will be assessed against those standards. These standards are likely to be the minimum acceptable. Assessment may be by external evaluators (independent inspection unit, consultants) or may be done internally (self-assessment).

Internally agreed quality standards

External standards do not exist for many areas of work, and even where they do exist may not be appropriate for a particular organisation. In this situation an organisation, ideally in consultation with its users, can develop its own criteria for what constitutes a good quality service. Assessment may be done internally or by external consultants.

It is important to guard against setting standards defined solely by professionals or others who do not actually use the services or activities. The process of setting quality standards may involve a long and complex process of determining, through discussions with users, what they consider to be a good quality service.

Setting quality standards is difficult, especially if people within the organisation do not agree about what the standards should be, or if they feel threatened by implementation of standards. But it is important for every organisation to be able to 'prove' it is doing its work well. Without such indicators, there is a risk that only quantitative or financial measures, or quality standards defined by (possibly inappropriate) outside bodies, will be used.

If undertaking self-assessment against internally defined standards it is essential to beware of in-built biases.

Negotiated standards

Standards may be agreed through negotiations between the funder/purchaser and provider. Such negotiations should always take into account the views of users.

Evaluation by external evaluators

To avoid allegations of bias, external consultants are sometimes brought in to assess the organisation or a service, using agreed standards (external, internal or a combination).

If standards have not been previously agreed, the consultants will be expected to evaluate against their idea of what the organisation or service should be. It is essential to ensure any standards or criteria they use are appropriate to the organisation.

User satisfaction

Questionnaires, interviews or meetings to assess user/client/consumer satisfaction must be carefully conducted if they are to give an accurate assessment of satisfaction. (Most people are reluctant to say anything negative, for fear of hurting people's feelings or jeopardising their future access to services; a minority, the grumblers, will complain about everything.)

Another way of assessing user satisfaction is through an analysis of complaints and what is done about them. While lack of complaints may be taken as an indicator of a good service, it often indicates a poor service in which there is no procedure for complaints or users are afraid to complain.

PROCESS INDICATORS

Process indicators focus on the ways in which decisions are made about the organisation and its services.

Involvement in policy decisions

For many organisations 'user involvement' or 'community involvement' is seen as being far more important than quantities and costs. But it is very difficult to assess levels of involvement (by users, workers, the community) in policy issues and other broad decisions made by the organisation.

For example, holding three 'community consultations' or 'user forums' is meaningless if participants do not have adequate background information, the meetings are dominated by professionals, participants do not have the confidence to speak, or interpreters, signers or other specialist provision are not available.

Despite the difficulties it is important for many organisations to try to develop ways to assess both quantity and quality of involvement, especially by users, in policy decisions.

Decisions about own services

Organisations need to develop clear policies, procedures and standards for assessing type and level of individuals' involvement in decisions affecting their own services.

Again it is important to ensure this is not simply a token exercise. (It is not uncommon to hear something like 'We talk to each client at least three times in the first month and give them opportunities to say what they want'. The key words here are *we talk to them* and *we give them opportunities.* There is no indication that the users are talking to us or taking the opportunity to tell us what they want, or that we are doing anything to provide what they want!)

OUTCOMES

Outcomes are **what happens as a result** of the organisation's work. They can only be assessed if there is some way to test or follow up what happens after a service has been provided. To assess some outcomes it may also be necessary to have information about what the situation was *before* the service was provided.

While some outcomes are easy to assess others, such as increased confidence, are extremely difficult.

Outcomes can be assessed by:

● objective indicators such as successful benefit claims, passing a test or getting a job after a training course, getting move-on accommodation;

● observation by workers, such as amount of participation in a group;

● users' own observations about what has happened to them as a result of coming to the organisation.

Short term outcomes

So long as the organisation is clear about what it is assessing and has procedures in place for collecting the information, it is usually not difficult to assess at least some immediate or short term results.

Longer term impact

In the longer term, the organisation might want to assess impact on individuals, groups or the community. This may require fairly sophisticated follow-up.

COMPARATIVE INDICATORS

Comparison with other providers

This involves comparing the organisation's numbers, time, costs, quality or whatever to someone else's. For this to be meaningful, like must be compared with like. There may be ethical implications about trying to prove how good one organisation is by knocking another.

Comparison with doing nothing

For some organisations or services it may be appropriate to compare what is being done and achieved with what the situation would be if the organisation or service did not exist.

IMPLICATIONS FOR ORGANISATIONS

Time spent thinking about appropriate performance indicators and how they might be introduced can help an organisation clarify:

● what it is trying to do and achieve;

● what it defines as a 'good service';

● how it might prove it is providing a good service;

● how these indicators might be incorporated in a contract or service agreement;

● which indicators it would not be appropriate to incorporate in a contract or service agreement.

It can thus help ensure that any indicators included in a contract are appropriate to the organisation and its users and are not being imposed by the purchaser/funder.

But use of performance indicators can also:

● put the organisation in a position of defining minimum standards it knows it can meet, rather than the higher standards it should be aiming for;

● divert the organisation into concentrating on easily measured services and outcomes;

● lead to pressure to adopt so-called objective, externally defined standards which are not appropriate for the organisation;

● lead to attempts to measure or assess aspects of an organisation's work which are too difficult, complicated or time-consuming to assess properly;

● take a phenomenal amount of time and effort, not only to define appropriate indicators, standards and targets but also to develop ways to collect information, collect it, analyse it, and redefine targets accordingly;

● lead to a situation in which information is collected without anyone being clear about how it will be used.

As with so many of the changes created by the contract culture, performance indicators have some good points. They may, in the long term, help the voluntary sector to provide higher quality, more responsive services. But they may also make organisations top-heavy, putting so much time and effort into defining and assessing services that there is little time left actually to provide them.

Chapter 14:

Managing people

Effective management of staff or volunteers involves a combination of common sense, sensitivity, confidence and good management practice in all areas of work. Some people seem to be naturally good managers; others need to acquire skills or sensitivity.

This short chapter covers:

- where responsibility for personnel management lies;
- what is involved in personnel management;
- workers' motivation;
- sample terms of reference for a personnel sub-committee.

Chapter 15 covers staff and volunteer recruitment and induction; chapter 16 looks at supervision, reviews and the management of work performance; and chapter 17 is about training for staff and volunteers.

Information on most personnel matters is available from the Institute of Personnel Management (35 Camp Road, London SW19 4UX) and ACAS (27 Wilton Street, London SW1X 7AZ). The Volunteer Centre UK (29 Lower King's Road, Berkhamsted, Herts HP4 2AB) provides information on volunteer management. It has an excellent booklet, *Volunteers First: The personnel responsibilities of people who manage volunteers* by Angie McDonough and Angela Whitcher (£1.50).

PERSONNEL MANAGEMENT IN CONTEXT

Personnel management is just one part of the overall management function which includes:

- managing the organisation's policies, objectives and long term planning;
- managing the day to day work of the organisation: deciding what needs to be done, when and to what standards, and ensuring it gets done;
- managing the people who do the work (personnel management): ensuring they have the necessary skills, information and time, and dealing with problems in work performance;
- managing the organisation's resources: being sure there is adequate money, space, equipment and materials to do the work.

These functions are considered in more detail in chapter 1 of this book.

Whose responsibility?

In voluntary organisations responsibility for managing paid workers is often very unclear, with responsibility constantly shifting between:

- the whole management committee;
- elected officers;
- a personnel or staffing subcommittee;
- a staff support group;
- senior staff (manager, project leader, coordinator, general secretary, director);
- 'middle management' or line managers (team leader, head of department);
- supervisory staff who oversee other people's work, but may not have other management responsibilities;
- staff or team meeting(s);
- individual workers, who often have considerable responsibility for managing themselves.

In groups which use volunteers there may be unclear boundaries between the volunteer organiser or placement worker, the manager of the department or team in which the volunteer is placed and the person who has day to day responsibility for supervising the volunteer.

The boundaries between staff and management committee, or between different levels of the staff structure, cannot be rigid; they change as managers and workers become more experienced and confident, or as experienced staff leave and the managers and management committee have to provide more guidance to new staff. However, the section on terms of reference for a personnel subcommittee, at the end of this chapter, should help organisations to allocate responsibilities.

Clarifying accountability

There is no right model, but every worker should know to whom she or he is accountable and what that accountability means in practice. For organisations which have a defined staff structure this is usually reasonably clear. For organisations where accountability is not clear, one way to clarify it is to ask:

'If this worker wanted to do something new or wanted to make a significant change in the way she or he does her or his own work, with whom would the change have to be agreed?'

If the answer is 'nobody', the next question is:

'If this worker's work was sloppy, shoddy and generally unacceptable, who would talk to her or him about it?'

If the answer is still 'nobody' (or just as bad, 'everybody', which in practice often means nobody) ask:

'Who *should* be dealing with issues like these in relation to this individual worker?'

Ultimately every worker in a voluntary organisation, both paid and volunteer, is accountable to the management committee or other governing body as a whole. But accountability to a large group is quite difficult to manage. It is usually better if each worker is directly accountable to one or two people.

Crunch points

The lack of clarity about accountability and responsibility for personnel management is especially acute at specific points in an organisation's development:

- after a group of volunteer committee members who have been doing everything themselves hire a worker or workers to do some of the work on their behalf;

- when a worker who has been doing a particular job takes on responsibility for managing other people doing it;

- when a small organisation which has not previously defined anyone as 'manager' or 'project leader' expands, and someone is given specific management responsibility;

- when the organisation has a coordinator without clearly defining whether coordination is a task or involves managing other people and their work;

- when an organisation reaches key points in its growth which may involve significant changes in how people communicate with and relate to each other (for small and medium sized organisations, these points are generally at around seven workers, 16 to 20 workers, and 35 to 40 workers);

- when the people responsible for management (either management committee, managers or members of a collective) fear they will be seen as authoritarian or will get it wrong if they exercise their managerial authority;

- when a confrontational workers versus management environment is created.

When any of this is happening, the management committee and managers, ideally in consultation with staff and volunteers, need to clarify responsibilities and ensure workers remain supported and able to get on with their work. If the issues are avoided or ignored, the result is likely to be low morale, internal arguments and conflicts, and poor work performance.

WHAT IS PERSONNEL MANAGEMENT?

Specific aspects of personnel management include:

- ensuring all workers (paid and volunteer) feel they are a valued part of the team and organisation;

- involving workers in discussions and decisions which affect their work or working environment, and ensuring they have adequate information and time to participate in those discussions (see chapters 4 and 5);

- ensuring workers know what they are supposed to be doing, how to do it and how it fits into the rest of the work of the organisation;

- helping workers plan work and reassess priorities if necessary;

- helping workers recognise and overcome intellectual, technical or personal difficulties affecting their work;

- ensuring workers have opportunities to learn, change and develop within their work;

- setting deadlines and informing workers about them, implementing procedures to monitor work against them, changing them as required;

- setting standards of performance (quality of work and/or behaviour) and implementing procedures to monitor them;

- dealing with poor timekeeping, poor work performance, and other potential or actual disciplinary matters;

- creating and maintaining a safe and pleasant physical environment (see the section on this in chapter 19);

- creating and maintaining a good emotional environment;

- helping sort out conflicts within the group (see chapter 18);

- dealing with workers' grievances.

MANAGEMENT STYLE

The organisational culture and the styles of key people involved in management will have significant impact on how people are managed. A top-down paternalistic organisation with a domineering chair and authoritarian general secretary will treat its workers very differently from an idealistic involve-everyone-in-everything organisation with a weak, unconfident chair and a coordinator whose main concern is to be nice to everyone and ensure everyone's needs are met. Neither organisation is likely to get the best from its workers.

Chapter 3, 'The good enough manager', explores issues around management style in more detail.

There is no right approach. In general people respond well to managers who are clear about what they are doing, consistent, fair, firm without being rigid, and understanding without being soft. They work best in environments where expectations are clear but flexible, and where people are genuinely valued, trusted and treated with respect. But within these statements is huge variation. Some workers learn best if they are told and shown exactly what to do; others prefer to work it out for themselves. Some want to be left to get on with a task; others want to discuss every stage with colleagues or manager.

The secret of being a good enough manager lies in getting it more or less right most of the time for most of the workers, and not expecting to be able to get it right all the time for everyone.

MOTIVATION

It sometimes seems one of the worst things that can be said about a worker in a voluntary organisation is that she or he is only doing the job for the money. Complete commitment is expected, 24 hours a day for seven days a week, 52 weeks a year. (One voluntary organisation, a residential community, reportedly told its workers they did not need to have holidays, because the organisation provided everything anyone could want!)

Good managers understand that people work, paid or unpaid, in voluntary organisations for a variety of reasons. These include:

- **earning money**;

- **commitment and idealism**: belief in what the organisation is doing or trying to achieve, desire to help or support people, desire to use skills or knowledge for 'a good cause';

- **personal development**: learning and using new skills, gaining confidence, building self-esteem;

- **creativity**: using imagination, expressing oneself, responding to challenge;

- **social contact**: being with other people;

- **convenience**: because the workplace is near the worker's home or children's school.

A range of less positive motivators can also be identified:

- **guilt**: because workers feel they would be 'letting the organisation down' if they were to leave;

- **egotism**: believing they are indispensible and the organisation could not survive without them;

- **fear** of moving on to another job or type of work;

- **inability** to find other work.

An understanding of *why* a staff person or volunteer is working in this particular job in this particular organisation and how she or he feels about the work is an essential starting point for supporting workers appropriately and dealing with performance or 'attitude' problems.

Work is the major criterion by which most people define themselves. If people are asked 'What do you do?' their first answer will nearly always be in terms of work. Even to the extent of saying 'I don't do anything, I'm at home most of the day looking after two children and I'm doing an Open University course and one day a week I help out at the local charity shop, but I don't actually *do* anything.' If work is unsatisfactory for any reason, workers will be demotivated and will not want to participate fully.

Motivation is not straightforward or static. A worker whose personal relationship has just broken up may want a routine job which provides money and social contact but very little scope for creativity; another in the same situation may want something completely demanding. Two years later the first worker may be more financially secure and emotionally settled and may be desperately bored and unhappy if work does not offer challenge and creativity; the second worker may be exhausted and need something easier for a while.

Many people come into voluntary organisations because of their commitment to a particular cause or type of work; over time the intensity of that commitment may wane but that does not necessarily mean they are less good as workers.

Managers who expect 100 per cent unquestioning commitment from their workers, or expect all workers to want to be creative and dynamic all the time, or scorn people who say they are in it for the money, are being unrealistic. Good management involves recognising individuals' needs and motivations and trying to ensure work can meet those needs in realistic ways.

Realistic is the key word there. Work may be the major criterion by which people define themselves, but it should not be the *only* one. Workers (and managers) who have no life other than work are on the path to burnout (see chapter 19). They do not do themselves any good and may also damage the organisation by setting unrealistic expectations for other workers.

Managers should also be honest about their own motivations. It is not unknown, even in the voluntary sector, for people to seek management positions because they want more money or the power they think is intrinsic in such positions.

TERMS OF REFERENCE FOR A PERSONNEL SUBCOMMITTEE

A personnel or staffing subcommittee is always directly responsible to the management committee or other governing body. It will usually include at least one senior staff member, the management committee chair or other senior officer, and another management committee member. Its terms of reference might include worker recruitment and selection, setting terms and conditions of work, ensuring workers are appropriately trained, ensuring adequate and appropriate supervision, and dealing with grievances and disciplinary matters.

In a small organisation these responsibilities might be undertaken not by a personnel subcommittee but by a management committee officer, with temporary groups set up as needed to negotiate contracts of employment, recruit and select new workers, or deal with disciplinary matters. In larger organisations many of the responsibilities may be delegated to a senior manager or line managers, a personnel officer or personnel department. In either case, or anything in between, it must be clear who can make decisions about various aspects of personnel management.

The ultimate responsibility for employment and for volunteers always rests with the management committee or other governing body (see chapter 2). *Voluntary But Not Amateur* chapters 2 and 3 cover the legal aspects of employment in considerable detail.

Key responsibilities

The most important responsibilities of a personnel subcommittee are:

- ensuring all members of the management committee or other governing body, even those not directly involved in employment, understand their responsibility as employers, and understand the main points of the organisation's employment contracts and policies;

- ensuring the organisation has clear personnel policies (see chapter 7).

Worker recruitment and selection

Specific responsibilities might include:

- gaining expertise and training in job recruitment and selection, including equal opportunities legislation and good practice (see chapter 15) and ensuring the organisation has and follows appropriate procedures;

- drawing up draft job descriptions and person specifications in consultation with relevant people, and getting them approved by the management committee;

- determining appropriate salary scales, and getting approval from the management committee or other governing body;

- setting up panels for shortlisting and interviewing, and ensuring management committee members and workers involved are aware of relevant legislation and good practice;

- presenting appointments to the management committee or other governing body for confirmation;

- deciding the most appropriate way to recruit, select and place volunteer workers.

Terms and conditions of work

Agreeing terms and conditions of employment is a responsibility of the management committee or other governing body. This agreement will usually be based on discussions or negotiations which have taken place between staff (often represented by a trade union) and the committee or its personnel subcommittee.

Except in genuine workers' cooperatives it is not appropriate (and in some cases is illegal) for staff to be directly involved in management decisions about their wages or contracts. If staff are on the governing body they should not directly take part in any decision or vote about these matters, though obviously they should be able to give their opinions.

Specific responsibilities of a personnel subcommittee might include:

- negotiating with the union or staff on terms and conditions of employment, and submitting agreed proposals to the management committee or other governing body for approval;

- drawing up the basic contract (terms and conditions of employment), and submitting it to the management committee for approval;

- ensuring staff and management committee understand the contract and implications;

- recommending salary changes, regradings, or changes in staff structure to the management committee or other governing body;

- drawing up the conditions for the probationary period for new staff;

- ensuring the organisation's redundancy procedures are legal, clear and workable; keeping staff, any recognised trade union(s) and the full management committee or other governing body aware of any possibilities of redundancy; recommending redundancy to the committee for agreement; and implementing redundancy procedures when required;

- drawing up contracts for volunteers and ensuring volunteers understand them.

Training

It is not the responsibility of a personnel subcommittee to decide the organisation's work and priorities. However, it has responsibility for ensuring workers have appropriate skills and knowledge to do the work. So responsibilities might include:

- drawing up the induction programme for new staff and volunteer workers (see chapter 15), or ensuring they have a proper induction;

- keeping the full management committee informed about probationary and induction arrangements;

- ensuring the organisation provides appropriate training for staff, volunteers and management committee members;

● ensuring there are adequate procedures for evaluating training.

Staff supervision and support

Chapter 16 looks in more detail at staff supervision and support. Broadly, a personnel subcommittee might have responsibility for:

● ensuring there are appropriate supervision procedures for all staff and volunteer workers;

● ensuring there are formal review/appraisal procedures for all staff, and for volunteers if required;

● ensuring staff and volunteers are adequately supported.

Supervision and reviews are usually carried out by those responsible for monitoring the worker's work performance. In some situations it might not be appropriate for support to be provided by them, because of the potential contradictions in simultaneously disciplining and supporting someone. However, it would be the subcommittee's responsibility to ensure adequate support procedures were in place.

Grievances and disciplinary matters

A grievance is a complaint by a worker; a disciplinary matter is a complaint by the employer. Chapter 18 looks at how grievances can be dealt with and chapter 16 looks at performance, which is a major cause of disciplinary action in voluntary organisations.

The subcommittee's responsibilities might include:

● ensuring the organisation's grievance and disciplinary procedures for staff and volunteers are legal, clear and workable, and submitting changes to the management committee for approval;

● receiving details of all disciplinary or grievance issues, taking the first steps to deal with such problems, and deciding the appropriate way of informing and/or involving the full management committee.

One advantage of having a personnel subcommittee is that it can deal with grievance or disciplinary matters with a considerable degree of confidentiality. If the worker then wants to appeal, the appeal can be to the whole management committee. If the whole committee deals with the issue all the way through, there is no body to which the worker can appeal.

Chapter 15:

Managing the recruitment process

If workers are recruited for jobs which are ill defined (so they do not know what they are supposed to do) or for which expectations and standards are unclear (so they do not know how well they are supposed to do the work), they are being set up to fail. The new workers become the battleground on which management committee members, managers or members of the collective fight out their differing interpretations of what the organisation is about, what needs doing and the standards of work required.

If workers are quickly or carelessly recruited the seeds are sown for later problems with performance (chapter 16). So this chapter covers:

● staff recruitment and selection;

● recruitment and placement of volunteers;

● the importance of contracts;

● guidelines for arranging induction.

The recruitment process and contracts of employment are covered in more detail in *Voluntary But Not Amateur* chapters 2 and 3.

STAGES IN RECRUITMENT AND SELECTION

At recruitment stage no one can know exactly what will need doing in a year's time or precisely how a job will develop. But it is the responsibility of those involved in recruitment to define the expectations as clearly and unambiguously as possible.

Good recruitment and selection procedures are an essential part of equal opportunities practice, because they help ensure the person best able to do a particular job is hired. The steps in good staff recruitment and selection are the same, regardless of the size or type of organisation.

● **Representative involvement**: be clear beforehand who will be involved in drawing up the job description, shortlisting and interviewing. Ensure everything is done by a representative group, well informed about the organisation, the job, equal opportunities legislation and the organisation's equal opportunities policy and procedures.

● **Task analysis**: draw up a detailed list of the tasks the person who gets the job will have to do. This helps in determining the qualities and qualifications genuinely required for the job.

● **Job description** (see below): produce an outline of the broad responsibilities (rather than detailed tasks) involved in the job.

● **Person specification** (see below): agree the qualities needed to do the job as defined in the task analysis and job description.

● **Advertising**: phrase the advertisement in a way that makes it clear what the job involves and the type of person needed, and choose the media most appropriate for the job and the desired kind of applicant.

● **Application form**: design a form which elicits information about the person's ability and willingness to do the job. Do not ask for irrelevant information. Make it clear on the form that applicants should consider the points in the job description and person specification when replying. Allow enough space on the form for applicants' answers, and indicate whether continuation sheets can be used. State clearly on the form the closing date for applications. For senior positions a supporting letter or CV (curriculum vitae) may also be required; if this is the case indicate the kind of information sought.

● **Background information**: provide applicants with clear, up to date and accurate information about the organisation, its work, its priorities and the job. Either the job description, the background information or a covering letter should indicate the closing date for applications and the shortlisting and interview dates.

● **Monitoring**: if an ethnic/gender monitoring form is used, design one which can be separated from the application before the shortlisting panel sees the applications, so race and gender are not used illegally to discriminate against or in favour of applicants. The monitoring forms should only be used after the selection process has been completed, to monitor the groups of people who applied for the job and how many of them were shortlisted and interviewed. The easiest way to do this is to assign a code number to each application form and monitoring form as they come in.

● **Shortlisting** (see below): assess applications on the basis of the person specification.

● **Informal contact**: decide beforehand whether candidates will be encouraged to come for an informal look around and chat, or whether there will only be the formal interview. Some people think informal chats encourage discrimination; others believe they encourage fair hiring practices. Whatever is done, it should be consistent for all applicants. Everyone should understand this contact is for the benefit of candidates and is not part of the selection process.

● **Tasks** or **sample work**: decide beforehand whether to ask for examples of previous work from shortlisted candidates (this can discriminate against people who have not been in work for some time). Decide whether to set a task for shortlisted candidates, either to do at home (and submit either before or at the interview), or to do immediately before or after the interview.

● **Decision-making**: be clear before the interviews how the final decision will be made (does it have to be unanimous? what if there is major dissension from the majority view? what if there is a tie?).

● **Interview** (see below): agree the areas that need to be covered and the questions to be asked.

● **Work programme**: be clear before the appointment, or certainly before the person takes up the post, about the work that needs doing in the first few weeks or months. Having a clear work programme makes it easier to plan the induction, helps the new worker settle in, and makes it easier to assess, at the end of the probationary period, whether the worker is suitable for the job.

● **Training and support**: be aware of the training and support necessary to give the new worker a fair chance of succeeding in the job. Be sure there is a thorough induction procedure, a clear probationary period, and fair reviews during and at the end of the probationary period.

JOB DESCRIPTION

A job description should give applicants as clear as possible an indication of what sort of work they would be doing. It should include:

● job title;

● main purpose(s) of the post;

● accountability (to whom the new worker is responsible);

● supervisory responsibility (workers whom the new person will supervise or manage);

● main responsibilities of the job, with a detailed breakdown if this is appropriate;

● starting date, if this is fixed;

● summary of the main conditions of employment, including starting salary, increments, pension arrangements, hours of work, holidays, probationary period, arrangements for supervision and staff reviews;

● closing date for applications, and dates of shortlisting and interviews.

In the list of job responsibilities include only tasks that are genuinely part of the job. The job description should not be so complex only a genius could do it, or so simplified that people apply for the job who are not able to do it.

PERSON SPECIFICATION

Drawing up a person specification is one way of ensuring the organisation meets its obligation to select employees on the basis of their relevant merits and abilities, rather than on subjective, unjustified or irrelevant criteria.

To draw up a good person specification it is vital to have a clear and accurate job description based on a careful task analysis. By knowing what the job involves, it is easier to assess the qualities needed to do it.

These requirements can be divided into five categories:

● **experience**: previous jobs, unpaid work experience, life experience;

● **skills, knowledge and abilities**: for example languages, driving, knowledge of specialist fields, ability to use equipment; plus some indication of the level of competence required, and whether the person must have the skills or knowledge beforehand or can learn them on the job (for example 'basic knowledge of WordPerfect word processing, or willingness to learn');

● **qualifications**: exams, certificates, degrees, diplomas (although some jobs such as social work require specific qualifications, most do not, and it is fairer to ask for the skills or knowledge represented by the qualification rather than asking for the qualification itself);

● **personal attributes**: such as strength, ability to lift, willingness to work in a hectic busy environment or on one's own;

● **personal circumstances**: such as being able to work weekends or evenings or to travel.

Each listed requirement must be justifiable in terms of the job description and task analysis. If it is not, it should not be part of the person specification.

If it is expected that a large number of suitably qualified people will apply for the job, it can be useful to include in the person specification not only the **essential** requirements, but also a list of **desirable** qualities. Only essential criteria should be considered in the first round of shortlisting. If large numbers of applicants meet all the essential criteria, the shortlisters can then judge them against a further list of agreed desirable qualities.

The people drawing up the person specification need to be clear how each requirement will be assessed during the selection process. This might be by:

● asking an appropriate question or questions on the application form;

● ensuring applicants know they should include information about this requirement in a supporting letter;

● taking up references and asking specifically about this requirement;

● asking candidates about the requirement at the interview;

● observing candidates' behaviour, for example in a group interview;

● giving candidates a task or test to assess their knowledge or ability.

If candidates are being observed or tested they should be told this is part of the selection process. Clear criteria should be agreed beforehand for assessing behaviour or performance and all candidates should be judged fairly against these criteria.

If a requirement cannot be assessed in some way, it should not be part of the person specification. There is no point saying the successful candidate must be reliable and honest if there is no way to assess these qualities.

EQUAL OPPORTUNITIES IN RECRUITMENT

In drawing up a person specification, shortlisting, interviewing or deciding whom to employ it is illegal to set requirements or use criteria which discriminate directly or indirectly against (or in favour of) people on the basis of their racial group, gender or being married. Under the Race Relations Act 1976, 'racial group' includes race, colour, nationality, national origin or ethnic group. Racial group, gender or marital status can be used as a factor in recruitment or selection only if it is a **genuine occupational qualification** for a job and can be justified in terms of the job description and task analysis.

'Improving the racial or gender balance of the staff' or 'making the staff more representative' does not in itself constitute a genuine occupational qualification. However, if particular racial or ethnic groups, men or women are under-represented within the staff group it is legal to **encourage** people from those groups to apply for a job.

Direct discrimination means discriminating against (or in favour of) people specifically because they are of a particular racial, national or ethnic group or gender. Indirect discrimination means setting criteria unnecessary for the job which disproportionately cannot be met by people of a particular group. For example, requiring O-level maths (rather than requiring 'ability to keep simple financial records') discriminates against people who did not go to school in England or had to leave school early.

Free pamphlets and leaflets about the legal aspects of equal opportunities in employment are available from the Commission for Racial Equality, Elliot House, 10-12 Allington Street, London SW1E 5EH (tel 071 828 7022) and the Equal Opportunities Commission, Overseas House, Quay Street, Manchester M3 3HN (tel 061 833 9244). Other free materials relevant to equal opportunities include:

- *Code of Good Practice on the Employment of Disabled People*, from the Employment Service, Rockingham House, 123 West Street, Sheffield S1 4ER;

- *HIV and Aids: Policy guidelines for voluntary organisations and small employers*, from LAGER (Lesbian and Gay Employment Rights), St Margaret's House, 21 Old Ford Road, London E2 9PL;

- *Declaring Convictions: A guide to the Rehabilitation of Offenders Act and applying for work with a criminal record*, from NACRO, 169 Clapham Road, London SW9 0PU;

- information on job sharing and other flexible working arrangements from New Ways to Work, 309 Upper Street, London N1 2TY (tel 071 226 4026).

Recruiting people with a disability

Organisations with 20 or more employees have a legal obligation to ensure three per cent of their employees are registered disabled. Most employers do not meet this obligation.

An organisation of any size with a commitment to equal opportunities has a moral obligation to make genuine efforts to recruit people with a disability for jobs they are able to do. Most organisations do not do this either.

Some jobs genuinely require physical mobility, good eyesight or other physical abilities, but most are suitable or could be adapted for people with various types of disability. Many premises are not accessible to people with serious mobility difficulties and cannot be adapted, but they are accessible to people with other disabilities.

If a job is *genuinely* not appropriate for someone with a particular type of disability, this should be clearly stated in the person specification. Beyond that, the organisation should be committed to interviewing applicants suitable for the job despite any disability they have, assessing them on the basis of their ability to do the job rather than their disability, and making necessary adaptations to equipment or premises to allow a person with a disability to do the job.

The Disablement Advisory Service and disablement resettlement officers can be contacted at local job centres. They provide advice, information and support to employers and employees. Funds are available for adaptations to premises or equipment to enable an individual worker to do a job; equipment is also available on permanent loan. The code of good practice mentioned above gives details of these and many other services.

SHORTLISTING

Even for a fairly low level job, shortlisting should be done by at least two people; for senior jobs four or more shortlisters might be involved. The shortlisters must be aware of the organisation's work, the job description and person specification, and any relevant background information about the job.

Before shortlisting, agree if there will be a maximum or minimum number of applicants selected. The maximum is determined by how many people can realistically be interviewed in the time the interview panel has available. Some organisations say they will interview all applicants who meet all the essential criteria; this can pose huge problems and take a disproportionate amount of the organisation's time if large numbers are then shortlisted. It is better to use additional 'desirable' criteria to narrow the field to a reasonable number.

Setting a minimum beforehand can make it easier to know how to proceed if only one or two applicants are suitable for the job. In this case the decision might be to interview the suitable applicant(s), or readvertise and hope for larger numbers of suitable applicants, or redefine the person specification criteria and readvertise. If the job is readvertised with the same person specification previous applicants would not have to reapply; this should be stated in the advertisement. If the person specification has been changed they should be invited to reapply.

To avoid one person's bias affecting other shortlisters, each person should shortlist individually, and keep a record of her or his views on a standard checklist.

The originals of application forms should be kept in a safe place and should not be circulated. If one photocopied set of applications is circulated to all shortlisters, enough time must be allowed for the set to circulate, and shortlisters must not put on the application forms any of their own comments, ticks, stars, exclamation points or anything else that might influence others who read it. If photocopying costs are not a problem, each shortlister should receive her or his own set of applications.

The checklist

Shortlisting is simplified if the person specification has been carefully drawn up and the application form asks the right questions. A grid can be devised with the person specification criteria listed down the left hand side and space for the names of applicants (and/or their reference number, if numbers are used) across the top. Horizontal and vertical lines are drawn to give a box for each criterion for each candidate.

The person specification criteria should be listed in a logical order. There are two main ways to do this.

● Criteria can be listed in the order of the questions on the application form, so shortlisters can fill in the shortlist form item by item as they go through the application. 'Essential' and 'desirable' criteria should be listed separately.

● Criteria can be listed in order of importance, with the most important essential criteria first, then the less important essential criteria, then a clear line or division followed by the desirable criteria in order of importance. (Some people say that either a criterion is or is not essential and therefore all are of equal importance, but the reality is that often some essential criteria *are* more important than others.)

Regardless of which type of listing is used, essential and desirable criteria should be clearly separated. The initial shortlisting should be on the basis of essential criteria only. If too many applicants meet all the essential criteria, the desirable criteria can be used to reduce the numbers.

Scoring

There are several approaches to shortlisting. Regardless of which is used, there should be a symbol or letters (perhaps NEI) to indicate there is not enough information to assess the applicant on a particular criterion. A consistent pattern of 'NEI' probably means inadequate questions were asked on the application form, or the person specification criterion was not one which could be adequately assessed by written questions and answers.

The simplest shortlisting method is a **ticks and noughts** system, with a tick to indicate if the criterion has been met and a nought (0) if it has not. (Avoid using a cross or X, as some people use this to mean 'met' and other use it to mean 'not met').

The applicants with all essential criteria ticked are shortlisted. If too many applicants meet all essential criteria, desirable criteria can be used to narrow the list to a more realistic number. If too few applicants meet all essential criteria, a decision will need to be made about whether to readvertise to attract more candidates, or whether to interview the candidates with the most ticks.

This method is straightforward, and some people feel it is the only fair way to shortlist: if a criterion is essential, either it has been met or it has not been met. But for many criteria it is too simplistic. It does not distinguish between relative levels of importance of essential criteria, nor does it allow for any recognition to be given to an applicant who almost, but not quite, fulfils a criterion.

A purely mechanistic 'met' or 'not met' approach may perpetuate discrimination by favouring people who have traditionally had access to educational and employment opportunities. Those whose experience has been less conventional may be excluded because they cannot fully meet the criteria.

A **points** system asks shortlisters to rate each applicant for each criterion on a scale of zero to three, zero to five, zero to 10 or whatever, with zero points if the criterion has not been met at all, the maximum number of points if it has been fully met, and intermediate points if it has been partly met. The applicants with the highest number of points for essential criteria are shortlisted.

This system can be complex to use: on the criterion 'Experience of living or working in a multicultural area', how many points does a shortlister give for 'I have lived and worked for five years in Birmingham'? It can also lead to misleading totals if some criteria are more important than others.

A **graded** system is similar to a points system but uses letters: A for fully met, B or C for partly met, and zero for not met. This avoids the temptation to add up points and come to a misleading total. The shortlister can quickly see which candidates have the most A's, and those with the most A's on essential criteria are shortlisted.

However, this system also does not distingush relative levels of importance. One way to get around this is to list the most important criteria first, and to give more weight to A's in the 'more important' category.

A **weighted points** system involves presetting a maximum number of points for each criterion depending on its relative importance. So for a very important essential criterion the maximum number of points which could be awarded might be 10, while for a less important (but nonetheless essential) criterion the maximum might be six. The applicants with the highest totals are shortlisted. It can be extremely difficult to work out a weighted points system but some people argue it gives the most accurate and objective assessment of the applications.

A **comments** system does not use ticks, numbers or letters but asks each shortlister to comment on each applicant's suitability. This can be difficult to compare among shortlisters.

Making the choice

Regardless of which system is used, the final decision about which applicants to shortlist is easier if each shortlister has been asked to use a simple code to indicate on the shortlisting form:

4: definitely interview;

3: maybe interview, tending towards the positive;

2: maybe interview, tending towards the negative;

1: definitely not interview.

If all shortlisters have given an applicant a '1' or '4' there will be little need for discussion about that applicant.

Shortlisted applicants should be notified of the interview date and time as soon as possible. Applicants who will definitely not be interviewed should also be informed. It may be advisable to keep a small number of applicants on a **shortlisting reserve list** for a few days in case some of the shortlisted candidates drop out. Take care not to forget to notify reserve list applicants after those few days that they have not been shortlisted.

The originals of unsuccessful applications and the shortlisting checklists should be kept in a safe place. Photocopies of unsuccessful applications should be destroyed. Shortlist panel members who are also on the interview panel should keep their copies of the application forms for successful applicants, and arrangements should be made to circulate application forms for successful applicants to other people on the interview panel.

TAKING UP REFERENCES

References might be taken up for all shortlisted candidates before interview, or for only the successful candidate after interview.

If a person specification criterion is going to be assessed on the basis of a reference, references will have to be taken up before the interview and will have to be considered before making a decision. Referees should be asked very specific questions to ensure they provide the required information.

One problem with taking up references before interview is that many people do not want their current employer to know they are looking for a new job. It is good practice to ask on the application form 'May we contact this reference before making an offer of work?' and 'Do you wish to be informed before this reference is contacted?' References should not be contacted if the applicant has indicated they should not be.

Unless references are being used to assess a person specification criterion they should be used only to *confirm* the selection panel's decision, not *influence* it. This is because references do not relate to the particular job for which the candidate is being interviewed, and are notoriously unreliable (the best references may come from an employer who is trying to get rid of a bad worker).

If references are being used to confirm the decision they can be taken up beforehand (unless the applicant has requested otherwise). Send the request in an envelope marked 'confidential' and enclose a stamped addressed envelope also marked 'confidential'. When the envelopes come back do not open them until the selection panel has made its decision. Only the references for the selected candidate should be read.

If the references are positive, fine: they have confirmed the selection panel's decisions. If the references are negative, the panel will need to consider very carefully whether to allow the references to influence their decision. They may need to follow up specific points with the candidate.

If references were not contacted before interview or were not received in time, any offer of employment should be made 'subject to references'.

There is no legal obligation to take up references, and some employers feel it is pointless to do so.

SELECTION INTERVIEWING

A selection interview can only be properly done if the whole recruitment procedure has been carefully planned. At person specification stage, some of the questions to be asked at the interview should already be clear.

Anyone involved in interviewing must be fully aware of what the organisation does overall, and this particular job description and person specification. If people are being brought in from outside the organisation, or if people are involved who are not fully aware of the job description or person specification, they must be fully briefed. No one can select properly if they do not fully understand what they are selecting for.

The interview panel should meet beforehand to decide the interview procedures and questions. They will need to be clear about all the following:

- arrangements for welcoming the candidates when they arrive, showing them around the building (if appropriate), offering them tea, showing them where lavatories are, showing them where to wait, offering them something to read, etc;

- who will call the candidates into the interview room, welcome them, introduce the interviewers, ask the first question;

- what questions will be asked and in what order;

- who will ask each question;

- whether any panel member can ask a supplementary or follow-up question, or only the person who asked the original question;

- what specific questions need to be asked of individual candidates, to get more information about points made (or not made) on their application forms;

- who will keep track of time to ensure all candidates are given approximately the same time, and to ensure the interview ends on schedule;

- who will answer questions asked by the candidate (this is especially important for questions involving terms and conditions of employment);

- who will close the interview, and what will be said to the candidates about when and how they will be notified about a decision;

- how the panel will keep a record of its views on each candidate (whether each member of the panel will keep her/his own notes during the interview, and whether these notes be discussed after each interview, or only after all candidates have been interviewed);

- if the selection procedure involves a test, whether it will be before or after the interview, who will administer it and who will assess it;

- whether references have been taken up beforehand or will be taken up afterwards;

- how the panel will make its final decision about who should be offered the post, whether the decision has to be unanimous or majority, and what happens if there is a tie;

- who will notify the successful candidate and the unsuccessful candidates;

- what will happen if the successful candidate does not accept;

- whether information will be given to all unsuccessful candidates about why they did not get the job, or only to those who ask, or not at all; and if information is to be given whether it will be verbally or in writing, and who will deal with it.

The venue

The room should be quiet and undisturbed (unplug the telephone). The candidate's seat should be nearest the door, and should not be facing into bright sunlight. The chair should be comfortable (but not soft), and should be the same height as the interviewers' chairs.

Sitting in a circle without a table creates an informal atmosphere but can be difficult if interviewers or applicants have a lot of papers, want to refer to the application form and want to take notes. Sitting around a table is probably easier (and can hide the candidate's shaking knees and nervous hands). The table should be tidy and uncluttered, with a glass and jug of water at the candidate's place. If a table is not used, interviewers should keep their papers tidily out of the way, and a small side table should be next to the candidate's chair. Interviewers should ensure candidates cannot see notes or application forms relating to other candidates.

Interview questions

Questions should be based on the job description and person specification and designed to elicit information about whether the person has the necessary experience, skills, knowledge and ability to do the job.

For each question, panel members should be clear about why the question is being asked, what kind of information or response it is designed to elicit, and whether there is a 'right' answer.

The interview should open with the candidate being welcomed and the panel members introduced. The interview format and timing should be explained. ('We'll have about half an hour to ask you questions, then 10 or 15 minutes when you can ask us anything you'd like.')

The first question should be relatively easy, with the intention of putting the candidate at ease, but should not be a time-waster like 'How was your journey?' One possibility is 'How does what you have been doing recently lead into this job?' There is obviously no right answer to this question; the purpose is to find out how the candidate thinks the job fits in with her or his current work or interests.

Avoid questions with yes/no answers (closed questions). Try for **open questions** which encourage candidates to give detailed information: not 'Do you know how to use WordPerfect?' but 'What experience have you had with WordPerfect or similar word processing packages?'

Interviewers frequently put words into the candidate's mouth, rather than letting candidates speak for themselves.

Ask 'How does your present or most recent job (or your studies, or whatever) relate to the sort of work you would be doing for us?' rather than 'This new job would really be a challenge, don't you think?' or 'Your present situation is quite different from what you would be doing here, isn't it?'

If candidates are asked how they would deal with a hypothetical situation, keep the situation fairly simple – not so complex the candidate can't remember all the details. Be clear beforehand what criteria will be used to assess the replies.

Questions requiring a detailed knowledge of the organisation or its practices should not be asked. Instead of 'How would you change our cataloguing system for welfare benefits information?' ask 'If you were updating and revising a cataloguing system for welfare benefits information, what criteria would you use?'

Questions which are discriminatory on the basis of race, ethnic background, nationality, gender or marital status must never be asked. Don't ask certain questions only to women, or to men, or to people of a particular racial or ethnic group. Don't ask irrelevant questions such as whether people have children. If it is *required* for people to be able to work evenings, weekends or during school holidays it is acceptable to ask candidates whether this would pose any problems – but all candidates must be asked, not just women or not just people who have volunteered the information that they have children. It is acceptable to ask all candidates (on the application form or in the interview) if they need a work permit to work in the UK, and if so whether they have one; the organisation should be clear beforehand whether it is willing to offer the post to someone for whom it would have to apply, as employer, for a work permit.

When interviewing candidates with a visible disability, or who have indicated on their application form that they have an invisible disability, focus on their *ability* not their disability. They would not have applied for the job if they did not think they could do it. It is acceptable to ask whether they would need particular equipment or support to enable them to do the job. If a person with a disability is hired, the employer can get a grant from the Employment Service to help cover the costs of new equipment or adaptations to equipment or premises to enable that person to do the job.

Successful interviewing

Don't trust to memory. Each panel member should write down her or his observations for each candidate, either during the interview or immediately afterwards. A sheet for each candidate listing the questions, with space for comments after each question, can be helpful.

Allow at least 15 minutes between candidates: time to write up notes, discuss the candidate briefly if this is being done between interviews rather than waiting till the end, go to the lavatory, make a cup of tea. Allow time for a lunch break as well.

An interview is a two-way process: for the panel to decide if this is the right person for the job, but also for the candidate to decide if this is the right job for her or him. Impressions count; if the interview is sloppy and badly prepared, candidates may think they can get away with sloppy work if they are hired.

Allow time for candidates to ask questions about the organisation, the job and conditions of work. Anything said at the interview is part of the contract of employment, so never promise anything unless authorised to do so.

Remember that the interview is not the end of the recruitment process. The organisation should have a clear work programme for the new worker, and should provide a planned induction to ensure all new workers get the information and training they need in order to do the job well.

Making the choice

The chair of the interview panel must ensure the choice is made on the basis of the application form, the candidates' responses to interview questions, and any other criteria (such as references or tests) that are going to be used as part of the selection process. Irrelevant information or opinions, or information that has not been gained as part of the selection process, should not be used.

If a choice cannot be made between two or more suitable candidates it may be necessary to call them back for a second interview, asking more detailed questions about their background and experience. This can be a difficult process, and care must be taken not to use the interview process as a battleground for disputes between factions within the organisation.

If no candidate is fully suitable a decision will have to be made about whether to readvertise (a costly and time-consuming process) or accept a candidate who is less than fully suitable. If the latter choice is made, **appropriate training or support must be provided to ensure the person can do the job.**

It is important to agree a procedure in case the chosen candidate does not accept the post. Usually second and third choices are agreed, with the chair of the interview panel authorised to offer the post to them if the original choice does not accept.

The chair of the interview panel must ensure records are kept detailing the reasons for selection or rejection of each candidate.

Notifying candidates

Usually the chair of the interview panel or other suitable person contacts the successful candidate by phone and offers the job. If the offer is conditional on acceptable references or medical checks this must be clearly indicated. The offer is then confirmed in writing, with details of starting date etc.

If the candidate wants time to think before making a decision about whether to accept, give a clear deadline for her or his final decision. If too long elapses, the organisation may lose the chance to offer to the post to the second or third choice.

Candidates who will definitely not be offered the post should be informed immediately in writing. There is no obligation to tell unsuccessful candidates why they were not selected. Nevertheless some organisations indicate the reasons in the rejection letter; others say they will give the reasons if the candidate contacts the chair of the interview panel (or other appropriate person) in writing. Information about why a candidate was not selected should be given only by someone who is authorised to do so.

At the end of the process the original application form for the successful candidate is the first item in her or his personnel folder. The originals of unsuccessful candidates' application forms, and the interview panel's final notes, should be kept in a safe place for a few months, in case there are any questions about the way the selection process was carried out. Photocopies of application forms should be destroyed.

RECRUITMENT AND SELECTION CHECKLIST

This checklist provides a general outline of the major steps in recruitment and selection; each organisation will have to add its own detail.

It refers to several roles: administrator, job description panel coordinator, shortlisting panel coordinator, interview panel coordinator, interview panel chair. In small organisations the same person may perform several or all of these roles; there is no problem with this so long as everyone is clear the roles involve different responsibilities.

Recruitment is a long, expensive and labour-intensive process. It is worth the effort to plan carefully and get it right first time.

Initial steps

● Current postholder gives notice of intention to resign, or management committee or other governing body decides to create new post.

● Management committee sets up panel to draw up task analysis, job description, person specification and advertisement and to decide where to advertise (**job description panel**). Depending on the size and type of organisation and the type of job this panel might include only management committee members, only workers or a combination. Users, clients or outside 'experts' might also be involved. One person should convene and coordinate the panel. It must be *absolutely clear* what decisions the panel can make and what has to be referred back to a personnel subcommittee or to the management committee or other governing body for approval.

● Management committee sets up **shortlisting panel** and **interview panel**. If the same people are on both it might be called a **selection panel**. One person named to convene and coordinate each panel. Ideally the same people should be on the job description and selection panels, but this is not always practical. There should at least be some overlap, so those involved in actually selecting the worker have some awareness of why the job description and person specification were drawn up in the way they were.

● People coordinating job description panel and selection panel ensure adequate liaison.

● Coordinators of the two panels draw up timetable for recruitment and selection, covering:

drawing up and getting approval for job description and person specification (allow enough time for consultation and for management committee approval if necessary);

advertising (allow at least 10 days for placing adverts, longer if publicity is to be circulated through mailings);

closing date for applications (two to three weeks after advertisements appear or mailings go out);

date(s) for shortlisting (can start immediately after the closing date);

date(s) for interviews (allow enough time after short-listing to notify candidates).

Drawing up a timetable at this stage enables people involved in shortlisting and interviewing to get the dates into their diaries, and also gives a clear indication of when a worker can realistically be expected to start.

● Timetable submitted to management committee for approval if required. Person who will be dealing with administration advised of relevant parts of timetable.

● Shortlisting and interview coordinator(s) ensure all panel members have had (or can quickly get) appropriate **training** in equal opportunities legislation, the organisation's equal opportunities policy and interviewing skills.

Defining the requirements

● Job description panel draws up **task analysis**, **job description** and **person specification**, and decides whether the post is suitable for job sharing. This should be done in consultation with those who will work closely with the new worker.

● Job description and person specification formally approved by personnel subcommittee or management committee, if necessary.

● Panel draws up **advertisement**, decides where to advertise and how to circulate within the workplace, and confirms that previously agreed closing date is still suitable (should be minimum of two weeks after advertisement appears, preferably three weeks for nationally advertised posts).

● Job description panel coordinator meets with shortlisting panel coordinator to clarify what has been decided and why.

● Person who will be responsible for arranging induction given copies of task analysis, job description, person specification and selection timetable.

Administrative work

● Administrator places advertisements.

● Job description panel collects, adapts or draws up **background material**, **application form**, **monitoring form** and other items to go to enquirers, and gives them to administrator. Job description panel disbanded.

● Administrator prepares, photocopies and collates sets of job descriptions, application forms and other material to go out.

● Administrator buys relevant publications (if copies have not been sent by the publisher), checks advertisements for accuracy, and takes steps to remedy any inaccuracies.

● Monitoring forms separated from application forms as they come in.

● Shortlisting panel draws up person specification checklist for shortlisting.

● Administrator photocopies application forms and person specification checklists and gives them to shortlisting panel coordinator.

Shortlisting

● Shortlisting panel coordinator distributes or circulates application forms and person specification checklists to panel members.

● Shortlisting panel meets for shortlisting.

● Administrator contacts people invited for interviews.

● If references are being taken up at this stage, selection panel coordinator writes to or rings referees.

● Administrator notifies applicants who have not been shortlisted, if panel decides to do this before interviews.

Interviews

● Interview panel meets to choose chair and decide format and questions for interviews.

● Delegated person checks room arrangements for interviews, arranges for candidates to be welcomed and arranges refreshments.

After selection

● Successful candidate informed verbally.

● Written confirmation sent, signed by management committee chair or authorised alternative. If references still have to be taken up, the offer of the job is made 'subject to references'.

● Interview panel coordinator takes up references if necessary.

● Administrator notifies unsuccessful candidates. Letter signed by management committee chair, chair of interview panel or senior manager.

● Person arranging induction gets details of person appointed, starting date and specific requirements for induction or training.

● Induction arranged, in consultation with all workers directly involved (see below).

● Mid-probation and end of probation reviews arranged (see chapter 16).

● Contract of employment issued within the first 13 weeks of employment.

ACCELERATED PROCEDURE

For temporary or short term (six months or less) posts, or for very part-time posts, or for posts which cannot be kept vacant because of risk to users/clients, this procedure may take too much time or be unreasonably expensive. In these situations it might be appropriate to speed up the procedure by:

- advertising only internally, through the local Job Centre and in the local press, in order to avoid the extra time required for weekly or monthly publications or the national press;

- giving only a phone number in the advertisement, rather than an address, so people have to ring for information and an application form and therefore receive it more quickly;

- setting a deadline only a week or 10 days after the advertisements are published, rather than two weeks or more;

- making it clear in the advertisement that the person must be available to start immediately (if this is genuinely required);

- having only two people involved in shortlisting and interview, rather than the three or four who might be involved for ordinary appointments.

All the other steps (a proper job description and person specification, shortlisting against the person specification and a proper interview) should be followed.

This accelerated procedure maintains the principles of equal opportunities recruitment – that jobs should be genuinely open to a wide cross-section of people in the community – without burdening the organisation with an unnecessarily cumbersome and time-consuming procedure.

If a temporary, short-term or part-time job subsequently becomes permanent or full-time, there are two approaches:

- it can be treated as a new position and advertised in the usual way, with the current post-holder eligible to apply;

- it can be offered to the current post-holder, provided she or he was properly recruited (even through an accelerated procedure) in the first place and provided the job description is basically the same.

Some people feel the second approach contravenes the principles of equal opportunities recruitment because if a permanent or full-time post had initially been advertised, different people would have applied. But the reality is that for small organisations, the time and financial cost involved in recruiting and inducting a new worker can be so onerous that the organisation is prevented from getting on with providing its services. This has equal opportunities implications of a different sort.

The organisation's recruitment and selection policy should give examples of situations in which an accelerated procedure can be used, and should also indicate what happens when a job is upgraded from temporary to permanent or from part-time to full-time.

RECRUITING AND PLACING VOLUNTEERS

Volunteers come into an organisation in four ways:

- being recruited to do a specific task or job defined by the organisation;

- volunteering, with the job or task(s) defined by the volunteer;

- offering specific skills, with the organisation deciding how to use those skills;

- volunteering to do anything that needs doing.

If volunteers are being recruited to do a specific job, a modified version of the procedure outlined for paid staff should be followed. If the post involves considerable responsibility the procedure should probably be nearly as formal as for hiring a paid worker; if the post is quite straightforward, such as stuffing envelopes, it is only important to define clearly the tasks involved and the time commitment expected.

If a person volunteers to do a specific task the organisation should be sure it actually wants the task done and can provide the necessary support and back-up. There is no point having a friendly graphic designer offer to design a new leaflet if no one has the time to write it, there is no money to get it printed, or the organisation has adequate supplies of its old leaflet.

If a person with specialist professional skills, such as accountancy or architecture, offers to help, ensure she or he is fully aware of the organisation's objectives, priorities and methods of working. An approach which is too slick or requires considerable money or time may not be appropriate for a voluntary organisation. Similarly, an approach requiring quick action may not be possible if major decisions must be referred to subcommittees and the management committee or other governing body.

It is not necessary to take up every offer of voluntary help. It is perfectly acceptable to ask someone to do something else which the organisation needs more urgently, or to ask her or him to wait and provide assistance later. It is better to do this than accept an offer and not be able to follow it through.

Most volunteers, however, want to do something for a 'good cause' and are not clear about what they can offer or what the organisation might need. In this case it is very important to have someone in the organisation with specific responsibility for getting the best from volunteers. This person must know at all times:

- what needs doing within the organisation;

- how urgent each task is, and what happens if a volunteer cannot be found to do it;

- what skills, knowledge or abilities are required to do it;

- how much time it will involve, and whether a regular or long term commitment is required;

- how the volunteer will be shown what to do;

- what additional training, if any, is available for the volunteer;

- who will organise the volunteer's work;

- who will supervise the volunteer's work;

- what will happen if the volunteer turns out to be unsatisfactory.

In addition, this volunteer organiser will need to know:

- who is available to do voluntary work for the organisation;

- what sort of work they want to do;

- what sort of work they are capable of doing;

- whether they are willing to be trained;

- how much time they have available, and how much notice they require;

- personal factors such as why they want to volunteer and how much supervision and support they are likely to need.

Problems around unsatisfactory performance by volunteers can be minimised by clearly defining the tasks that need doing, and ensuring the volunteer knows what needs doing and is able and willing to do it.

Problems can also be minimised by providing appropriate training, supervision and support for volunteers, and by offering volunteers opportunities to be involved in discussions and consultations about their work and their part of the organisation.

Information about volunteering and how to support volunteers is available from:

- local volunteer bureaux;

- local councils for voluntary service or other voluntary sector coordinating bodies;

- the Volunteer Centre UK, 29 Lower King's Road, Berkhamsted, Herts HP4 2AB (tel 0442 873311);

- Advance, 444 Brixton Road, London SW9 8EJ (tel 071 978 8577).

When recruiting volunteers it is important to be aware of possible implications for unemployment benefit, income support and other benefits. Leaflet FB26 from any Department of Social Security office has details.

It is also important to ensure volunteers are adequately insured for any work they do for the organisation. There is some information about this in chapter 2, and the Volunteer Centre UK (address above) can provide detailed advice.

SECONDMENT

Secondment is the temporary loan of an employee from business or industry to a voluntary organisation. The secondment might be for a very short period or for as long as two or three years.

Secondment should always be seen as a **two-way process** giving benefits to both parties. The voluntary organisation gets the benefit of business, financial or other specific skills. As for the benefits to the secondee, it is worth quoting the Institute of Personnel Management (so it's not the voluntary sector blowing its own horn). According to the IPM, community organisations offer *'a rich environment for individuals to test and stretch themselves because such organisations are likely to:*

- *be used to managing with limited resources, forcing a secondee to recognise actual costs and to operate with little support;*

- *be small, allowing a secondee to gain an overview of the organisation's objectives and activities, as well as to see a process through from start to finish;*

- *be less hierarchical and more consultative, facilitating good communication skills and giving greater opportunities for a secondee to make decisions;*

- *be at the sharp end of many of the challenges facing our society, requiring immediate responses to daily problems which broaden a secondee's perspective;*

- *operate in a very dynamic environment, fostering initiative and creativity and encouraging the secondee to take calculated risks;*

- *be run by committed and enthusiastic staff with different backgrounds and opinions, thus widening the secondee's outlook and promoting good negotiation skills.'*

As with any volunteers, secondees need a clear indication of what the organisation expects from them and a good induction.

Information about secondment is available from IPM (35 Camp Road, London SW19 4UX, tel 081 946 9100) and Action Resource Centre (102 Park Village East, London NW1 3SP, tel 071 383 2200).

CONTRACTS

Terms and conditions of employment

Employment legislation specifies that every employee who works 16 hours or more per week is entitled to a written contract (statement of terms and conditions of employment) within the first 13 weeks of employment. It is good practice to provide this contract for all employees, including part-time staff, as soon as they start work.

Voluntary But Not Amateur chapter 3 gives details of employment law as it relates to contracts and provides an example of a contract.

In management terms the contract is important because it should define clearly, for the employee, the manager and the management committee or other governing body, what is expected of the worker and the organisation. These expectations should include:

- how many **hours** the employee is required to work each week, the extent to which individual workers can determine when they work and the extent to which their times are set contractually or by a manager or staff meeting, whether flexitime is allowed and if so whether there are core hours which must be worked;

- whether **overtime** work is allowed, whether it can be paid or time off in lieu (TOIL) is given, if there is a maximum amount of TOIL that can be stored up and whether it has to be taken within a specified period;

- **holiday** entitlement (and how it is determined for part-time or job share workers), how much notice is required to take time off for holidays, whether notice has to be in writing or can be verbal, what happens if a worker falls ill on holiday, whether accrued holiday time can be held over from one year to the next, what happens if the worker leaves while still owed holiday time;

- whether additional time off can be taken for **religious holidays** other than Easter and Christmas, and if it is paid or unpaid;

- arrangements regarding time off due to **sickness**, including whom to notify, maximum time allowed, what happens if that time is exceeded, and sick pay arrangements;

- arrangements for **compassionate** or **dependants leave**, whether there is a maximum that can be taken, and if it is discretionary who decides what is allowed and whether it is paid or unpaid;

- what workers should do if they have a **grievance** (complaint) or want to appeal against a disciplinary procedure;

- how **disciplinary** matters must be dealt with.

A clear, workable contract, and an expectation that the conditions set down will be followed, can help prevent difficulties around poor timekeeping, excess time off and similar situations.

Contracts for volunteers

It is good practice to offer contracts to regular volunteers, setting out what the organisation can offer (expenses, training, supervision and support, a reference if work is satisfactory) and what the organisation expects (commitment to specific tasks and/or times, punctuality, confidentiality). Model contracts for volunteers are available from the Volunteer Centre UK (address above).

ARRANGING AN INDUCTION

Induction is a planned training programme to enable workers to get to know the organisation, their colleagues, their job and other organisations or agencies doing similar or related work.

Every organisation needs to develop its own procedures for ensuring staff and volunteers are adequately and appropriately inducted. It is worth spending the time to develop an **induction core programme** which can then be adapted for new workers.

Induction should not be rushed, avoided, ignored or cancelled. It is an essential step in ensuring workers know what is expected of them and are able to meet those expectations. Even in the smallest organisation the induction should be planned, with named individuals doing specific sessions. If it is left to new workers to 'pick things up as they go along' they are likely to do so haphazardly, incorrectly or not at all.

It is not difficult to plan an induction if it is built around a core programme and a thoughtful analysis of the new worker's job description and the relative importance or urgency of the various tasks. The process should ensure the new worker understands what needs to be done, why it needs to be done and how to do it before having to start a task.

For permanent full-time workers in fairly complex organisations the induction period should be at least four weeks. In small organisations two or three weeks may be sufficient; for very straightforward jobs in small organisations one or two weeks may be enough.

It is best if one person has responsibility for arranging the induction timetable, writing it up, and making sure everyone involved knows what they are supposed to be doing and when. Someone should also have responsibility for liaising with the new worker about induction, suggesting additions or changes and dealing with queries or problems.

During the induction period new workers should have some easily achievable tasks and some fairly open-ended ones, so they always have something to do. For all tasks, it is important to be clear about whether the new worker is supposed to do them on her or his own or with someone else.

There are many small ways to help new workers fit in. If the organisation has pigeonholes for post and messages (and all organisations should), make one for the new worker before she or he starts. For the first few days, ensure the new worker is invited to lunch and that provision is made, if appropriate, to include her or him in informal groups.

The induction pack

Before the new worker starts, an induction pack should be made up including:

- the induction timetable;

- a list of staff and their job titles, and a list of regular or long term volunteers and what they do;

- details of how to contact union representatives, health and safety representative, first aid person etc;

- a list of management committee officers, members and subcommittees;

- the latest annual report, current leaflets and other basic written materials;

- essential policies, such as equal opportunities, health and safety, confidentiality;

- essential procedures, such as timekeeping, petty cash, notice required for holidays, procedures when ill;

- minutes of the last two staff meetings;

- other information as appropriate (see chapter 2, 'Information for management').

It is a good idea to provide similar information, perhaps less detailed, for regular or long term volunteers.

An induction core programme

A core programme can provide a starting point for deciding what needs to be included in the induction for individual staff members or volunteers.

Scheduled events

Draw up a timetable covering the induction period and put into it all the relevant scheduled events, including:

- staff or project meetings;

- team, workgroup or worksite meetings;

- meetings of users, members, clients or residents;

- union shop or branch meetings, if appropriate;

- in-house training events;

- work-related social events;

- management committee or subcommittee meetings, if appropriate;
- other meetings or events.

Indicate whether these are obligatory or optional.

Also include:

- individual supervision sessions (see chapter 16).

Long term timetable

At the end of the induction timetable add later events such as mid-probation and end of probation reviews (see chapter 16), future training events and important meetings.

Tasks

Go through the job description and task analysis, and decide how quickly the new worker has to, or can reasonably be expected to, start to take on each task. Mark each one, for example:

A = immediate, very urgent, first week or two;

B = moderately urgent, say in three to four weeks;

C = can wait for four to six weeks, until the worker is settled;

D = longer term.

Decide what the worker needs to know for each group of tasks, and schedule it accordingly. The worker should not be forced to take on too much too soon, and should not be

expected to carry out tasks until the organisation has provided the necessary training or background information.

Allow enough time for reading and absorbing the written information provided in the induction pack as well as relevant files, books, old minutes and other information.

Day one

The first day's induction should include:

- welcome;
- explanation of induction, with the person in charge of induction;
- tour of the workplace, introductions, lavatories, kitchen or tea facilities, fire alarms and extinguishers, fire exits, first aid boxes, accident book;
- brief history of the organisation, brief description of the overall structure and (if appropriate) team or workgroup structure, explanation of how the new worker's job fits into the workgroup and the organisation;
- invitation to lunch;
- time with a committee member or another worker talking informally about the new person's job and what it will entail, including time to observe others at work or start with straightforward tasks;
- quiet time for the worker to settle in at her or his desk (or wherever), chat or read.

Remainder of week one

It is probably still too early for the worker to absorb complicated information about the organisation, so the remainder of the first week should concentrate on basic systems and procedures:

- communication and information: reception, pigeonholes, incoming and outgoing post, incoming and outgoing calls, visitors, noticeboards;

- basic equipment: switchboard, photocopying, typewriter or word processor, computer, fax;

- basic financial procedures: petty cash, cheque requisitions and authorisation, salary arrangements;

- timekeeping, time off in lieu, arranging leave, notification of sickness or other absence;

- how staff, project or team meetings work and what they cover, how to get items on the agenda, how minutes are taken and circulated;

- the role of the management committee or other governing body and subgroups;

- supervision and review/assessment procedures, staff training;

- people who use the organisation: members, users, clients;

- activities, services and facilities provided by the organisation;

- the work of staff whose jobs are directly related to that of the new worker;

- tour of other sites, if relevant;

- time for reading, listening, chatting;

- basic information and skills for the worker's tasks and responsibilities;

- time to start straightforward tasks.

Week two

By the second week the worker should understand the basics of what the organisation is about and how it functions, and be ready to take in more general information, such as:

- who makes what kind of decisions;

- the role of the union;

- more on the history and philosophy of the organisation;

- health and safety policy and procedures;

- other policies and their implementation, such as equal opportunities, confidentiality, open door, alcohol or drugs on premises;

- how other parts of the organisation work;

- anything left over from the first week;

- more time for reading and absorbing;

- more detailed information and skills for the worker's tasks and responsibilities.

Weeks three and four

By this time the worker should be gaining the specific skills and knowledge required for the job. This might include:

- detailed explanation of the organisation's funding and fundraising;

- financial and bookkeeping procedures;

- lessons on how to use the computer;

- information about organisations doing similar work;

- information about organisations with which the worker will be liaising or working jointly;

- suppliers;

- clarification of what the new worker will be doing in the next month or two and what still needs to be learned;

- clarification of what the new worker can decide or do on her or his own and what needs to be checked with someone else.

By the end of the induction period new workers will not know everything that needs to be known about their jobs. But they will have a solid understanding of the organisation and how it works, and perhaps more importantly, will feel the organisation actually cares about them and their work and is willing to put considerable effort into ensuring they can do their work properly.

THE PROBATIONARY PERIOD

A probationary period overlaps with, but is completely separate from, the induction. Induction is a training and learning process; a probationary period is an opportunity for the employee and employer to decide whether they are suited to each other.

Formal reviews should be held midway through the probationary period and shortly before the end (see chapter 16). If work is unsatisfactory the worker should be told clearly what the problems are and what standards are required.

At the end of the probationary period the management committee or other governing body should formally confirm the appointment, unless work is still unsatisfactory in which case the probationary period may be extended. In some organisations a senior manager is able to confirm some appointments or extend the probationary period.

Even if the worker has been given and signed a contract of employment, either side can terminate employment during the probationary period, provided proper notice is given. Indeed, either side can terminate employment even without a probationary period.

Some organisations do not allow workers to sign cheques, have access to large amounts of cash, have keys to the premises or work on their own with vulnerable clients until they have satisfactorily completed their probationary period.

Chapter 16:

Managing workers' performance

'She's always late ...'

'Every time he does something I have to redo it ...'

'There's no way we can send out a leaflet that looks like that. She can never be bothered to do anything properly, can she?'

'I don't think she's really understood the latest benefit changes. I'm sure she's giving clients inaccurate advice ...'

'He's months behind on his filing and none of us can find any of the papers we need ...'

'She's a real perfectionist, always wants everything done to absolutely impossible standards ...'

Does it sound familiar? The reasons for these situations are similar whether the organisation is large or small, rich or poor, structured hierarchically or collectively:

- the emphasis (implicit or explicit) is on individualism: staff or volunteers think they can do whatever they want, rather than what the organisation as a whole needs or wants;

- no one is clear what expectations or standards are reasonable (or everyone has her or his own idea of what is reasonable);

- no one is clear who has responsibility for setting those expectations and standards (or everyone has her or his own idea about whose responsibility it is);

- there is an underlying assumption that 'we all know what needs doing and how to do it properly';

- in some groups there is an aversion to anything managerial;

- many people who now have responsibility for managing voluntary organisations have little or no experience of managing or being managed in a work setting;

- managers feel isolated and unsupported, and transfer this feeling to the workers they are supposed to be supporting;

- there is a great reluctance to be seen to be criticising colleagues;

- many colleagues are also personal friends so it becomes even more difficult to be seen to be criticising them;

- there is an equally great reluctance to praise people.

In small groups which raise all their own money, unclear expectations and standards may not be a problem. But in groups which are responsible to funders, donors, members or the community, the management of perfor-

mance must be a major issue. It takes on even more importance if the group enters into contractual obligations to provide or undertake specified work to agreed standards (see chapters 12 and 13).

Staff and volunteers do their jobs well if they are committed and enthusiastic, feel valued, know what they are supposed to do and how to do it, and get credit for doing it well. This is more likely to happen if managers are aware of factors which motivate and demotivate workers (see chapter 14) and if the organisation has a clear staff/volunteer development policy encompassing induction, supervision, support, formal reviews or appraisals, and opportunities for training and learning. The policy should also include, where appropriate, members of the management committee and other committees.

LAYING THE GROUNDWORK

The basis for managing performance lies in:

- clear procedures for recruiting staff or for recruiting and placing volunteers, based on what needs doing in the organisation and the person's ability and willingness to do it;

- planned induction for all staff and volunteers, based on what they need to know about their job, the organisation and the broad area of work;

- clear procedures for deciding what needs doing, deadlines and standards;

- clear procedures for conveying that information to the staff or volunteers who will be doing the work;

- clear procedures and responsibility for monitoring work to be sure it is being done, and is being done adequately;

- clear procedures and responsibility for dealing with work which is not being done or being done inadequately;

- training and support to help workers do their jobs or do them better.

Chapter 15 covered recruitment, selection and induction. This chapter looks at supervision, support, reviews and disciplinary issues, and chapter 17 is about training.

A good book on voluntary sector supervision and related issues is *The RTI Practical Guide to Supervision* (Research Training Initiatives, 1991; 94 pages; ISBN 1 873488 00 9; £17.95 from RTI, 18-20 Dean Street, Newcastle upon Tyne NE1 1PG).

SUPERVISION

Supervision has two meanings:

● to manage workers directly in the performance of a specific task or tasks;

● to provide a structured opportunity for workers to discuss their work.

In this section 'supervision' is used in the second sense. In many voluntary organisations supervision is haphazard, taking place 'whenever we need to sit down and talk about things'. There is no clear procedure for dealing with potential or minor problems before they become major. And the bigger and more real the problems, the more reluctant people are to sit down and talk about them – until they explode into a crisis.

The voluntary sector is full of stresses and people need a chance to talk about how they are affected by them. All workers at every level in the organisation should have regular opportunities to discuss their progress, actual or potential problems and their feelings about work.

In most organisations this should be every four to six weeks (more frequently during the first few weeks for new workers) and scheduled on a regular basis. Depending on the type of organisation and work, the session might last anything from 15 minutes to an hour or more. Sessions should not be cancelled except in an emergency, and if cancelled or missed should be rescheduled.

Who supervises whom?

In traditionally structured organisations the supervisor will usually be the line manager. Situations in which it is less clear who should supervise include:

● organisations with only one worker;

● organisations or teams which work non-hierarchically;

● when a manager considers it is her or his job to manage the work, but not the people who are doing the work;

● when there is no one to provide supervision to those at the top of a hierarchy.

In these cases supervision might be provided by a management committee member. In groups which work non-hierarchically, workers could be supervised by each other (co-supervision), either individually or in small groups.

Another possibility is external or non-managerial supervision, which is discussed later in this chapter.

Purposes of supervision

The main purposes of supervision are to:

● monitor work and work performance;

● evaluate work and performance;

● clarify priorities;

● share information about work;

● provide an opportunity to discuss how the worker and supervisor feel about the work;

● recognise and deal with existing or potential problems;

● discuss how outside factors are affecting work;

● provide a framework for discussing and agreeing change.

Monitoring work and work performance involves looking at what has been done, what needs to be done, and how it is being done. This includes checking workers have done everything they were meant to (and to the agreed standards) since the last session, clarifying work to be done before the next session, ensuring workers are accountable (answerable to someone for what they do), and helping them get an overview and sense of direction for their work and the work of the organisation as a whole.

Evaluation means assessing whether the expectations and standards that were set were realistic. This can involve considering whether workers performed well and whether the job or task was worth doing, identifying strong and weak points, encouraging workers, and identifying training and support needs.

The creation of a **framework for change** can mean limiting workloads and helping workers set priorities, identifying potential or actual problems and looking for ways to prevent or resolve them, and encouraging a sense of responsibility and commitment to the organisation and the job.

The purpose of these sessions is not to give supervisors or managers an opportunity to insult or criticise workers. It is to enable two people to take time out and look together at how the work of the organisation can best be done and how workers can best be supported in doing that work.

Common difficulties

The most frequent problem with supervision is that people, especially those new to management, do not know how to supervise or do not want to do it. This is exacerbated by lack of:

● information about the worker's job;

● clear standards or reference points against which to monitor or evaluate work and work performance;

● commonly agreed procedures for arranging and carrying out sessions;

● agreed procedures for taking notes and acting on recommendations made in the session;

● a clear policy about confidentiality;

● organisational commitment to supervision;

● a clear distinction between supervision and disciplinary procedures.

Often there is no consistency of approach from session to session, or between supervisors. A broad framework of questions makes it easier to standardise approaches (see 'Preparing for a supervision session', below).

If there is no clear way to record recommendations the session can easily become a chat which does not change or achieve anything. A one-page form with a few headings ('priorities for the next X weeks', 'things for worker to do', 'things for supervisor to do') can make it easier to standardise note-taking. This form then becomes the starting point for the next session. If desired, the worker and supervisor can sign and date the form.

Sometimes changes agreed in a supervision session involve other people so cannot be implemented immediately. It is therefore essential to decide, in the session, who will have responsibility for passing on information to the appropriate people.

Information obtained in a supervision session should not be conveyed to others without the agreement of both the worker and supervisor. Discretion should be expected; if supervision is to be effective, workers must be certain that information given in a session will not be misused.

If supervision is seen as a low priority within the organisation people will not put very much energy into it, and the work of the organisation as a whole will suffer. Ideally, scheduling should be flexible enough to allow for more frequent sessions at times of change or individual or organisational stress. However, the reverse should not happen: cancelling sessions when 'everything is going well'. Sessions which unavoidably have to be cancelled should always be rescheduled.

Because most people in voluntary organisations are exceedingly reluctant to implement disciplinary procedures, they may issue veiled warnings in supervision sessions then say these were the first stage in a formal disciplinary action. **If a disciplinary warning is being issued, it must be clearly defined as such.** Saying 'you really are going to have to get here on time in future' to someone in a supervision session does not constitute a verbal warning.

Overcoming resistance

In organisations where there has been no supervision there can be great resistance, especially from workers who are very well established in their position. As with any planned change, the introduction of supervision needs to involve discussion and consultation. Some organisations have found it helpful to photocopy all or part of this chapter and distribute it as a discussion document.

For workers who are very established and possibly quite conservative and worried about change, a regular one to one session can provide opportunities for them to air their concerns in an environment where they will be seriously listened to. The manager in this situation gains a valuable insight into the views of people with a long term commitment to the organisation.

For senior managers who feel they 'know it all' and do not need supervision, or are too busy, supervision can provide a respite from the day to day rush, a chance to stand back and look at the broader picture and to discuss problem issues.

Managers and workers sometimes feel there is no need to provide this sort of session for part-time workers or for caretakers, domestic workers, clerical workers or others who are not directly involved in service provision. For these workers supervision might be less frequent, or for a shorter session. But a regular one to one session is a way of maintaining morale, showing the organisation values all its workers, and ensuring people who may be marginalised within the organisation have genuine opportunities to contribute.

Preparing for a supervision session

Supervision sessions are much more useful if the worker and supervisor have thought beforehand about the situation. Workers might want to consider questions such as:

- What have I done since the last session that I am pleased about? How has my work improved? What factors have helped me work better?

- What have I done since the last session that I am unhappy about? Why did I do it in that way? What would help me do it differently in future?

- Have I done what I set out to do at the last session? If not, why not?

- What do I want to do before the next session? What will the emphases and priorities in my work be? How do they fit into the priorities of my workgroup, team and the organisation?

- Am I happy with the amount and type of work I have to do and the conditions in which I work? If I am unhappy, what could improve the situation for me?

- Is anything or anyone at work creating a problem for me? How could this be dealt with?

- Are situations or people in my personal life affecting my work? Do I need support to deal with the effects on my work, or with the situations themselves?

The supervisor should consider a similar set of questions:

- What has the worker done since the last session that I am particularly pleased about? How has her/his work improved? What factors might have helped her/him work even better? How can I help the worker build on this success?

- What has the worker done since the last session that I am unhappy about? Why did it happen? What could I or other people in the organisation have done to prevent it or make it better? What can we do to prevent such things happening in future?

- Has the worker done what was agreed at the last session?

- Am I satisfied with the quantity and quality of work?

- What do I think the worker should be concentrating on before the next session? How will this fit in with the worker's own priorities?

- Does the worker seem to be overworking or underworking? Are there problems about timekeeping? Is the worker keeping up with essential administration, maintenance and other routine tasks?

- Am I aware of any particular problems for this worker, at home or at work, that I should bring up?

Effective use of sessions

The setting should be private and undisturbed (unplug the phone and put a 'do not disturb' sign on the door), and as comfortable and relaxed as possible.

Key factors in making supervision successful are:

● preparation;

● not simply moaning or discussing in general terms;

● focusing on how matters could be improved, rather than on what is wrong;

● not getting sidetracked;

● remaining patient and calm, **asking** questions, **listening** to what is said;

● agreeing specific recommendations for change, even if they are only very small steps;

● writing down the recommendations and using them as the starting point for the next session.

The emphasis should always be positive. Blame, rumour and hearsay have no place in good management.

Supervision is much easier if the organisation has clear objectives and priorities, the worker and supervisor know what they are and how they affect the worker's job, and the worker has a clear job description.

The supervisor should be able to assess other people's work, offer suggestions for improvements and be able to build on the worker's suggestions for change. The supervisor should also be able to accept criticism.

And for supervision to work effectively, both people must feel confident that the supervisor has the authority to act in that capacity. If she or he does not have the authority to implement recommendations that come out of the session, the worker and supervisor should agree the steps that need to be taken for implementation. This is especially important if the supervisor is not the worker's manager.

At the end of the session, the date of the next session and anything that needs to be done should be confirmed.

Identifying responsibility for problem areas

The roots of problems at work can be divided into six broad categories:

● poor individual management;

● inappropriate or inadequate skills, knowledge or ability;

● lack of motivation or commitment to work;

● breaches of conditions or rules;

● poor organisational management;

● factors outside the individual's or organisation's control.

For the first three, responsibility rests jointly with the supervisor and worker to try to identify what the problems are, why they are happening, their effects, and what can be done to improve the situation.

For the fourth (breach of conditions or rules) responsibility rests with the supervisor to explain what has been done wrong and what rule has been broken, and to listen to the worker's reasons for her or his action. They then need to look jointly at the reasons for the rule and effects of infringement, and decide how to proceed.

Problems arising from poor organisational management should not be made the responsibility of individual workers. If no one is clear about standards and expectations, or if there is simply too much work and no one is willing to set priorities, it is unfair to castigate individuals. In this case the purpose of the supervision session should be to identify causes of the problems and to agree action that can be taken by the supervisor and other managers.

When factors outside the individual's or organisation's control are affecting workers and work, the supervisor's responsibility is to provide the necessary support to enable the worker to deal with the situation.

Dealing with typical problems

In dealing with problems relating to work it can be helpful for the supervisor to have fairly clear (but flexible) objectives for what needs to be achieved in the long term and during the session.

For example if the problem is **unreliability**, chronic **lateness** or **lack of honesty** about work, the long term objective might be being able to trust the worker to get on with the job. Objectives for the supervision session might be to:

● state clearly what has gone wrong;

● try to find out why it has gone wrong;

● establish the need for reliability;

● encourage the worker to take responsibility for her or his own arrangements;

● discuss and agree how to avoid this problem in future;

● explain what will happen if the situation does not improve;

● clarify priorities;

● review the past month;

● plan next month.

Or if the problem is **poor planning**, **poor work organisation** or **difficulties in prioritising**, the long term objectives might be for the worker to be able to plan her or his own work and set her or his own priorities within the framework of team and organisational priorities. Objectives for the session might be to:

● establish the need for organisation and planning;

● establish the worker's particular problems;

● discuss whether the workload is realistic;

● be sure the worker understands why tasks are necessary or important;

● clarify priorities;

● discuss strategies such as workplans and to-do lists (see chapter 11);

● agree a strategy.

If the worker has **difficulties working with certain people** (clients, users or colleagues), the long term objective might be for the worker to be better able to get on with those people. Objectives for the session might be:

- recognition and acceptance of the problem;

- understanding why it is a problem;

- discussing possible courses of action for improving the situation;

- agreeing the first steps.

Note that the supervisor has not come into the session with fixed ideas of what has to happen to sort out the problems, but does have a clear idea of the **steps** involved in coming to an agreed plan.

SUPPORT

Supervision and support are separate but overlapping managerial functions. Supervision deals with the work itself; support deals with the worker. In reality, of course, they cannot very easily be separated.

Purposes of support

A support session aims to:

- give workers a safe setting in which to express themselves, let off steam and discuss their feelings about work;

- help workers explore possibilities for work and career development;

- look at how outside situations are affecting work, and help workers consider appropriate support.

Common difficulties

The most common problems in trying to provide support within work are:

- unclear boundaries between work-related and personal support;

- actual or potential conflicts between support and supervision;

- questions of confidentiality.

The unclear boundary between work and the worker's personal situation is always a problem. When and how should a supervisor intervene if a worker is quite clearly drinking a lot, but work performance is not visibly affected? When and how should a supervisor intervene if a worker is weepy, snappish or bad tempered? The unclear boundary is made worse when people's personal life overlaps to a large extent with their work life: when their work colleagues are also their friends or lovers (or ex-lovers).

Personal problems should come into work only if they are directly affecting work. If they are discussed in a work setting, the objective should be to help the worker find outside support and/or resolve the problem in some way. Except for a few specific types of self-help groups, voluntary organisations do not exist to provide therapy or counselling for their workers.

One way to visualise this distinction is to put work life and personal (non-work) life into separate circles, and to imagine a supervision session as a square around the circles. (People who do not think that work and non-work

lives should be separated should read chapter 19, especially the section on burnout.)

Traditional management would see supervision as relating solely to the tasks the worker is supposed to be performing:

In many voluntary organisations, there is such a reluctance to manage that supervision focuses solely on the worker's personal situation:

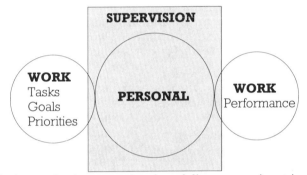

Or the worker's personal and work lives are so inextricably intertwined that any discussion of one overlaps totally with the other:

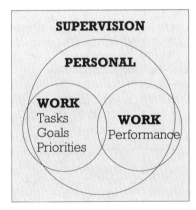

Obviously personal lives affect work lives, and good supervision takes this into account. It includes within supervision those aspects of personal life which are directly affecting work, but excludes other personal factors:

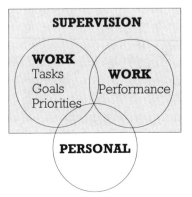

If people do not want to talk about their personal life at work, or if things are going well, the area of overlap may be very small; if a worker is going through a major trauma the area of overlap may be, for a while, quite large. In any case, it should be clear to both supervisor and worker that it is not the supervisor's role to deal directly with those personal situations.

Even when the overlap problems are sorted out, there can be an inherent contradiction between task-oriented supervision (which may have to be very strict about a person's performance) and support (which wants to be understanding about why the person's performance is inadequate). Care must be taken either to separate the support and supervision functions or, if they are not separated, to be aware at all times of this potential conflict.

Confidentiality

If confidentiality is an issue (for example if a worker is having serious personal problems and does not want colleagues to know the reasons) this should be discussed and agreed between the supervisor and worker. A plan may be needed to implement changes without directly telling other people why those changes are required.

In some cases, however, the supervisor will not be able to guarantee confidentiality. An example is a worker who does not want anyone else to know she is pregnant. If she only wants a couple of weeks in which to decide whether to have the pregnancy terminated before telling anyone, there is probably no problem about the confidentiality. But if she is already four months pregnant and the organisation needs to start making arrangements to hire someone for maternity cover, the request for confidentiality is unreasonable in terms of the organisation's needs.

A supervisor or manager should not agree to confidentiality before someone says what it is they want kept secret. If someone says 'I can only tell you this if you agree to keep it confidential' the best response is something like 'I can't agree to that before I know what it is. But I can promise to use my best judgment and discretion in deciding whether to tell anyone else, and to consult you as far as I can before I do.'

Matters which significantly affect work, colleagues or the organisation as a whole may need to be discussed with the supervisor's own manager, the personnel subcommittee or the chair of the management committee or other governing body. Great tact should be used in disclosing personal information, and no one should be told more than they need to know in order to deal with the work-related effects of the situation.

Support in a crisis

A crisis or serious problem in the worker's personal life will inevitably affect work. The manager's responsibility in this situation is:

● to be available to listen;

● to suggest possible sources of support, advice or practical help;

● to help the worker decide what and how other people at work should be told;

● if appropriate, to offer a reduced or altered workload;

● if appropriate, to offer sick leave, compassionate leave or other time off.

A useful booklet is *Someone to Talk to at Work: An employer's guide to problems in coping*, which is free (with a 9x6 inch 28p stamped addressed envelope) from the Mental Health Foundation, 8-10 Hallam Street, London W1N 6DH.

Some guidelines for supporting a worker who is very distressed are to:

● acknowledge the seriousness of the situation, rather than ignoring it or treating it lightly;

● let the worker know people are willing to listen and provide support;

● be prepared to listen and allow the worker time to cry or talk;

● not be afraid to talk about personal matters if the worker wants to, even if it seems inappropriate;

● not be embarrassed about the strong emotions that people sometimes express when they are distressed;

● remember it is not the role of the supervisor to provide therapy or counselling, but it is appropriate to suggest other sources of such help;

● close the session sensitively, reassuring the person that it is alright to have talked about personal matters and that everything will be treated confidentially unless the worker and supervisor have agreed otherwise;

● not hold the worker to things she or he may have said in the pain of the moment;

● treat in absolute confidence any personal matters which have been discussed which do not directly affect work, and use great discretion in disclosing those matters which do affect work.

NON-MANAGERIAL SUPERVISION

The kind of supervision discussed in this chapter is often referred to as **managerial supervision** because it is directly linked to the management of the organisation as a whole, and to the management of the individual's work within the organisation.

Non-managerial supervision involves a supervisor who has no direct link with the management of the individual's work, and may not even have a direct link with the organisation.

Another model for non-managerial supervision is a **support group**, where the function is to provide support for the worker rather than to manage her or his work.

Situations when non-managerial supervision is appropriate include:

● providing support for workers in high-stress jobs, where it might not be appropriate for the manager or a management committee member to do so (sometimes called **external supervision**);

● providing support for the senior manager, where there is no management committee member able or willing to do so;

- providing professional insight, especially in situations involving complex in-depth casework and especially where the manager does not have the necessary professional experience (sometimes called **therapeutic supervision** or **casework supervision**).

Even where there is non-managerial or casework supervision, there should still be managerial supervision. Without managerial supervision, the person's work is essentially unmanaged. This may not pose problems while work is being done well, but difficulties can arise when the worker's performance is inadequate and no one has responsibility for doing anything about it.

Non-managerial supervision is expensive in terms of workers' time, and often in terms of money. It should be provided by the organisation only if there is a justifiable reason for doing so. Other workers who feel they need external support should consider personal counselling, therapy, self-help groups or other sources of personal support.

Links with the organisation

The relationship between the non-managerial supervisor and the managerial supervisor must be very carefully worked out. Non-managerial supervision can provide opportunities for workers to talk and think through situations, but the responsibility for implementing changes still lies within the organisation.

Sometimes the non-managerial supervisor has absolutely no links with the organisation or the worker's manager; everything said in the non-managerial supervision session is confidential and it is the worker's responsibility to implement, through the normal managerial channels, any changes.

At the other extreme there may be direct links, with the non-managerial supervisor conveying to the manager what has been said and agreed in each session. Clearly very complex issues of confidentiality and responsibility need to be considered here.

VOLUNTEERS

Regular or long term volunteers should have the same opportunities for supervision and support as paid staff. The process may need to be adapted for their particular situation.

It can be awkward to 'supervise' very long term volunteers, or people from business or industry who are on secondment. But after the initial awkwardness and resistance both parties usually find these sessions very fruitful, both for the volunteer and the organisation.

For shorter term or casual volunteers it is often helpful to have regular brief one to one sessions, primarily to get feedback from the volunteers about how they are feeling, to ensure they are formally praised and thanked for their work, and to provide a regular setting within which problems can be addressed.

If the organisation uses volunteers with special support needs (for example people who have never been in paid employment, or who have learning difficulties or mental health needs) adequate extra time must be allowed for induction, support, supervision and training.

Unsuitable volunteers

Some volunteers may lack the skills or knowledge needed by the organisation. In most cases this can be overcome by providing training, or by developing new tasks suitable for the volunteer. But some volunteers may need more training or support than the organisation can justify giving. It is important to acknowledge this, rather than ignoring it and allowing a volunteer to become a net drain on the organisation.

Telling a volunteer that she or he is unsuitable is unlikely to be a comfortable task. It will be easier if a clear explanation can be given about what the organisation can offer volunteers, what it needs from volunteers, and why this volunteer cannot be accommodated. It might be possible to suggest another organisation more suited to the volunteer, but this should never be done if the volunteer is unlikely to be rejected there too.

While it may seem cruel to turn away volunteers, it is probably more cruel in the long term to keep people whose confidence will be undermined because they constantly get things wrong and are resented.

REVIEWS OR APPRAISALS

Supervision sessions deal primarily with day to day, week to week or month to month problems or issues. Staff reviews or appraisals are different because they:

- are held less frequently;

- may be more formal;

- can take a longer view, providing an opportunity for workers and supervisors to look in more depth at how workers feel about their jobs, their career development and the organisation as a whole;

- might be done by a senior manager or member of the management committee along with or instead of the usual supervisor;

- are part of a formal management review structure (which might not be the case for supervision sessions, especially if they are done by someone from outside the organisation).

Reviews should generally be held:

- midway through the probationary period, so the new worker, supervisor and manager become aware of any difficulties;

- shortly before the end of the probationary period, so the appointment can be confirmed, or the worker can be given a chance to improve before the end of the time if there are small but serious difficulties, or the probationary period can be extended if there are continuing major difficulties;

- six months after the end of the probationary period;

- annually thereafter.

One person in the organisation (either a worker or management committee member) should have responsibility for keeping track of when reviews are due and notifying the worker and the person who will be doing the review.

The terminology of reviews

Staff reviews are often called something else, or are confused with something else. As with so much management jargon there is no agreement about what is meant by words and concepts, and distinctions between the processes listed below are often unclear.

- **Supervision**: an ongoing process, looking at relatively short term issues related to an individual's work.

- **Organisational review**, **organisational evaluation**, **strategic review**, **programme review**: looks at what the organisation has done and wants to do. Might lead to a development plan or strategic plan (see chapters 8 and 9).

- **Process review** or **process evaluation** (also sometimes called organisational review): looks at the ways people communicate and the ways decisions are made within the organisation or team, and at whether organisational or team structures and procedures need to be changed.

- **Job evaluation**: assesses the relative demands of jobs within the organisation, often against an externally agreed framework for this type of work. Usually undertaken when salary scales within the organisation are being reconsidered.

- **Job review**: assesses whether the work done by an individual worker has changed and if so, how the job description should be changed to reflect this.

- **Salary review** or **reward review**: assesses whether a salary is appropriate for a particular job (especially after there has been a job review). If in doubt, a job evaluation might be necessary.

- **Performance review** or **performance appraisal**: assesses how well or badly work has been done and whether targets have been met. The term might relate to individuals, a specific service or the team or organisation as a whole. Individual performance reviews may be linked to salary increases (**performance-related pay**).

- **Training needs analysis**: assesses the training required or desired to enable workers as a group or individual workers to do their job better or to develop.

- **Staff review** or **staff appraisal**: as used in this book, it is similar to supervision but longer term, looking at bigger issues. It incorporates aspects of individual performance review but goes beyond what the worker has done and how well; it also includes individual training needs analysis and possibly job review. The focus is on how the individual can develop within the organisation.

The linking of staff reviews to salary increases is a complex issue. It is difficult for workers to be honest in assessing their progress and problems if they know a salary increase depends on what they say. In small voluntary organisations it is nearly always better to have agreed salary levels and agreed annual rises (say, inflation plus 3 per cent each year) rather than trying to link rises to performance or productivity.

Preparing for a staff review

As with supervision sessions, staff reviews are more effective if everyone involved has spent some time on preparation. One way to encourage this is with a standard set of questions for the worker, manager and supervisor (if different from manager).

The questions should form the basis for this review, but the review should not be a question and answer session. Before the review, the worker and manager should think carefully about which questions are relevant and make a note of any particular points they want to cover during the review.

Changes since the last review

- What are you most pleased about since the last review?

- How close do you feel you have come to meeting the goals set at the last review?

- What has improved since then?

- What has got worse since then?

For the mid-probation review:

- How do you feel about working here?

- How has the job met or not met your expectations?

Your own job

- How do you feel about your work as a whole?

- Are there particular aspects of your work you are happy or unhappy about?

- Do you think you have too much or too little work?

- Do you understand which tasks take priority?

- Do you think you need additional skills or experience to help you carry out your work better?

- How could we help you get those skills or experience?

- Can you use the equipment you need for your job?

- Can you produce necessary written material?

- Do you feel you do a fair share of the routine work, like washing up?

The rest of the organisation

- Are you getting the information you need from me?

- Are you getting the information you need from other workers, other teams and the management committee?

- Do you feel there are enough opportunities to participate in decision-making about your work, and about the organisation overall?

Our policies and procedures

- Do you feel you understand our philosophy and approach?

- Do you feel comfortable about how your job fits into this philosophy?

- Do you feel you understand what's going on locally and nationally that might affect us?

- Do you have ideas about how we should develop as an organisation?

Jerry has a bit of a problem with the boundary between work and his private life...

- Are there topics you would like to have discussed at staff forums?

Relations with other people

- Are there any users/clients/members you feel particularly good or bad about working with?
- Are there any workers you feel particularly good or bad about working with?
- How do you feel about your working relationship with your supervisor?
- How do you feel about your working relationship with me?
- How do you feel about the workers you have to supervise?
- Are you getting the support you need within the organisation? If not, what more do you need?

Relations with other organisations

- Are you in contact with other organisations or agencies you need to know about?
- Do you understand how our work fits in with, and differs from, the work of other organisations?

Your long term plans

- How would you ideally like to see your job develop?

- Have you thought about your long term career plans for yourself?
- Are there ways the organisation could help with your career development?

Following up the review

A staff review follow-up sheet might include sections with the following headings. Any follow-up point should include the timescale and who will do it. The timescale might be immediate or very long term.

- Changes in the job
- Changes in the organisation's procedures
- Other organisational changes
- Training and other opportunities for learning
- Other tasks or objectives.

The follow-up sheet should end with a note of the month when the next review will be held.

It should be typed up (if necessary) and two copies signed by the worker and manager. The top copy goes to the worker and the second signed copy in the worker's personnel file, with photocopies, if required, for the worker's manager and/or supervisor.

The follow-up sheet should be reviewed as appropriate at supervision sessions, and should form the starting point for the next review.

Even people who are very antagonistic to the idea of staff reviews are often won around after the first year or two. A typical comment is 'I never realised how much I've achieved and changed in the past year.'

IF THERE ARE STILL PROBLEMS

Even with good supervision and review procedures and opportunities for training, some workers may still not perform adequately. What has gone wrong, and what can be done about it?

Inability to do the job

The worker may be incapable of doing the job or specific tasks within it. Can the difficult parts be done by someone else? Can the overall job be changed? Would additional training or support help? Can the worker be transferred to another post?

If there is at least one 'yes', the option should be explored. But if the answers are all 'no', the worker may have to be let go. Dismissal is highly unpleasant and no one wants to be involved in it. Every effort should be made to avoid getting into a situation where dismissal is necessary. But if the work has to be done and the person cannot do it, it damages the organisation, the person involved and the other workers to keep that person in post.

If an employee can be shown to be incapable of doing the work the dismissal is 'fair' and the employee cannot bring a case of unfair dismissal against the organisation.

Lack of commitment to the work

The worker may not want to do the job properly. There may be a problem of motivation (see chapter 14) or stress or burnout (see chapter 19). If the worker will not do anything to deal with the cause of the difficulty, the only solution is for her or him to be given a clear indication of what must be done and to what standards, and to be warned that disciplinary procedures will result if work does not become satisfactory. This is not pleasant but a worker who does not want to work can too easily undermine everyone else's commitment and enthusiasm.

Poor management

Many aspects of poor organisational management can contribute to poor performance and lack of motivation.

- The supervisor may not be able or willing to manage the worker, so supervision sessions, reviews and other procedures are used ineffectually (or are not used at all). The manager needs training and support (see chapter 22).

- The supervisor may not have authority to implement changes required to help the worker improve her or his work. Lines of communication need to be created between the supervisor and those who have authority to implement change.

- The organisation may be unclear about what it expects from the worker. It may be giving mixed messages, and/or expecting too much. ('We want you to spend a lot of time on outreach work talking to young people in the community' ... 'We want you to be accessible at the office every day so there is someone for the young people to talk to whenever they drop in.')

- The organisation may have conflicting or too many priorities. ('The financial report has to be ready to go out with the management committee papers tomorrow' ... 'Jane is on a training course, you'll have to cover for her welfare advice session this afternoon' ... 'Don't forget the new desk is being delivered this afternoon, you'll have to clear the old one so it can be taken out as soon as the new one comes.') Individuals and the organisation as a whole have to learn more about planning (chapter 8) and time management (chapter 11).

- Workers may feel unappreciated and unsupported within the organisation. Unless appropriate support is given, workers are likely to work at the minimum acceptable level and feel alienated from the team or organisation.

If the manager is unable or unwilling to manage or if the organisation is unclear about its priorities, the worker is being set up to fail. When this happens, the organisation fails as well.

AND IF THERE ARE *STILL* PROBLEMS

Disciplinary procedures

Disciplinary action should only be started if informal discussions and supervision sessions with clear targets for improvement have proved ineffective, or if there is misconduct or a breach of rules which is too serious to be dealt with informally.

A disciplinary action is an important matter which affects the morale of everyone concerned: the worker, the manager and colleagues. But it can be equally demoralising if disciplinary action is not taken when everyone is aware that work is not being done properly or a worker is constantly breaking the rules and being allowed to get away with it.

Voluntary But Not Amateur chapter 3 explains some of the legal aspects of disciplinary procedures. Detailed information is available from ACAS (27 Wilton Street, London SW1X 7AZ, tel 071 210 3000).

Every stage in the disciplinary procedure must clearly indicate:

- what is wrong;

- what needs to happen to make it right;

- what the deadline is for improvement;

- how improvement will be assessed and by whom;

- what will happen if the necessary improvement does not occur.

Disciplinary action relating to poor work performance is undertaken if informal chats and supervision sessions with clear targets for improvement have not produced the desired results. The disciplinary action usually starts with one or two **verbal warnings**. Even though these are called verbal, a written note should be given to the worker and a copy placed in the worker's personnel file. They should clearly indicate they are the first stage in disciplinary action.

If performance does not improve, the next step may be more verbal warnings, or one or two formal **written warnings.**

Minor breaches of rules, for example consistent lateness which does not directly affect the organisation's services to users, are usually dealt with in the same way.

A more serious infringement of rules or policies, for example taking the organisation's minibus without authorisation, might start at the written warning stage.

A worker and manager may disagree about whether performance is adequate or whether misconduct has occurred. They need to discuss this, but ultimately it is a management decision, not the worker's, to start disciplinary action. If the worker disagrees with the action, she or he must have the right to appeal to someone who has not been directly involved in giving the warnings. The disciplinary procedure will set out how to appeal.

Final warnings and dismissal

If performance still does not improve or rules continue to be broken, the next stage will be a **final written warning**, making it clear that dismissal may follow failure to improve. The worker must have the right to appeal.

If the final warning is held on appeal to be justified, and if the worker's conduct does not improve sufficiently, the next stage is notice of dismissal. The worker must be given the amount of time specified in the contract of employment or the minimum time allowed by law (or must be given pay in lieu of this period of notice, if the organisation does not want the worker to continue working during the period of notice). The worker must have the right to appeal.

Gross misconduct

Very serious misconduct is usually dealt with through suspension on full pay while the incident is investigated. This step must only be taken in very serious cases such as theft from the organisation or a user, violence, or gross racism or sexism. Any incident of gross misconduct must be investigated and dealt with urgently, perhaps bringing in independent people from outside the organisation to help with the investigation.

If the gross misconduct is proved the worker can be immediately dismissed with no notice and no pay in lieu of notice, unless the contract of employment says otherwise.

Fair and unfair dismissal

All employees, no matter how long they have been employed or how many hours they work per week, have the right not to be dismissed for any reason to do with their race, ethnic origin, national origin, nationality, gender or marital status. A worker who believes she or he has been dismissed on any of these grounds can bring a case of unfair dismissal against the organisation.

Apart from that, employees do not get any employment protection until they have worked for an employer 16 hours or more per week for two years, or eight to 16 hours per week for five years. Before the two year/five year mark, any employee can be dismissed at any time for any reason, or indeed for no reason, and will have no recourse in law. This means a worker who does not work out satisfactorily during the probationary period, or one who consistently breaks rules, can be dismissed at any time within the first two years/five years. The organisation has a moral obligation to follow its own disciplinary procedures before dismissing anyone within this period, but the worker cannot do anything if the organisation does not follow its procedures.

After the two years/five years employees can claim **unfair dismissal** if they believe they have been dismissed without good cause or if the organisation's disciplinary procedures were not followed.

So if a worker is dismissed after the two year/five year period the organisation must be able to prove:

● the employee is unable to do the work for which she or he was hired (if the work no longer exists and the worker cannot do new work the organisation should make the worker redundant, rather than terminating the employment);

● *or* the worker is unwilling to do the work;

● *or* the worker has continued to break rules even after warnings;

● *or* there has been gross misconduct;

● *and* in any of those cases, the organisation followed its disciplinary procedures;

● *and* those procedures conform to the ACAS guidelines for disciplinary procedures.

With good recruitment, selection, induction, supervision and review procedures and a good staff training programme the likelihood of having to terminate an appointment should be minimal. But it does happen, and when it does it must be dealt with as quickly and as fairly as possible.

Disciplinary procedures for volunteers

An organisation which regularly uses volunteers should have a simple, fair procedure for dealing with disciplinary problems. This usually follows the organisation's disciplinary procedure for paid staff but with fewer stages. The Volunteer Centre UK can advise.

Chapter 17:

Managing training

Job-related training can be defined as systematic instruction or practice to help individuals learn how to do their work, or do it better. It overlaps with, but is different from, education, which has wider aims. A broader definition of training is 'all organised occasions which are aimed at encouraging the development of individuals and/or organisations'.

As well as formal training, there are many opportunities for **learning**. A worker who receives a clear agenda for a meeting, watches a good chair in operation and receives clear, accurate minutes a few days later is learning far more about running meetings than could be taught on an 'effective meetings' course.

Training is sometimes seen as the magic answer to all the ills of the voluntary sector. Unfortunately short courses, no matter how good they are, cannot convey vast amounts of information, ideas or skills to people. All they can do is introduce new ideas and provide basic awareness and skills which can then be developed by the people who have been trained.

Training cannot solve problems caused by bad management, inadequate policies or procedures, or lack of resources. But it *can* make people more aware of how to recognise and deal with those problems.

Training cannot be a substitute for management. Managers and workers must make decisions and take action, and must have procedures for doing so. A training session is not an appropriate place for managerial decision-making, although it can give participants time to think through situations and come up with ideas which can then be fed back into the appropriate decision-making structures (such as team or management committee meetings). If it is felt that decisions have to be made within a 'training' context, it is more appropriate to think about facilitation or consultancy (see chapter 22).

Good training makes people more confident and competent in their work. Bad training, or training for which unrealistic objectives have been set, can leave people feeling frustrated or hopeless.

This chapter looks at:

- types and purposes of training;
- how to develop a training policy;
- training needs analysis;
- where to find information about courses;
- how to develop in-house training;
- national vocational qualifications (NVQs) and their implications.

More information is available in *Tackling Training: Practical training guidelines for voluntary organisations* (London Voluntary Service Council, 1989; 28 pages; £4.95 from LVSC, 68 Chalton Street, London NW1 1JR).

TYPES OF TRAINING

Training may take place within the organisation (in-house), outside, or jointly with other organisations. The trainers may be people from within the organisation or from outside.

Training includes:

- induction for new workers, volunteers and committee members;
- on the job training;
- practical demonstrations;
- opportunities to 'shadow' or work with experienced workers;
- workshops, seminars and discussion groups;
- speakers or films at meetings;
- lectures;
- conferences or residential events which are educational (designed to develop knowledge and understanding);
- visits to or from other organisations;
- one-off training sessions, lasting anything from an hour to several days;
- linked or modular courses, consisting of several sessions over a period of days, weeks or months;
- courses lasting a year or longer which may lead to a qualification;
- a formal programme of reading;
- opportunities for 'distance learning', using books, audio tapes, video or television programmes and/or correspondence.

FUNCTIONS OF TRAINING

Used appropriately, training can help workers or committee members learn more about:

- their specific **job** or **tasks**, so they can do their existing job, do it better, or take on new work as the job or organisation changes;

- relevant **legislation** or other requirements for their work;
- **organisational and management skills**, so they can manage themselves, their work and the organisation (this includes, for example, chairing meetings, taking minutes, time management, goal-setting, teamwork, staff supervision);
- the **history and philosophy** of the organisation;
- the **political, social and economic setting** in which the organisation operates;
- **policy development and strategic planning**, so they can develop, implement or review policy or plan major changes in the organisation;
- **personal skills and awareness**, so they can function more effectively as individuals and therefore work more effectively (this includes, for example, assertiveness training, stress management, communication skills);
- **interpersonal and group skills and awareness**, so they can more sensitively and effectively provide services to their whole community or client group.

Training can also play a major role in individuals' **career development**, enabling them to progress within the organisation.

TRAINING POLICY

Regardless of the size or type of organisation, training will be more effective if there is a clear and coherent training policy. This will determine how much should be included in the budget for training. The amount available will affect, in turn, policy decisions about how the money should be spent.

A training policy should cover objectives and priorities, access to training, equal opportunities considerations, in-house training, external training and extended or long term training.

Objectives and priorities

This section covers why the organisation provides training and what it is expected to achieve. It might include:

- purposes of training;
- how it relates to the organisation's objectives;
- criteria used to determine the budget;
- how individual training needs are assessed;
- how group, team or organisational training needs are assessed;
- who decides priorities, and what criteria are used;
- who decides how much time can be devoted to training;
- who decides who should go on specific sessions or courses;
- who decides how much can be spent on them;
- who sets objectives for them, and who assesses whether the objectives have been met.

Access to training

This covers:

- whether in-house training is open to people other than full-time or permanent workers (for example part-time or temporary workers, long or short term volunteers, management committee members, organisational members, users, or people from outside the organisation);
- whether people other than full-time or permanent workers are eligible to go on external courses.

Equal opportunities considerations

Two separate aspects are:

- how training will provide opportunities for staff, volunteers, management committee members or other members who have traditionally missed out on training opportunities, for example women, people from minority ethnic groups and people with disabilities;
- how training will help individuals and the organisation to challenge oppression and oppressive behaviour.

In-house training

It is helpful to consider in-house and external training separately, since different people may be involved in the decision-making. Policy issues include:

- who decides what training is offered in-house;
- who decides the objectives;
- who decides whether to use an in-house trainer or someone from outside;
- who briefs and liaises with the trainer;
- who decides who attends;
- what happens if all workers are expected to attend a training event (does the organisation close? is locum cover provided?);
- under what circumstances a creche is provided;
- who evaluates the training, and against what criteria;
- who decides whether or how work performance or behaviour is expected to change as a result of training, and who evaluates whether it has changed.

External training

- how much information the organisation should receive about training, and from which sources;
- who should collect and monitor the information;
- how training information is made available to staff, volunteers, management committee, users and members;
- how individual workers are notified about relevant courses;
- who decides whether a worker can go on a course;
- whether there should be a limit on the number of days or amount of money each worker can have for training each year;

- who arranges cover while the worker is away;

- who deals with course applications and other paperwork;

- who pays for transport, meals, accommodation or childcare;

- how external courses should be evaluated;

- who decides whether and how work performance or behaviour is expected to change as a result of training, and evaluates whether it has changed;

- how what is learned on the course is fed back into the team or organisation;

- whether course materials, such as books, belong to the worker or the organisation.

Extended or long term training

Some organisations allow workers to attend courses lasting a year or more. These may be part-time day or evening courses for which time off is given (paid or unpaid), or full-time courses accommodated by giving unpaid leave or a sabbatical. The training policy should cover:

- under what circumstances workers can get time off to attend a long term course;

- whether the course has to be directly work-related;

- whether the time off will be paid or unpaid;

- whether the organisation will pay fees and/or for course materials;

- if the organisation pays for a course or allows paid time off, whether the worker has to stay with the organisation for a specific time afterwards, and what happens if she or he does not come back for the required period;

- whether study leave will be given and whether paid or unpaid, for workers who take courses in their own time.

TRAINING NEEDS ANALYSIS

A training needs analysis (TNA) is a systematic attempt to find out what training is needed or wanted by individuals, teams and the organisation as a whole.

Most training needs become apparent through good supervision and review procedures (chapter 16). Others become clear by various types of questionnaire, for example asking people to list courses they think important for themselves or the organisation and rate each one on a scale from 1 (I'm interested in it, but it's not very urgent) to 5 (very urgent). A TNA might ask for:

- skills (knowing **how to do** something) to help the worker carry out her or his work or do it better;

- knowledge (knowing **about** something) to help the worker do her or his work or do it better;

- personal development courses (for example stress management or assertion) that a worker needs or wants;

- self-management courses (for example time

management, basic administration) that a worker needs or wants;

- management training;

- training to develop awareness of specific groups' needs or to develop work which challenges discrimination or oppression;

- areas in which the team or workgroup needs training;

- areas in which the organisation as a whole needs training;

- training which could help future development as a team or organisation;

- training which could help the worker's career development.

It is important not to raise people's expectations. Make it clear that priorities will have to be decided, and there are limits to the amount of training that can be provided.

FINDING OUTSIDE COURSES

A few years ago it was so difficult to find relevant courses that voluntary sector workers or managers had to make do with training designed for the commercial or statutory sectors. Now it is much easier to find appropriate courses. The best places to start are:

- London Voluntary Service Council's Training Unit (68 Chalton Street, London NW1 1JR, tel 071 388 0241) which runs its own short courses, provides a detailed listing of courses relevant to the voluntary sector in Greater London, and maintains a database of information about freelance and other trainers;

- the Local Development Team at the National Council for Voluntary Organisations (Regents Wharf, 8 All Saints Street, London N1 9RL, tel 071 713 6161), which organises short courses outside London;

- the Directory of Social Change (Radius Works, Back Lane, London NW3 1HL, tel 071 431 1817), which runs a range of courses and conferences on voluntary sector management, finance, fundraising and related topics;

- large national organisations, umbrella bodies or networks for particular types of work, for example MENCAP, National Federation of Housing Associations, Richmond Fellowship, MIND, Oxfam, Volunteer Centre UK;

- local councils for voluntary service or other coordinating organisations, for information about courses in a geographical area;

- local adult education institutes, community education centres, colleges or the Workers Educational Association;

- funders, to see if they run courses specifically for organisations they fund.

The LVSC Training Unit and the Local Development and Mangagement Development Teams at NCVO can provide information about commercial training agencies which provide courses for the voluntary sector.

Course information should clearly indicate the course objectives and content and for whom it is intended. There is usually little point going on courses if these details are not given; it is probably a sign that the training organiser and trainer have not clarified why the course is being run and what it can realistically achieve.

IN-HOUSE TRAINING

In-house training ensures everyone who attends gets the same information and has the same experiences, and the session can be tailored to the specific needs of the organisation or team. If several workers need the same or very similar training it is usually less expensive to provide in-house training than to send them all on external courses.

Before employing a trainer it is essential to be very clear about why training is needed, what workers are expected to understand or be able to do as a result, who needs to participate, available time, premises and funds.

Information about training providers (voluntary organisations, commercial agencies and freelance trainers) is available from the places listed above.

When contacting trainers, explain what the organisation does, what kind of training is wanted and why, how many people would attend, how much time is available and when the training is needed. Then ask the trainers:

- whether they are interested in this work;

- what other training they have done, and for whom;

- their approach to this type of training;

- how they would ensure equal opportunities considerations are taken into account in the training;

- their fees, whether there is an additional charge for preliminary meeting(s), and how expenses are charged.

Unless it is a straightforward 'off the shelf' course, the trainer will arrange a meeting to discuss the course content and objectives in more detail and to agree fees, starting and finishing times, procedures for getting handouts photocopied, equipment or materials required, special provision for participants with language difficulties or disabilities, and evaluation procedures.

Within a few days the trainer should provide a written course programme. Some trainers provide a formal contract giving details of fees, dates and times and other essential information. If the trainer does not do this, the training organiser should confirm these details in writing.

NATIONAL VOCATIONAL QUALIFICATIONS

Increasingly formal training and other types of learning are being linked with national vocational qualifications (NVQs). Unlike traditional education, NVQs are not based on what people **know** but on what they can **do** as part of their work. People gain NVQs by showing competence in a range of work activities at different levels.

NVQs will be nationally recognised and equivalent to qualifications in other European Community countries. They will be transferable from the voluntary to the public and private sectors, as part of a continuing structure leading to further qualifications.

They are currently assessed at four levels:

● **Level 1**: work activities which are primarily routine and predictable, or provide a broad foundation;

● **Level 2**: broader and more demanding work activities involving greater individual responsibility;

● **Level 3**: more complex and non-routine work activities involving, in some cases, supervisory competence;

● **Level 4**: complex, technical and professional work activities, including supervision or management.

Level 3 is considered roughly equivalent to A-level. In due course higher levels (5 and 6) may be developed.

NVQs are developed by more than 140 independent **lead bodies** for different sectors or occupations including, for example, care, housing, legal, administration, management. The lead bodies produce **competencies** from which an awarding body (usually a professional body) can create an NVQ. The NVQ is then accredited by the National Council for Voluntary Qualifications (NCVQ) or SCOTVEC in Scotland. Their criteria include:

● there must be no time limit on gaining the qualification;

● it must be modular;

● there must be no requirement to attend any particular course or college;

● there must be no other requirements relating to how the qualification is gained.

The assumption is that assessment against defined standards of competence will be carried out in the workplace by an **assessor** (probably the candidate's line manager). Another appropriate member of staff, such as a training officer, will provide internal verification of the assessment. There is then further assessment and verification by the awarding body.

Obviously this model for assessment is not appropriate for small organisations, or for those where there is no line manager. In some areas of work consortia are being formed to provide national coverage, a 'pool' of assessors and verifiers, and supervised work placements if necessary. Information about these and other aspects of NVQs are available from the Management Development Team at the National Council for Voluntary Organisations (Regents Wharf, 8 All Saints Street, London N1 9RL, tel 071 713 6161).

Accreditation of prior learning

Because NVQs are competence based they can enable people to gain a qualification even if they have never attended a course or had a job. This is done through accreditation of prior learning (APL), which recognises skills already gained through employment, volunteering, personal and home roles, even if those skills are not being used in current work.

Implications for the voluntary sector

The voluntary sector has often provided a route to employment for people who do not have traditional qualifications (GCSEs, A-levels, degrees) or who have not followed a traditional career path. NVQs will enable people who came into the voluntary sector in this way to gain formal recognition of what they know and can do. This should make it easier for them to move on to other jobs in other sectors or other European countries, without feeling that volunteering or working in the voluntary sector is somehow second best.

But there is a risk NVQs will work the other way. Especially with the new emphasis on providing defined services to agreed standards under contracts, voluntary sector employers might start requiring NVQs as 'proof' that new workers can work at the necessary level, thus excluding people from employment opportunities if they do not already have NVQs. Voluntary sector employers need to ensure this does not happen.

As NVQs are established, voluntary organisations may need to develop new patterns of training, perhaps with other organisations or local colleges, as a way of helping workers gain competence in particular skills or types of work.

BEING REALISTIC

Training does not exist in isolation. It should be part of a comprehensive staff/volunteer development policy which includes induction (see chapter 15) and regular supervision, support and formal reviews (chapter 16).

Training cannot work miracles. It is unlikely to enable workers or management committee members to perform tasks today they could not do yesterday, or to change deeply rooted attitudes or beliefs, or to turn people who hate managing into skilful managers. However, it can provide a starting point.

Training is not the same as **facilitation** or **consultancy**, which focus on specific situations or problems in organisations and look for ways to deal with those situations. Chapter 22 looks at these in more detail.

Chapter 18:

Managing differences and conflict

In any relationship or group there will be differences. People think differently, have different values, interpret information in different ways. Differences are the basis on which individuals, relationships and organisations grow and change. Sameness may seem attractive but it leads, in the long term, to complacency and stagnation.

In effective organisations or teams there is a shared sense of **unity**, of commitment to common objectives and ideals. But there is also a shared sense of **diversity**. Differences are welcomed, there are clear opportunities for people to express and discuss their differing views, and people are committed to finding ways to operate which value everyone's contributions and beliefs.

This does *not* mean everyone can always get what they want. People must recognise they are working together as a group and sometimes may have to do things they do not want to do, go along with decisions with which they do not fully agree or even, if the group goes in a completely unacceptable direction, sever their connection with the group.

Conflict arises when differences cannot be satisfactorily dealt with. Differences become conflict if:

● people are unwilling to accept the validity of differing values, priorities or views of what is 'right' or 'important';

● individuals or the group as a whole have different or unclear standards for action, behaviour or performance and common standards cannot be agreed;

● something (money, attention, workload, responsibility) is, or is perceived to be, unfairly distributed;

● people feel an individual or collective need to win, be right, get their own way or dominate;

● people succumb to fear, distrust and the need to define anyone different or unknown as 'other', 'outsider' or 'enemy';

● the people involved do not want to change;

● there are unclear or nonexistent procedures for discussing and resolving differences before they escalate into conflict.

Conflict is difficult but if managed well can provide an opportunity for a group and all the people involved to learn, grow and change.

It is a mockery to talk about 'equal opportunities' or 'commitment to the community' if people are unwilling to value everyone's ideas, opinions and contributions.

The differences or conflicts which people say they are concerned about (the 'presenting problem') are not always the real problem. Sometimes conflict resolution involves looking beyond the presenting problem to discover what else is happening within the group. If the underlying causes of conflict are not uncovered and dealt with, conflicts will continue to erupt.

This chapter includes:

● questions that need to be asked when (or preferably before) conflict occurs;

● various approaches to conflict resolution;

● guidelines for dealing with conflict.

One of the best books on avoiding and dealing with conflict in organisations is *Managing Conflict: The key to making your organization work* by Dean Tjosvold (Team Media, 1989; 130 pages; ISBN 0 9621542 0 2; $14.95 plus $3 postage from Team Media, 1555 118th Lane NW, Minneapolis, Minnesota 55433, USA).

POSITIONS AND ISSUES

When problems, disagreements or conflicts arise people's first response is usually to define their own position. Conflict resolution is then seen as a process of negotiating among the defined positions to find a solution to the immediate problem.

That kind of conflict resolution is important. But it is more productive, in the long term, for the whole group (not just the people directly involved in the conflict) to look beyond the presenting problem to underlying issues or confusions. This takes time and commitment, but it can make it easier to deal with the presenting problem and prevent related problems from arising.

It is, of course, even better to sort out what the group is doing and how it is doing it *before* problems arise!

The most common underlying issues can be divided into four broad categories:

● policies, objectives and priorities;

● inadequate resources to meet needs or demands;

● structures and procedures;

● personal, historical and hidden issues.

Examining these issues, perhaps by using a series of questions such as those below, should reveal the roots of conflict and help clarify how it can be eased or prevented.

When exploring sources of conflict it is important to remember that no one has a **monopoly on truth**. Issues which seem absolutely clearcut from one perspective are always less clear when other points of view are considered. People involved in conflict resolution must be willing to listen to, and take seriously, different viewpoints even if they are unpleasant or difficult.

Policies, objectives and priorities

If the organisation or group has problems in this area, chapters 7 and 8 may help.

● Does the group have clear objectives (what it wants to achieve) and priorities (what is most important for it to achieve) for the long, medium and short term, and for the immediate future? Does everyone involved know and understand them? Does it have clear criteria for setting priorities? How are differences of opinion about objectives and priorities dealt with?

● What does the constitution say about what the organisation was set up to do? What does it actually mean? (People often interpret clauses in constitutions and similar documents very differently.) Is there a conflict between constitutional objectives and the organisation's actual work?

● Does the group have clear policies about its work? What are they? What do they mean? (Even something as supposedly clear as an equal opportunities statement of intent can be interpreted in many different ways.) Do policies need to be clarified?

● Is there a need for new policies?

Pressure on resources

Chapters 8 and 11 provide guidelines on how to deal with problems in this area.

● What needs, pressures and demands (from users, members, community, staff, volunteers, funders, management committee or others) is the group expected to meet?

● Can other organisations or agencies meet those needs? Is this organisation trying to be too many things to too many people, and creating a risk of organisational and individual burnout?

● What resources (money, people, time, premises, commitment, energy) are available within the organisation or could be made available to meet the needs? Are resources being used as effectively as possible? Is the organisation creating problems for itself by taking on more than it can realistically cope with?

● What are the priorities for existing and potential resources? Is there a conflict because the organisation is constantly responding to immediate demands, and can never meet its longer term objectives?

● Are people in the organisation realistic about what it can and cannot take on? And about how much time has to be allowed for administration, meetings, communication, fundraising and all the other essential infrastructure?

Structures and procedures

Chapters 4 to 6, 14 and 16 may help to deal with problems in this area.

● How clear are boundaries between individual workers, the staff group, volunteers, the management committee, individual officers, subcommittees, users or clients, members? Is everyone aware of what they can and cannot do, and which decisions they can and cannot make?

● Are the procedures for decision-making as set down in the constitution being followed? Is there a conflict between constitutional procedures and what actually happens?

● How clear are the lines of communication? Do the appropriate people get the information they need to make informed decisions?

● Are meetings held regularly? too infrequently? too often? Are they run well, with a clear agenda, good chairing and decision-making, and clear minutes? Do people attend and participate?

● Are there clear procedures for setting job expectations and standards of performance, monitoring whether they are being met, and dealing with the situation if they are not?

● Are there clear, workable procedures for dealing with day to day problems, grievances and disciplinary issues? Do workers and management committee members know what they are?

Personal, historical and hidden issues

These problems are more difficult to manage, because they are rooted in individuals rather than in the organisation. If a group is under stress or badly managed these problems may occupy a disproportionately large amount of everyone's time and energy. This is unproductive: it makes workers feel bad, the group cannot get on with what it is supposed to be doing, and the group and the workers in it soon get a reputation for 'not being able to get their act together'.

The rest of this chapter and chapter 19 focus on this type of problem.

Some of the questions that need to be asked are:

● Where are the hidden hierarchies and/or power struggles in the group? How can they be brought into the open, acknowledged, and dealt with? (Hidden hierarchies are informal and emerge because of age, level of involvement in the group, level of knowledge, personal power or friendships. They exist in all groups, whether they have formal hierarchies or work non-hierarchically.)

● What part does 'ownership' play in what is going on? ('Ownership' in this context refers to personal or emotional investment. People who are too emotionally involved often feel the group *absolutely must* do what *they* think it should do. There is no scope for anyone else's views or ideas.)

● What part do racism, sexism, and other unacceptable prejudices and oppressive behaviours play? What needs to happen for these to be recognised, acknowledged and changed? How can this be done in a way which is constructive rather than destructive for the group and the individuals involved?

- Are allegations of racism, sexism and other unacceptable prejudices and oppressive behaviours dealt with in a way which recognises their seriousness and importance, but without overwhelming the group or organisation? (Sometimes when there is a race or gender element in a conflict that gets all the attention, while other fundamental problems are ignored.)

- Does the group have a history which is still causing problems? Do past grievances still need to be resolved?

- Are personal disagreements and distrust getting in the way of work? How can the people involved be helped to get beyond this and commit themselves to working together?

This list does not cover all the possible causes of conflict within groups, but it provides a starting point for identifying actual or potential problems and beginning to do something about them.

Unfortunately, it is not easy to examine these underlying factors when tempers are high, individuals feel fragile and the group seems to be collapsing. It may need someone outside the conflict to help the group get a perspective on what is happening, how the immediate problem can be resolved and how underlying difficulties can be overcome.

The section below describes some of the processes of conflict resolution and chapter 22 looks at how to call in a consultant or other outsider.

APPROACHES TO CONFLICT RESOLUTION

Even when dealing with only one broad type of conflict – disputes within organisations – the terminology of conflict resolution is imprecise, inconsistently applied and confusing. But there are significant differences in approaches to conflict resolution or dispute settlement, and the terminology must somehow reflect these. The definitions in this section may help to clarify which processes are most appropriate for various types of disputes.

The desired outcomes

- **Resolution**: agreement on how a conflict should be dealt with.

- **Solution**: a specific step or series of steps to end the conflict.

- **Reconciliation**: building or rebuilding a good relationship between parties who have been in conflict. Reconciliation is not the same as conciliation. Reconciliation is the responsibility of the people involved in the conflict.

The processes

Most day to day conflict resolution involves only the parties to the dispute. But more serious conflicts may require an **intermediary** or **third party**: a person or group not directly involved in the conflict, who intervenes to help the parties in conflict reach a resolution.

- **Crisis intervention:** (1) intervening in a fight or heated conflict by separating or protecting people or getting help; (2) intervening in a situation which is on the verge of becoming heated, by asking people to calm down or asking what is happening. Crisis intervention may not directly be part of the conflict resolution process but gives people a chance to calm down and become more rational.

- **Facilitation**: helping people to listen to, communicate with and respect each other. A **facilitator** focuses more on communication than on resolution of the conflict.

- **Conciliation**: the process of working towards resolution. It does not have to involve an intermediary but if it does that person or group is called a **conciliator** or **mediator**.

- **Mediation**: conciliation with an intermediary.

- **Advocacy**: intervening or negotiating on behalf of one party. An advocate supports one party in the conflict; a conciliator or mediator should not overtly support either party.

- **Negotiation**: discussing each party's needs, demands and interests and agreeing which aspects of each should be incorporated into a solution. A **negotiator** may or may not be involved.

- **Arbitration**: a legal or quasi-legal process in which the parties to the conflict agree beforehand to accept the decision of the **arbitrator**.

- **Adjudication** or **litigation**: settlement of a dispute through formal legal processes.

STEPS IN CONFLICT RESOLUTION

Regardless of the process or processes used and regardless of whether an intermediary is involved, the goal of conflict resolution is agreement on specific actions which can be taken by some or all of the parties to the conflict to deal with a particular situation. This requires:

- ensuring each party in the conflict has an opportunity to clarify and define the issues as they see them;

- giving each person the opportunity to say why they want something to be done about the situation;

- identifying common interests and, if possible at this stage, common goals;

- defining issues on which agreement is essential and/or possible;

- clarifying facts, opinions and values about each issue;

- defining and discussing suggestions for resolution of each issue;

- agreeing a specific solution and the steps to implement it;

- being sure all parties are willing to implement the solution, even if they do not fully agree with it;

- agreeing a procedure for reviewing the situation to be sure it is working, and/or for dealing with people who do not do what they have agreed to.

KEEPING IT WITHIN THE GROUP

In an organisation facing conflict the first reaction is usually to try to handle it internally. Three broad approaches can be identified:

- pretending it's not happening, or ignoring it;

- imposing a solution;

- enabling the people in conflict to work towards their own solution (with or without third party involvement).

If these approaches are not effective, an independent third party may have to be called in from outside to start a process of mediation.

Pretending it's not happening

Denying a conflict exists may keep things quiet in the short term, but the conflict will not go away and is likely to keep resurfacing, often in ways completely unrelated to the real problem. It may be painful to admit and deal with a conflict but it is nearly always even more painful, in the long term, to pretend it is not there.

When people admit a conflict exists but refuse to do anything about it, they may be **suppressing** it. 'We can't be seen to be arguing,' they say, or 'There's no point in trying to do anything, because we would never come to any sort of agreement.'

Suppression may be appropriate for minor conflicts which do not directly affect people's work or their working relationships. After all, there is no point putting huge amounts of time or energy into dealing with differences which are irrelevant and which people do not care about very much.

Suppression is *not* appropriate just for the sake of being seen to be 'one big happy family'. Conflicts suppressed for this reason will erupt in other ways.

But in situations where power is very unevenly distributed, suppression may be the only viable option. A person low in the organisational hierarchy may feel, with considerable justification, there is simply no point in trying to deal with a conflict with a powerful and intransigent person higher up the hierarchy. This is an issue of **survival**, rather than conflict resolution. But eventually the person who is trying to survive will have to make a choice: to find a way to address and deal with the problem, to accept that she or he cannot do anything about it, or to get out of the organisation. If the person cannot make one of these choices, the inevitable result will be individual or organisational stress (see next chapter).

Solutions imposed on people in conflict

The use of formal or legitimate power or authority means a person or group of people who have the right to do so find a way of dealing with the conflict, and impose that solution on those involved. People who have this right might include, for example, a project leader, a management committee chair or a staff meeting. They might exercise the power in an authoritarian way or in a caring and sensitive way, or anything in between. In a group, a solution might be agreed by voting or by consensus.

The significant point is that the solution is external to the people directly involved in the conflict. They do not come up with it themselves.

There is nothing intrinsically wrong with power or authority being used in this way, so long as the parties to the conflict accept the right of the person or group to make and impose such a decision. But the people in conflict may not have very much commitment to implementing such a solution, nor will it necessarily resolve any underlying conflict.

Sometimes solutions are imposed by people who do not actually have a right to do so, but who for some reason have power or 'clout' in the organisation. Such a solution might or might not be acceptable, depending on who is imposing it and whether the people involved in the conflict are willing to accept it.

DIY conflict resolution

Neither denial, suppression nor imposed solutions get to the root of a problem. It is nearly always better for the people involved to come up with their own solution.

Do it yourself conflict resolution does not mean the person with the most power putting others in a position where they have no choice but to agree to her or his solution. Conflict resolution means discussing, negotiating and coming to a joint solution through a process of compromise or consensus.

For this to work, all parties must:

● want to find a solution;

● be willing to talk rationally to each other;

● be willing to **listen** to each other;

● be willing to explore a range of solutions, not just their own;

● be willing to accept a solution even if it does not meet all their needs and wants.

A quiet, neutral venue and a time specifically committed to discussion can make this easier.

Compromise starts from each party stating their concerns and what they feel they need and want, and then indicating what they are (or are not) willing to give up. Compromise only works if all parties have relatively equal power (or relatively equal matters to hold on to or give up). If power is not equal, a false sense of balance may be created: 'I'll agree not to reprimand you in front of the other secretaries any more, if you agree to bring me cups of tea whenever I ask for them.'

Compromise can also lead to solutions which are unworkable because no one is really committed to them, or because aspects of the solution are combined in an unworkable way.

Like compromise, **consensus** starts with each party stating their concerns, needs and wants, but then the approaches diverge. In working towards a consensus

solution, people's differences are respected and the goal is to try to find a solution which recognises and is sensitive to those differences. Each party states what is important to them, and why. Both or all parties then work together to try to find a solution, possibly something quite new and unexpected, which takes into account what is most important to each of them.

It can take a great deal of time and skill to draw out people's ideas; without this, people can become locked into a narrow view based on their existing positions (which means it becomes a compromise rather than a consensus solution).

Consensus also needs a deep awareness of power within the group or organisation, and a commitment to sharing rather than abusing it. In working towards a consensus it is easy for hidden (or not so hidden) power to be used so that the solution is actually imposed by the most powerful person(s), while giving the impression that everyone is participating equally.

Neither compromise nor consensus is appropriate when the decision has to be on an either/or basis. But beware of defining something as either/or when in fact it could be resolved in a different way by compromise or consensus.

DIY conflict resolution does not work when one party (or all of them) behaves irrationally, refuses to listen, or insists on having her or his own way. DIY conflict resolution can also be hindered by other people in the group who have a vested interest in keeping the conflict going, and who stir things up or say 'that would never work' whenever a solution is in sight.

The three first steps approach

A very simple starting point for DIY conflict resolution is for each person involved to write their answers to the following sentences:

1. The problem is ...

2. Effects of this problem are ...

3. I think it is important to do something about this because...

4. Some causes of this problem are ...

5. Things I could do to deal with or help improve this situation are ...

6. Things I think other workers [or committee members, or whoever] should or could do individually are ... [name the people]

7. Things we should or could do as a group are ...

8. Things other people (from outside the group) should or could do are ... [indicate who should do it]

9. The first three steps to deal with this problem are:

   a. To ...

   b. To ...

   c. To ...

If the people involved in the conflict can broadly agree on the problem (even if they disagree on the causes or effects) and can understand why each wants to do something about it, they might then be able to agree on some steps to start dealing with it. So the only questions the people need to discuss are numbers 1, 3 and 9 – but the others need to be filled in so people can get to number 9 in their thinking.

Helping people find their own solutions

Someone from within the group may be able to act as a facilitator or mediator, encouraging the people in conflict to move from their fixed positions and work towards an agreed solution. The facilitator or mediator will help the people involved in the conflict to define the problem as they see it, clarify its importance, and work towards solutions acceptable to both or all parties.

A person in this position should seek to be:

- aware of her or his own biases, prejudices and feelings, and able to keep them separate from the process of conflict resolution;

- committed to finding a solution acceptable to all parties;

- able and willing to listen;

- able to ask appropriate questions and elicit necessary information;

- able to recognise and build on points of agreement;

- aware of the differences and overlaps between facts, opinions, values, prejudices, judgments, feelings and fantasy;

- aware of cultural, ethnic, social, gender and class differences in perception and presentation of conflict in general or of particular issues;

- willing to explore underlying issues as well as the immediate or presenting problem, if this is appropriate;

- able to recognise negativity ('that will never work' 'people like that will never change') and challenge it;

- creative;

- patient;

- realistic – and idealistic;

- willing to maintain confidentiality if this is required;

- supported in her or his own life, so she or he does not get overwhelmed by the conflict.

CALLING IN AN OUTSIDER

If the people involved in the conflict cannot sort it out themselves and there is no one in the group with the authority (or willingness) to impose a solution, it may be necessary to involve someone from outside. This outsider may simply help the people involved in the conflict find their own solution, or may be asked to devise one.

The section in chapter 22 on using a consultant will be useful when considering whether to ask someone from outside.

Solutions facilitated by a third party

If people are more concerned about communicating than about finding an immediate solution, facilitation may be appropriate. An outside **facilitator** can help equalise the power in situations where one party is stronger than the other, and can encourage people to break out of the dead-locked positions they get themselves into when they are trying to sort out disputes on their own.

A **mediator** will be more directly involved in resolving the conflict. A mediator is usually independent and impartial, but does not have to be if everyone involved knows and is willing to accept her or his partiality. The mediator may (or may not) suggest solutions but does not in any way impose a decision. If the parties in conflict cannot agree on a solution, the situation is left unsettled.

There are two main forms of mediation. In **face to face mediation**, the parties meet together with the mediator. If the mediator acts as a **go-between**, she or he deals with each party separately to attempt to reach an agreement.

People from another part of the organisation can act as facilitators or mediators, provided they are not directly involved in the conflict. But they must be very clear about their role, and must not get caught up in the conflict or misuse their authority.

Community mediation schemes now exist in some areas. They may be voluntary or community groups, or set up and run by statutory agencies. Some deal only with disputes between neighbours or disputes in a specified geographical area; some also deal with conflict within organisations and may be able to help.

Solutions imposed by a third party

If neither facilitation nor mediation is successful, it may be necessary to resort to legal or quasi-legal processes.

An **arbitrator** will encourage the parties to the dispute to participate in the resolution and reach voluntary agreement, but the arbitrator has the final say about what should happen.

As a last resort, court procedures may be needed.

KEEPING IT IN PERSPECTIVE

When dealing with conflict there are four important points to remember.

- Conflict is not innate but differences are. Conflict arises when differences cannot be accepted and accommodated.

- Conflict does not have to be negative and destructive. It can be used creatively and positively.

- Conflicts can only be resolved if the people involved want them to be. Without this commitment, another dispute will arise as soon as this one is settled.

- Conflict resolution only works if the people involved accept the solution for themselves. An imposed solution may work in the short term but the conflict will soon resurface in some way.

Chapter 19:

Managing stress

Stress management has much in common with time management (chapter 11). Not only does poor management of one lead, inevitably, to poor management of the other, but the same excuses are used to avoid tackling either. So people talk endlessly of how much they are suffering from stress or how little time they have, but somehow never quite get around to doing anything about it.

Stress management also has much in common with conflict resolution (chapter 18), for stress and conflict go hand in hand. Indeed, poor management of any sort is likely to lead to stress.

This chapter looks at:

● causes and effects of stress;

● how stress affects individuals and groups;

● how to recognise warning signs of stress and burnout in oneself and others;

● what people responsible for management can do to reduce stress within a team or organisation.

For people who want to know more, most good bookshops have a wide range of publications on personal stress (in the health section) or workplace stress (usually in the business section). Each book will have a different perspective, so it's worth spending some time finding those which seem most appropriate to your own situation. Some favourites are:

● *Stress and Relaxation* by Jane Madders (Macdonald Optima, 1988; 126 pages; ISBN 0 356 14504 2; £6.99 from bookshops);

● *Coping with Stress: A practical self-help guide for women* by Georgina Witkin-Lanoil (Sheldon Press, 1987; 106 pages; ISBN 0 85969 438 0; £3.99 from bookshops);

● *Beating Job Burnout* by Dr Donald Scott (Sheldon Press, 1989; 96 pages; ISBN 0 85969 597 2; £3.99 from bookshops).

WHAT IS STRESS?

Stress can be defined in terms of both causes and effects. In physics, stress is any force capable of producing strain or deformation in an object. In biology, stress may be defined as anything which causes change in the organism (two definitions are 'any influence that disturbs the natural equilibrium of the living body' and 'situations leading to continuous behavioural adjustment'), anything which causes difficulty for the organism ('any kind of burden, pressure or hardship'), or anything which threatens the organism ('anything constituting a threat, real or apparent, which would adversely affect the organism').

Situations, events, people or objects which cause stress are called **stressors**.

Stress is also defined in terms of its effects: 'the reaction of the mind and body to change' or 'the result of imbalance, when a person's perceived or actual capabilities and resources are insufficient to meet the demands of the situation'. Or even 'the wear and tear induced in the body by the adaptive day to day struggle of the organism to remain normal in the face of potentially harmful agents'.

Effects of stress may be positive in the short term (helping people to think more clearly in panic situations or to get the energy to work creatively) but if there is no respite the effects become negative or harmful. Perception of a stressor leads to the body's **sympathetic** system taking over and releasing hormones (adrenalin and noradrenalin) which prepare the body to respond to the stressor. If the effects of these hormones are not released through some sort of activity (fight or flight: lashing out at the stressor or getting away from it) they are likely to produce anger, twitches or other negative responses.

People can tolerate quite high levels of stress if they feel they are doing something about the stressor, and if they give themselves time for their bodies to get back to normal between stressful events. This return to equilibrium is governed by the **parasympathetic** (rest and digest) system.

If someone is under constant stress, with inadequate opportunities to 'rest and digest', the adrenal glands eventually pack up. This leads to overtiredness, insomnia, headaches, muscular weakness and a craving for sweet starchy foods.

Within work settings probably the most useful definition of harmful stress is **changes in a person's physical, mental or emotional condition or in behaviour, caused by constant pressure to perform in ways which are incompatible with perceived or actual ability, time or resources.**

DEALING WITH STRESS

There are no easy answers in dealing with stress. People have to decide what is right for them, and what they are willing and realistically able to do. The basic guidelines are:

● recognise and acknowledge what is causing the stress, without pretending, making excuses, or blaming someone or something else;

● recognise and acknowledge present and potential effects;

- decide whether **you** (not someone else, but you) can do something to change the stressor;

- decide whether you are willing to do it;

- if you cannot (or are not willing to) change the stressor, decide whether you can (and are willing to) change the way you react to it, for example by not getting so angry or hurt about it;

- decide whether you can (and are willing to) reduce its negative effects on you, for example by taking time to relax so you are not so tense;

- if you really cannot (or will not) do anything to change the stressor or yourself then accept it, because worrying about something you cannot or will not change only makes it worse;

- decide what you can realistically do to help yourself manage or cope with the stressor or its effects, by setting realistic time-limited objectives and getting as much support as you can;

- **do it**;

- keep yourself strong and relaxed: allow yourself to relax (long baths, music before bedtime), give yourself treats and incentives, say no to anything that would increase the pressure, and don't punish yourself if you don't do as much as you intended.

Alcohol (except in very small quantities), cigarettes, medications or illegal drugs may help in the short term but are not, in the long term, appropriate for dealing with stress. They may create addictions which cause even greater trauma to the body and mind.

STRESSORS

The first step in dealing with stress, whether individual or within groups, is to be clear about the cause or causes. Often attempts to deal with stress are unsuccessful because people try to deal with something quite minor while ignoring major stressors.

Individual stressors can be divided into four broad categories:

- work-related (this can also apply to lack of work);

- non-work or home situations;

- self-generated;

- external.

Work-related

Clearly, **unemployment** can be highly stressful. But **employment**, even in a 'good' job, can also be stressful if the worker feels constantly dissatisfied or frustrated, knows there are no hopes for promotion or significant change, or is not sure she or he is in the right job but does not know what else to do.

Even if a worker likes her or his job, the **team** or **organisation** can be stressful if there are conflicting demands, unclear objectives or inadequate resources; if there are constant changes with inadequate consultation or planning; or if it gets caught between meeting the needs and expectations of the community at large, users,

members, the management committee and/or the funders. Other organisational causes of stress are poor work environment (noise, clutter, glare, general grottiness), poor time management so everything is always done at the last minute, insecurity about funding, and poor supervision and support procedures.

An individual's **job** can be stressful if there is too much or too little work, the work is too difficult or too easy, the worker has to take decisions without proper information or authority, there are constant deadlines over which the worker has no control, or the worker has to take responsibility for the lives of other people.

Stress can be caused by **relationships** at work with managers, subordinates, colleagues, management committee, users, members, or people from other agencies.

Non-work and home situations

Conflict between work and home demands is a frequent cause of stress among voluntary sector workers. Family's or flatmates' expectations may seem unrealistic, or may be realistic and lead to guilt because they cannot be met. There may not be enough time for basic tasks like shopping and laundry or to participate in social events, and there certainly is not enough time to cope with major tasks like repairing the roof or redecorating the flat.

There is often too great an **overlap** between personal and home life, so a great deal of 'personal' time is actually filled with working at home, attending meetings, and talking about work on the phone or at social events. Or personal time may be taken up with other voluntary activities which demand a great deal of time and energy.

A difficult **living situation**, such as sharing with uncongenial people or living in temporary accommodation, can lead to huge stresses, as can **money** problems caused by financial mismanagement or simple lack of money.

Too much or too little **physical or emotional contact** can cause stress: an unsatisfactory sex life, lack of friends, or inadequate or excessive physical contact or emotional demands from family or friends.

Self-generated

Self-inflicted stressors are created by people mistreating themselves. They include **physical maltreatment** which causes stress and makes it more difficult to deal with other stressors, for example skipping meals or eating on the run, not getting enough exercise, not sleeping enough, smoking, drinking more than a pint of beer or two glasses of wine or two measures of spirits per day, or dependence on caffeine from tea, coffee or cola drinks.

Unwillingness to relax is so prevalent within the voluntary sector that it might almost be called an occupational disease. People do not take lunch breaks, do not leave work at a reasonable time, do not take time off in lieu, sometimes do not even take holidays. They do not allow themselves time for mini-breaks during the day when they can relax, when they do leave work they often rush off to other meetings or engagements, and when they get home they collapse in a heap. Then they wonder why they do not sleep well and wake up exhausted the next morning.

Stress can also be **self-generated** by people who set themselves unrealistically high or unrealistically low goals or standards; in either case they end up feeling inadequate. Another way of self-generating stress is to refuse to do anything about other stressors!

External

External stressors are factors which really are beyond immediate control: traffic, public transport, pollution, noise, decisions by funders, legislative changes. But stress is reduced by doing something about the stressor, so involvement in political or campaigning groups can help (and might even lead to change!).

And if stressors themselves cannot be changed, people can change the way they react to them. Even situations over which individuals have no control do not have to cause them harmful stress.

EFFECTS OF STRESS

The effects of harmful stress can be divided into four broad categories: physical, emotional, intellectual and behavioural.

Physical conditions which may be a result of stress and should be viewed as potential warning signs include headaches, backaches, neckaches, muscular twitches, tiredness, indigestion, cravings for sweet or starchy food, palpitations, chest pains, diarrhoea lasting more than a few days, and insomnia. **If these warning signs are ignored they can lead to serious physical conditions.**

Long term physical effects of stress include migraine, ulcers, heart attack, high blood pressure, angina, diabetes, impotence in men, menstrual disorders in women, asthma, arthritis, eczema, psoriasis and hair loss.

Prolonged stress weakens the immune system, which makes people more prone to colds and flu as well as more serious illnesses. There is evidence that some cancers are related to this suppression of the immune system. Stress is especially dangerous to people who are HIV positive or whose immune systems are suppressed because of other illnesses.

Anxiety, irritability, frustration or depression not related to a specific cause, a feeling of hopelessness, withdrawal from people, aggressiveness, and unjustified levels of anger are **emotional effects** of harmful stress. As with physical effects, these are warning signs that something needs to be done about stressors or reactions to them.

In the very short term, stress focused on a particular task (for example, a deadline) can be positive and help people think creatively. But if stress continues or is more diffuse it can lead to **intellectual disfunction**. This might manifest itself as forgetfulness, inability to pay attention and absorb information, confused thought processes, inability to concentrate, inability or unwillingness to make decisions, or loss of memory.

Behavioural changes include being uncharacteristically aggressive or withdrawn, drinking more alcohol than usual, eating more or less than usual, changes in behaviour while driving, or being consistently late for or missing appointments.

STRESSFUL SITUATIONS

Not everyone reacts to stressful situations in the same way. Many people are familiar with 'A' and 'B' type personalities, with A the highly stressed executive type destined for an early heart attack, and B the laid-back placid type. But it appears that in dealing with stress there are not just A and B people, but seven different types.

These 'types' are all stereotypes; no one fits completely into one, two or even three categories. But being aware of how people react to stressful situations can make it easier to understand what causes harmful stress in different people and how to manage it most appropriately.

Ambitious people are the classic A type. They like change and challenge and work best under pressure. If there are no deadlines or other pressures, they will create them. Unless they find opportunities to relax and ease the pressure on themselves, they are likely to suffer from harmful stress, most likely physical effects.

Anxious people turn everything into a source of harmful stress, constantly worrying about what might go wrong. Unless they learn to put things in perspective and stop worrying about everything, they too are likely to feel the effects of harmful stress, but most likely the emotional or intellectual effects.

Traditionalist people are relaxed so long as they are dealing with tasks with which they feel comfortable. But they suffer from stress if they have to react to changes beyond their control or if their routine changes.

People-centred people are fine so long as they get lots of attention and support. They find it stressful if they have to work on their own or do not get constant recognition for their work.

Isolates, on the other hand, dislike working with other people and find it stressful to have to relate to colleagues or the public.

Placid people are the classic B type. They do not like stressful situations and will try to avoid them, or will avoid getting tense about them when they do happen. Most of their stress is caused by being around other people who are highly stressed.

Adventurous people take on activities like motorcycle racing which would cause very high stress for other people. These activities do not cause much stress for them, but they can cause a lot of stress for other people. Adventurous people are likely to become bored and frustrated, and therefore stressed, in routine jobs.

THE STRESS CYCLE OF ORGANISATIONS

Regardless of what causes it, its effects or how people react to it, **stress is bad for organisations**.

This whole book has been about managing stress by:

● understanding the pressures on the voluntary sector and what good management means (chapter 1);

● understanding and clearly allocating management responsibilities (chapter 2);

- developing consistent but flexible managerial styles appropriate to the organisation and the people within it (chapter 3);

- establishing clear structures and procedures for communication and decision-making (chapters 4 to 6);

- setting clear and realistic policies and objectives and keeping them under review (chapters 7 to 9);

- ensuring people understand changes within the organisation (chapter 10);

- effectively managing time (chapter 11);

- understanding how organisations and individuals may be affected by new funding relationships and the resultant pressures (chapters 12 and 13);

- establishing clear job expectations and standards, and providing appropriate supervision, training and support for workers (chapters 14 to 17);

- dealing effectively with differences and conflict (chapter 18);

- effectively managing and controlling money and information (chapters 20 and 21);

- dealing with unconfident or inadequate managers (chapter 22).

Organisations and teams in which stress is not managed succumb, inevitably, to a **stress cycle**. And once they are in this cycle, it is very difficult indeed to get out.

The stress cycle may be triggered by unclear objectives or policies, unwillingness to set priorities, unclear structures or procedures, workers' inability to do their job, pressures from users or funders, political pressures, or workers suffering from unresolved stresses in their non-work lives.

If time and energy are not managed properly, the result is

overwork. Even for people who enjoy (or say they do not mind) working overtime, it leads to exhaustion, frustration and eventually resentment at having to work so much. Just as importantly, overwork can lead to frustration and resentment in people who do not want to work so many hours and feel they are put under pressure by their workaholic colleagues or bosses.

When people feel frustrated or resentful they lose interest, stop caring, get fed up with users or members. Conflicts occur, which of course means unproductive use of even more time and energy. People start feeling the physical and emotional effects of stress, which leads to sickness and absenteeism among a significant proportion of workers. Intellectual disfunction means decisions are not thought through or clearly made, tasks are done inadequately and important responsibilities are forgotten or ignored.

At this stage, the organisation or team is in a dire situation. A radical overhaul is needed, to look at objectives, priorities, communication, decision-making, job descriptions and support for workers – in fact, to look at all the issues indicated in chapter 18.

If this overhaul does not take place the organisation may stagger along, but the price will be high. Major conflicts may rip the organisation apart, with no one having the commitment or energy to do anything constructive about them. Workers become burnt out, a euphemism for what used to be called a nervous breakdown.

Even workers who remain relatively unaffected by this cycle are by this stage drawn into it. Because people affected by the stress cycle are operating so inadequately, other workers must step in to fill the gap. And this means, of course, that they become overworked, resentful, alienated ...

THE BURNOUT PATH

Chapter 18 looked at how organisations can avoid getting into a stress cycle. Individuals, too, can recognise the factors (in and outside of work) causing them stress, and can take steps to deal with them. But what can be done about the harmful influence of a worker who is on the path to burnout and does not recognise anything is wrong?

Workers on the burnout path may be constantly busy doing vast amounts for the organisation. But they get less and less personal satisfaction from their work, and therefore do it less and less well. Despite the constructive nature of what they are doing, these workers, volunteers or committee members have a destructive effect on the group. This is because they complain constantly about how much they have to do, and are so wrapped up in what they are doing that they become impatient, critical or rude when other people have other priorities. Other people feel guilty about not being able or willing to give so much time or energy to the organisation. And eventually the person is likely to collapse, leaving the organisation in the lurch.

In *Planning Together: The art of effective teamwork* (Bedford Square Press, 1988; £11.95 + £1.50 p&p from Plymbridge Distributors Ltd, Estover Road, Plymouth PL6 7PZ), George Gawlinski and Lois Graessle give a checklist for recognising burnout:

- not sleeping well at night;
- feeling low in energy all day;
- feeling exceptionally tired after work;
- increasing use of alcohol or other drugs at lunchtimes and immediately after work;
- having frequent colds, flu or back trouble;
- suffering frequent headaches;
- frequent absences from work;
- being unable to concentrate on work;
- being unable to listen attentively to colleagues or clients;
- postponing work, visits or meetings;
- loss of positive feelings towards users;
- not wanting to go to work;
- becoming easily upset by other people's comments, whether made directly or indirectly;
- suspicion of everyone else's intentions;
- increasingly working to rule;
- strong resistance to any change in working conditions;
- a sense of failure;
- conflict at home with partner, family or flatmates.

Karoshi is a Japanese word describing death from overwork. That is the ultimate burnout.

Getting off the burnout path

There are four major ways to minimise the possibility of burnout. Each requires a recognition by the worker that she or he is on the burnout path, and a willingness to do something about it – for her or his own sake and for the sake of the organisation.

The first step is to **take time to relax**. There are all kinds of complex reasons why people push themselves to be constantly busy and constantly achieving. It is important to take proper breaks, eat meals at the times the body expects them, go for walks, find a quiet time and space, get exercise to release the pent-up stress hormones, and relax.

Although people on the burnout path do not want to believe it, a person who uses time well during an eight-hour day with lunch and tea breaks and spends the evening at a concert gets more done than a person who slaves through an unplanned 10-hour workday with no breaks.

The next step is to **get enough sleep**. No one can use time effectively if they are exhausted. Insomnia, poor sleeping, waking up at four o'clock in the morning thinking about work are all warning signs of stress and should not be used as excuses to sleep even less. Quiet music, a warm bath and a milky drink before bed all help people sleep better.

Support systems are essential. All workers and volunteers should have regular supervision sessions in which workloads and work pressures can be discussed (see chapter 16) and action taken. Personal support systems away from work are also important.

The only way actually to get off the burnout path is to **reassess priorities**. This means deciding which tasks absolutely must be done, and which of those absolutely must be done by the person who is under such stress. If they all seem essential and no one else can (or will) do them, that person is heading for burnout. If even the priorities exercise in chapter 11 does not succeed she or he should:

- make a list of everything that has to be done and the time available for doing it;

- call an urgent meeting of the workgroup, team, management committee officers and/or personnel subcommittee;

- distribute the list to the people who have been invited to the meeting, asking them to prioritise the tasks and revise the timescales;

- sit down with them and listen to what they say;

- stop making excuses for doing nothing to change the situation.

THE WORK ENVIRONMENT

The offices, workshops and public spaces in which people work can have significant effects on their stress levels. With a bit of energy and time (and money, if available) it is nearly always possible to improve the work environment.

- **Start at the entrance**. Be sure the approach is tidy and attractive, the door is well painted, clean and clearly signposted, and the entryway is clear.

- **Make it friendly**. Plants are nice, but be sure someone is willing to look after them. Posters, photographs or pictures, especially if they are relevant to the organisation's work, make the walls interesting, but not if they just add to the clutter. Magazines on a low table in the reception area and toys in a carpeted corner make the place more welcoming.

- **Reduce mess, clutter and chaos**. Everyone should be expected to clean up after themselves (including in the kitchen and lavatory), leave desks tidy when they go home, and put away tools and equipment. Provide adequate wastepaper baskets or dustbins, and ensure they are emptied regularly. Set up a rota for putting milk bottles out or taking them back to the shop. Keep noticeboards tidy and up to date by setting up a rota or giving one person responsibility. Keep steps and exits clear at all times; this is a health and safety requirement. Have a monthly, quarterly or annual clear-up day.

- **Keep it clean**. Clean the windows regularly. Wash down the paintwork from time to time. Be sure floors are swept, vacuumed or mopped.

- **Provide adequate storage facilities**: filing cabinets, shelves, lockers, storage boxes. If possible, put anything not in regular use in a basement or other storage area.

- **Reduce, isolate or insulate noise**. Put the photocopier, computer printer and other noisy equipment as far as practicable from desks. Buy acoustic hoods for printers. Turn the telephones down. Separate the reception area from places where people are trying to concentrate. Consider carpets, partitioning, soundproofing, a quiet room for people who have to concentrate.

- **Improve the lighting**. Change fluorescent tubes as soon as they start to flicker. Provide gooseneck or anglepoise lamps at people's desks.

- **Be aware of computer and visual display unit hazards**. No one should work at a computer or word processor keyboard for more than an hour without a 15-minute break. Position the keyboard and VDU to reduce arm and eye discomfort. Lights should be fitted with glare diffusers and windows should have curtains or blinds to cut down glare.

- **Invest in good chairs**. For people who sit at desks all day, inadequate seating is a major contributor to backache. Get proper chairs; they are expensive but it is often possible to buy them secondhand at office furniture shops.

- **Ensure adequate ventilation**. If noise and pollution levels are not too high, open the windows. Be sure there are enough fans.

- **If people must smoke**, limit it to specific parts of the office or building.

- **Sort out the heating**. Be sure it works. If possible, position people who like a warm room away from doors and near radiators, or provide them with individual heaters. Put people who like it cooler near doors and windows. (There is no way to satisfy everyone, but repositioning desks or workspaces can help.)

- **Keep copies of users' manuals** and maintenance and repair instructions or procedures near equipment, so people know how to use it and what to do if it stops functioning. (Keep the originals of the manuals safe in a filing cabinet.)

- Be rigidly strict about observing **safety regulations** around dangerous equipment.

TAKING RESPONSIBILITY

Organisational stress and individual burnout are the responsibility of everyone who allows them to happen. Workers or managers who refuse to deal with their own stress, or who recognise signs of stress in colleagues and do not do anything about it, are contributing to a potential breakdown: their own, their colleagues' or the organisation's.

Chapter 20:

Managing money

Money management can broadly be divided into two overlapping categories: financial responsibility and financial accountability. This chapter covers:

- what 'responsibility' and 'accountability' mean for voluntary organisations;

- financial record-keeping;

- computerising the accounts;

- responsibilities of the treasurer and/or finance subcommittee;

- how to understand accounts and financial reports;

- how to prepare for audit (an annual independent check on whether the organisation has spent its money properly and kept appropriate financial records).

This chapter can only provide a general introduction to financial management. For more detailed information new or small groups should refer to:

- chapter 7 in *Voluntary But Not Amateur*;

- *How to Manage your Money, if you have any*, 3rd edition (Community Accountancy Project, 1992; 31 pages; ISBN 0 9508555 1 0; £3 + 50p p & p from CAP, 489 Kingsland Road, London E8 4AU);

- *Money Management for Community Groups* (Sheffield Training Group and Sheffield City Council, 1990; 113 pages; £10 from Sheffield City Council Communications Unit, Publicity Department, Old Town Hall, Sheffield S1 2HH).

Larger or more established organisations should refer to:

- *Organising Your Finances: A guide to good practice* by Maggi Sikking (Bedford Square Press, 1987; 64 pages; ISBN 0 7199 1176 1; £3.95 + 50p p&p from Plymbridge Distributors Ltd, Estover Road, Plymouth PL6 7PZ);

- *Accounting and Financial Management for Charities* by Michael Norton and Hilary Blume (Directory of Social Change, 1989; 112 pages; ISBN 0 907164 18 8; £7.95 from DSC, Radius Works, Back Lane, London NW3 1HL);

- *Charity Accounting and Taxation* by Robert Vincent (Butterworths, 1991; 284 pages; ISBN 0 406508 801; £37.50 from Butterworths & Co, 88 Kingsway, London WC2B 6AB);

- a subscription to *NGO Finance: Professional information for non-governmental organisations*, £25 per year from Subscription Department, PO Box 247, Haywards Heath, West Sussex RH17 5FF.

FINANCIAL RESPONSIBILITY AND ACCOUNTABILITY

Put simply, financial responsibility means:

- not taking on obligations the organisation cannot meet;

- being sure the organisation has enough money to pay its bills on time;

- actually paying the bills on time;

- keeping proper records of all money which comes into and goes out of the organisation.

Even if an organisation acts responsibly and keeps all the necessary records, it may have problems with its **accountability**: being clear about who has the right to know what the organisation is doing with its money, and how much control those people have over financial decisions.

Legally, the management committee or other governing body is responsible for the financial undertakings of a community group or voluntary organisation. (If the organisation is a charity, the trustees will have this responsibility. Usually the trustees are the same as the management committee; see chapter 2.) To make proper decisions, the committee or trustees need adequate and comprehensible information about:

- the group's budget (what it expects to receive and spend during a fixed period or for a specific project);

- its cashflow projections (when it expects the money to come in and go out), and how any shortfalls will be covered;

- its income and expenditure (what it actually receives and spends);

- its assets (the value of what it owns, and money owed to it);

- liabilities (what it owes).

Staff or volunteers with responsibility for bookkeeping, financial administration and/or financial decision-making are always accountable to the treasurer, and through the treasurer to the finance subcommittee (if there is one) and the management committee or other governing body as a whole.

The committee is, in turn, accountable to the membership if it is a membership organisation, and must provide accounts to the members each year. A good committee will go beyond this, ensuring the accounts are presented in a way members can understand, and providing opportunities for members to ask about them.

Legal accountability

If the organisation is a limited company it must send audited accounts annually to the Registrar of Companies. The accounts are kept on file and are available to the public, but unless there is a complaint of fraud the Registrar will not question them. Industrial and provident societies and friendly societies must send audited accounts to the Registrar of Friendly Societies, who will check the accounts to be sure funds have been properly used.

An organisation registered as a charity must send its accounts to the Inland Revenue if it claims any of the tax benefits charities enjoy. The Charities Act 1992 requires all registered charities which are not registered as companies to keep accounts, have them independently examined or audited, and submit annual accounts to the Charity Commission. (Charities which are also companies are already required, under company law, to prepare a full set of accounts and have them professionally audited.)

For charities which are not also companies, the type of accounts and audit depends on the charity's annual income.

● Income up to £25,000: a simplified receipts and payments account and statement of assets and liabilities must be prepared, and the accounts must be examined by a qualified auditor or 'an independent person who is reasonably believed by the trustees to have the requisite ability and practical experience to carry out a competent examination of the records'.

● Income between £25,000 and £100,000: a full set of accounts (in accordance with the Charities Act regulations) must be prepared, and must be examined by a qualified auditor or an independent person.

● Income over £100,000: a full set of accounts must be prepared and professionally audited.

Unregistered charities with an annual income of less than £1000 must prepare simplified accounts; unregistered charities with income over £1000 must follow the same rules as registered charities. Slightly different rules apply to exempt and excepted charities.

Details of accounting requirements for charities and other voluntary organisations are available from the legal department of the National Council for Voluntary Organisations, Regents Wharf, 8 All Saints Street, London N1 9RL (tel 071 713 6161).

The Charity Commissioners may at any time scrutinise any charity's accounts, to be sure the charity's funds have been spent in accordance with its aims and objects and no funds have been spent for purposes not allowed under charity law. If funds have been misused the Commission and Inland Revenue can remove the privileges of charitable status from all the organisation's funds or from funds which have been used for purposes the Commission judges to be non-charitable.

Accountability to funders

Any grant-aided organisation should ensure it has, in writing, a statement of how much control the funding body expects to exercise over the grant and in what way, and how much information it wants, how often and in what form. It is important to be clear whether the funding body wants complete accounts or only accounts covering its grant, and whether it wants accounts quarterly, annually or on completion of a one-off project. The same principles apply to work paid for under a service agreement or contract rather than a grant (see chapter 12).

If the funder demands a representative with voting powers on the management committee, clarify how much power that person has to take part in decisions not directly related to the funding. Clarify, too, what will happen if decisions with which the funding body subsequently disagrees are made when the representative is absent.

RECORD-KEEPING

Information required

Financial responsibility involves keeping records ('accounts' or 'books') of how much money has come into the organisation, where it has come from, and how it has been spent. This process is called **bookkeeping**. Along with the books the organisation must keep documentation, such as invoices or receipts, to prove the money was spent in the way shown. The books and proofs will be used to draw up regular **monthly and/or quarterly accounts**, **financial reports** (sometimes called **management accounts**) and the **annual accounts**.

The books and financial documentation must be kept for seven years.

The organisation must register with the Inland Revenue for PAYE ('pay as you earn') if it:

● pays workers, even on a casual basis, who earn more than the minimum national insurance (NI) threshold (£54 per week in 1992-93);

● pays workers, even on a casual basis, who work in another job as well (even if they earn less than the NI threshold in either or both jobs).

The organisation must deduct tax and national insurance from the earnings of all workers who earn more than the tax/NI thresholds, and pay the tax and NI to the Inland Revenue every month. PAYE records must be kept for at least three years.

If an organisation receives income from sources other than grants, donations, subscriptions and investments it *may* need to register for value added tax (VAT) if this income is more than the VAT threshold (£36,600 in 1992-93). This applies even to charities. There is more about this in chapter 12, but specialist advice is always required when dealing with VAT. VAT involves keeping very detailed records.

Grants and donations are not subject to corporation tax but organisations which receive income from other sources, such as trading or property rents, may have to register for and pay this tax.

Charities which reclaim tax on covenanted donations must also keep special records.

Using the information

Good financial record-keeping is essential for financial planning. This includes **budgeting**, which involves working out how much money the organisation expects to spend and receive for a fixed period and being sure these amounts match up (balance).

Financial planning also involves **forecasting**: adjusting the budget during the period, to take account of changes in income or expenditure. Without good financial records, it is impossible to budget or forecast.

With the move to service agreements and contracts it is becoming even more important for organisations to be clear not only about their overall costs, but also about the cost of each service or activity within the organisation. This is covered in *Costing for Contracts* by John Callaghan (Directory of Social Change, 1992; ISBN 0 907164 81 1; £8.95 from DSC, Radius Works, Back Lane, London NW3 1HL).

COMPUTERISING THE ACCOUNTS

Computerised accounts programs can simplify the processes of adding up, and spreadsheet programs can make it much easier to allow for many different scenarios when planning budgets. But computerising the accounts is not a magic answer, because:

- it is unlikely initially to save much time, and in the first six months will involve double time because the organisation has to keep paper (manual) systems *as well* until it is absolutely certain the computer systems are working properly;

- the person responsible for inputting data must still understand basic bookkeeping at the same level as required for manual systems, or at a more complex level if the computer program is more detailed than the manual accounts;

- it is still necessary to have detailed systems for keeping information before it is entered on the computer, and for storing documentation;

- it can be expensive to update programs, especially those relating to wages, tax and national insurance.

Before computerising accounts it is *essential* to get approval from the organisation's auditor, and it is *highly advisable* to get advice about programs from a computer consultancy which specialises in voluntary organisations.

RESPONSIBILITIES OF THE TREASURER

In a small group, the treasurer may deal with all aspects of finance and funding. As groups grow or take on paid staff, some responsibilities may be delegated to a volunteer or paid worker, or some may be shared within a finance sub-committee (see below). Even if the financial decision-making and work are carried out by the treasurer, finance subcommittee and/or finance worker or workers, final responsibility for financial matters always rests with the management committee or other governing body as a whole.

The treasurer's responsibilities can be divided into six broad categories:

- general financial oversight;

- funding, contracts, fundraising and sales;

- financial planning and budgeting;

- financial reporting;

- banking, bookkeeping and record-keeping;

- control of fixed assets and stock.

The checklist below can be used to decide which tasks should be carried out by the finance worker or treasurer, and which require the involvement of the finance subcommittee or whole management committee or other governing body.

General financial oversight

This category covers broad responsibility for the organisation's financial decision-making. It includes:

- ensuring funds are used in accordance with the constitution and committee decisions;

- ensuring use of funds complies with conditions set by funding bodies;

- ensuring workers and members of the management committee or other governing body know enough about financial administration, bookkeeping and the accounts to be able to do their work properly and make decisions for which they are responsible;

- advising on financial policy issues, for example what expenses can be claimed and the procedures for claiming them, the circumstances (if any) under which staff can receive advances on their salary payments, financial implications of new activities, or the organisation's policy on charging for its services;

- advising on contracts of employment (if there is no personnel subcommittee) and on other contracts;

Looks like Skip's gone over budget again...

- making financial decisions on behalf of the management committee between meetings, and reporting such decisions to the committee as appropriate;

- liaising with the bank or other financial institutions on behalf of the organisation;

- preparing accounts for audit, and discussing them with the auditor as required;

- deciding on security measures to ensure cash or cheques are not misused.

Funding, contracts, fundraising, sales

This area of responsibility involves ensuring the organisation has enough money to carry out its activities. The sources of this money can be divided into **funding** (grants which are applied for from statutory authorities, trusts and other sources), **contracts** or **service agreements** to provide activities or services (see chapter 12), **fundraising** (activities such as membership drives, appeals, jumble sales or special events undertaken by the organisation or its members to raise money), and **sales** of goods or services.

Responsibilities in these areas include:

- collecting and acting on information about statutory, charitable, business and other funding sources;

- completing and submitting funding applications;

- coordinating funding applications;

- liaising with funding agencies;

- drawing up tenders or proposals for contracted services;

- coordinating fundraising activities;

- running fundraising activities;

- ensuring money received for special projects is spent for that purpose, and if necessary is separately accounted for;

- ensuring goods or services to be sold are priced appropriately.

Financial planning and budgeting

The treasurer has overall responsibility for financial planning, including:

- in consultation with the appropriate workers and funders, preparing budgets for ongoing work and special projects;

- presenting budgets to the management committee or other governing body for approval;

- keeping track of actual income and expenditure as compared to budgeted income and expenditure, and adjusting financial forecasts as appropriate;

- in case of cashflow problems (not having enough money to pay bills when they are due), deciding priorities for paying and negotiating for late payment if necessary.

Financial reporting

The treasurer is responsible for ensuring the management committee or other governing body has enough informa-

tion to make its decisions. This means:

- reporting regularly, in writing, to the management committee on the organisation's financial position;

- preparing and presenting financial reports and accounts when required;

- presenting the end of year financial report (draft annual accounts) to the management committee or other governing body;

- presenting the audited accounts to the annual general meeting;

- ensuring members at the AGM have a basic understanding of the annual accounts and the budget for the current year.

Banking, bookkeeping and record-keeping

Although the treasurer may not actually do the tasks involved in getting money into and out of the bank or writing up the books, she or he is responsible for:

- advising on which banks or other financial institutions the organisation should use and what type of bank accounts it should have (note that every decision to open, close or change a bank or other account *must* be approved by the management committee or other governing body);

- serving as a signatory for the organisation's bank accounts (all changes of signatory *must* be approved by the management committee or governing body);

- ensuring there are proper systems for receiving and paying out cash and cheques;

- setting up appropriate bookkeeping and petty cash systems, and ensuring related documentation is kept;

- ensuring membership subscriptions are collected and proper membership records are kept;

- ensuring other moneys due to the organisation are collected, guidelines exist for action to be taken in cases of non-payment, and such action is taken if required;

- ensuring receipts are issued, if required, for money received by the organisation;

- ensuring all income (including cash) is paid into the bank;

- ensuring all bills are paid;

- ensuring everyone handling money for the organisation keeps proper records and documentation.

Control of fixed assets and stock

The treasurer has broad responsibility for ensuring the organisation maintains proper control of its **fixed assets** (major equipment, vehicles, buildings and other property owned by the organisation), its **materials or supplies** (goods which get used up in running the organisation) and its **stock** (goods such as publications waiting to be distributed or sold, or timber waiting to be used in a carpentry training workshop). This responsibility includes:

- ensuring the organisation keeps proper records of materials and supplies used in its work;

- ensuring systems are set up and maintained for stock control and reorders;

- undertaking or overseeing regular stock checks;

- ensuring the organisation keeps proper records of its equipment and vehicles, including date of purchase, supplier, value, model and serial number;

- ensuring the organisation keeps proper financial records relating to property (buildings and land) it owns or uses;

- ensuring that the organisation has all necessary insurances and keeps them up to date.

FINANCE SUBCOMMITTEE

A finance (or finance and funding) subcommittee can spread the workload of the treasurer, ensure more democratic control of finances, and help train new committee members. It should include at least the treasurer, another management committee member, the manager and/or financial manager, the person who deals with accounts and bookkeeping, and the person or people with major responsibility for funding and fundraising.

The subcommittee should have clear terms of reference, indicating the responsibilities and authority of the subcommittee itself, the treasurer, staff members and the management committee as a whole. The terms of reference might include any or all of the points listed above under treasurer's responsibilities.

The terms of reference should be clear about whether individuals (treasurer or manager) or the subcommittee can make decisions about particular matters or can only make proposals or recommendations for final decision by the management committee.

Some organisations have a separate fundraising subcommittee which takes responsibility for funding applications and/or fundraising activities. Others have set up a contracts subcommittee or contracts working party to deal with the introduction of contracts or service agreements.

LOOKING AT ACCOUNTS

'Accounts' has several meanings:

- money kept in a bank or other financial institution (the organisation's bank accounts or building society accounts);

- arrangements with a supplier to sell goods or provide services on credit (for example, an account with a stationery supplier or the gas board);

- the books in which an organisation's financial transactions are recorded;

- summaries of the information in the books, presented in a standard format so people know about the organisation's financial transactions and position.

This section considers this last type of accounts.

These accounts may be drawn up monthly, quarterly or annually. In themselves they tell relatively little; it is the **interpretation** of them which is significant. But many people on management committees or other governing bodies do not believe they are competent to make such an interpretation.

The person who draws up the accounts, whether finance worker, treasurer or accountant, has an obligation to present the information in a way people can understand. This may mean simplifying the presentation, adding notes in plain English (or other language, as appropriate for the group), or offering a training session on how the accounts are set out and how to use them.

For housing associations and other organisations dealing with complex financial transactions, accounts and financial reports will necessarily be more difficult. Committee members may need training to ensure they have a basic understanding of financial issues and information.

Listed below are questions that can make it easier to look at a financial report or set of accounts without panicking or glazing over. Some need to be asked only once, but others may need to be asked occasionally or even every time the accounts are circulated.

What the accounts cover

If some very basic points are not clear there is no way that anyone, no matter how experienced, can understand the accounts. If the following points are unclear, **ask the treasurer or finance worker**. If one person does not understand the accounts, probably other management committee members or workers do not understand them either.

- Do the accounts cover the whole organisation and all its work, or only part? Some organisations have different sets of accounts for different departments or areas of work. If this is the case it can be difficult to get an overall picture, especially if money is transferred between accounts.

- Do they cover all income and expenditure, or only revenue? Some organisations have separate accounts for **capital equipment** (purchase of vehicles or equipment expected to last for at least a year or having a resale value) and for **revenue** (running costs, such as wages, administration, rents, materials, stock, professional fees). If the organisation owns property it might also have a separate **property account**. If it has a large sum of money in an interest-earning account this might be separately reported as a **capital account**.

- What is the financial period (the period covered by the accounts)? It might be a month, a quarter, the financial year to date (covering the period since the beginning of the financial year), or a year.

- Do the accounts cover two overlapping periods? They might, for example, include figures for last month and the year to date. This enables people to have current as well as cumulative figures. Clear headings are essential; a vertical line between the two columns can make it easier to consider the two sets of figures separately.

- Do the accounts include comparative figures from an earlier period? This helps people compare current figures with figures from a similar period, to see if income and expenditure are going up or down. The accounts might include, for example, figures for last quarter and the previous quarter, or figures for last quarter and the same quarter in the previous year, or figures for last year and the previous year. Again, clear headings are essential and a vertical line between columns can make it easier to compare the figures.

- Do the accounts include a **budget**? This lets people compare actual income and expenditure against budgeted (anticipated) income and expenditure. The budget figures given might be for the period covered by the accounts (which makes it quite easy to compare) or for the whole financial year (which makes it more difficult, because people have to work out how much of the year has gone by and whether too much or too little of the budget has been met in the period). If budget figures are given for the period covered by the accounts, there might be a third column for **variance**. This is the difference between the actual and budgeted amounts. If the number in the variance column is in brackets (£123) it means the income is that much *less* than budgeted or expenditure is that much *more* than budgeted; if the number is not in brackets it is that much *more* than budgeted for income or that much *less* than budgeted for expenditure.

- If the accounts include a budget, is it balanced? A balanced budget is one in which anticipated income is equal to anticipated outgoings. If expected income is more than expected expenditure, the excess may be shown as 'surplus to be transferred to reserves' in order to balance the budget. (This means it is anticipated there will be money left over at the end of the financial period, and it will be kept in reserve rather than spent.) If anticipated income is less than anticipated expenditure, the difference will be shown as a **deficit**. (It might be labelled 'shortfall' or 'to be found'.) If a deficit is shown, ask how the organisation expects to cover it.

- Do the accounts include a **forecast** or **projected outcome**? This is a revised budget, based on the reality of what is happening during the year. For example an organisation might budget to receive £300 in donations, but receive an unexpected cheque for £1000 during the year. The forecast might then be adjusted upwards, to £1300. Or a mild winter might mean the budget for heating costs is adjusted downwards.

- Do you understand the categories into which income and expenditure are divided? These are called **analysis headings** and help to show exactly where income comes from and where expenditure goes.

Although most accounts are divided into 'income' and 'expenditure', they might technically (and confusingly) actually be a 'receipts and payments account' rather than an 'income and expenditure account'.

A **receipts and payments account** is a simple statement of the money received and paid out by the organisation. A receipts and payments account works like this:

Balance brought forward (amount of money at the beginning of the financial period) *plus* **receipts** (money which came in during the financial period)

equals

Payments (money spent during the financial period) *plus* **balance on hand** (amount left at the end of the financial period).

The balance on hand is sometimes called the balance carried forward (C/F). The balance carried forward at the end of one financial period becomes the balance brought forward (B/F) at the beginning of the next financial period.

An **income and expenditure account** is based on the receipts and payments account, but is adjusted to include money owed to the organisation and owed by it. But, confusingly, the headings on a receipts and payments account might be labelled 'income' and 'expenditure'!

The financial situation

A **financial report** or **management accounts** can be anything which informs people of the financial situation. For most small voluntary organisations an appropriate financial report for the management committee includes:

- a receipts and payments account, showing the balance on hand at the end of the financial period;

- a simple outline or statement of how much money was owed to the organisation at the end of the financial period and what for;

- an outline or statement of how much money the organisation owed and what for;

- an indication of any financial problems or situations requiring a decision by the finance subcommittee and/or management committee or other governing body.

This additional information is needed to make sense of the receipts and payments account. For example, the balance on hand might be £2500. But what if the organisation owes £1000 to the Inland Revenue and £1500 in overdue rent? What if the organisation has been promised a £3000 grant which has not yet arrived? A balance on hand does not by itself give a useful picture of the financial position.

If this information is not given, you may have to ask:

- Were we owed anything at the end of the financial period? And how much did we owe in unpaid bills?

Income

Having established the basic facts about what the accounts cover, you can look more closely at the details. Start with the income (or receipts), which will be divided into several categories.

- Do you understand broadly where the income has come from?

- Are there separate categories for grants received for capital and revenue?

- Is too much lumped into a meaningless category like 'miscellaneous', 'other' or 'petty cash'?

- Are there any amounts which seem to you disproportionately large or small? (For example, a tiny amount for 'fundraising' when you know the organisation has had several successful fundraising events.)

- If figures for a comparative period are available, is current income broadly in line with them, after allowing for inflation and planned growth or contraction? If not, why not?

- If budget figures are given, is actual income broadly in line with budgeted? If not, why not? Does the organisation need to take steps to generate more income?

- Have all grants due for the period been received? If not, what is being done to chase them?

- If the accounts show income owing to the organisation as well as income actually received, how much of the money has not yet come in? What is being done to chase it?

Expenditure

Next look at the expenditure (payments) figures, which will also be divided into several categories.

- Do you understand broadly where the expenditure has gone?

- Is there too much lumped into a meaningless category like 'miscellaneous', 'other' or 'petty cash'?

- Are there any amounts which seem to you disproportionately large or small? (For example, a huge amount spent on phone and postage or on cleaning costs.)

- If figures for a comparative period are available, is current expenditure broadly in line with them, after allowing for inflation and planned growth or contraction? If not, why not?

- If budget figures are given, is actual expenditure broadly in line with budgeted? If not, why not? If expenditure is higher than expected, does the organisation need to consider cutting back? If expenditure is lower than budgeted, does the organisation need to spend more to ensure a funder does not 'claw back' unspent grant?

- Are there any major items of expenditure which may occur during the year but have not yet been budgeted for? Does the budget for expenditure need to be adjusted?

Comparing income and expenditure

If the organisation is to survive income must be in line with, or more than, expenditure.

- During the financial period, has the organisation had in more than it has spent out? This will be called something like **excess of income over expenditure**. Or has it spent out more than it had in? This will be called something like **excess of expenditure over income**.

Excess of expenditure over income is usually shown in brackets like this (£574.65). If the organisation had in £1000 during the month but spent £1574.65, its excess of expenditure over income was £574.65. Putting the amount in brackets makes it immediately clear to anyone looking at the accounts that £574.65 is a negative or minus amount. The traditional way of showing a negative amount was to write it in red, which showed up easily in books normally written in black. (Hence the saying 'in the red' when someone is in debt, and 'in the black' when they are in credit.) But red does not show up on photocopies, so another system is needed to show negative amounts. A minus sign (-) is not used in handwritten or typed accounts because it can be too easily confused with a dash. Some computerised accounts do not use brackets; they use a **trailing minus sign** after a negative number.

Petty cash

Some items, such as bus fares, must be paid in cash, but cash expenditure should be kept to the minimum. Whenever possible cheques should be used, because they provide legal proof of payment and a legal record of what has been paid to whom.

Often the accounts only show money which goes through bank accounts; they do not show money which comes in or is spent out in cash. This is acceptable only if the amounts involved are small. It is much better to show all petty cash in the agreed analysis categories.

- Is there a large amount indicated for petty cash expenditure? If so, ask for petty cash expenditure to be included in the analysis categories in future.

- Are you satisfied the petty cash system is working well, with proper controls? If not, ask for details of who has access to cash, who can authorise cash expenditure, and how much cash is kept on the premises.

Cashflow and the financial position

Cashflow means just that: the flow of money (cash or cheques) into and out of the organisation. A simple receipts and payments account might show the organisation has had in much more than it has spent and has thousands of pounds in the bank. But the organisation might still have cashflow problems if it owes even greater amounts in wages, telephone bills and rent.

- How long ago was the end of the financial period? Has the financial position changed significantly since then? A grant or a large bill might have come in since the end of the financial period, so the financial report might need to be updated by the time the committee discusses it.

- How much money is owing to the organisation? In the financial report this might be called the organisation's **debtors**: people who are in debt to the organisation. Are necessary steps being taken to get the money?

- Are there any doubts or uncertainties about grants due during the rest of the financial year? Does the organisation need to make contingency plans in case grants do not come in as budgeted?

- How much money does the organisation owe? In the financial report this might be called **creditors**: people who have, in effect, extended credit to the organisation. Creditors include recurrent costs such as salary payments, taxes and national insurance, rent, telephone, photocopier as well as one-off or occasional expenditure.

- Are payments to the Inland Revenue for tax and national insurance up to date? (Some organisations try to deal with their cashflow problems by not paying the Inland Revenue on time. Not only is this bad practice, it is also illegal.)

- If the organisation has more money than it currently needs, is it invested in an interest-earning account or some other form of investment? Are the investments bringing in a reasonable return? The organisation's auditor or another accountant can advise on high interest accounts and other investments, including those which take into account ethical considerations.

- Is there enough money to pay the bills which are due? If not, what will the organisation do? Can it make a concerted effort to bring in the money owed to it? Does it need to negotiate with some creditors for late payment? Does it want to use its **reserves** (money set aside for the future)? Does it need to ask the bank for an **overdraft**, allowing the organisation to spend more than it has in its bank account?

If the organisation has short term cashflow problems an overdraft will ease the crisis, but constant overdrafts are not a good form of financial control. First of all they are expensive, which can often make the organisation's longer term financial problems even worse. Besides, the bank will probably want security for the overdraft, in the form of **collateral** (the organisation's assets) or **personal guarantees** from committee members. **Committee members who give personal guarantees become personally responsible for the overdraft if the organisation cannot pay it**.

If the organisation does not have a reasonable prospect of ever being able to pay its bills, it is in trouble. If it is not incorporated (as a company limited by guarantee or an industrial and provident society) the members of the management committee or other governing body could be held personally liable for the organisation's debts. It needs urgent advice from a qualified accountant or auditor.

If the organisation is a company limited by guarantee it may be unlawful under the **Insolvency Act 1986** for it to carry on operating. The company's accountant or auditor should be contacted immediately. If the organisation carries on despite being in such financial difficulty, individual directors (committee members) could lose their limited liability and be held personally liable for the organisation's debts. (This is explained in chapter 2.)

Forecasts

A forecast is a budget which has been revised on the basis of what has happened to income and expenditure since the beginning of the budget period and what is expected to happen in future.

- Do the forecasts for income or expenditure need to be adjusted upwards or downwards?

- What are the implications of this change?

- Does the organisation need to take steps to ensure future budgets are more accurate?

Balance sheet

A receipts and payments account is a relatively simple statement of how much money the organisation had in and spent during a financial period.

An income and expenditure account is adjusted to include how much the organisation is owed (as part of income) and owes (as part of expenditure) at the end of a financial period.

A balance sheet is different. It is designed to show what the organisation is worth on a particular day (the last day of the

financial period). It includes **assets** (everything the organisation owns) and **liabilities** (everything it owes). A balance sheet shows the organisation's **net worth** at a particular point in time; it does not show what happened over a financial period.

Assets may be fixed or current.

- **Fixed assets** are property, equipment or other major and tangible items owned by the organisation. The treasurer will need to agree with the auditor how the value of fixed assets is worked out and adjusted every year. This will be based on **depreciation**: a way of spreading the cost of the asset across its useful life (in the accounts only, not in reality). Assets such as computers and minibuses are typically depreciated across three or four years. The treasurer or finance worker should be able to explain how the value of fixed assets is calculated to committee members, organisation members and workers.

- **Current assets** include the value of stock (materials, supplies or goods), debtors (money owing to the organisation), investments (shares) and cash (money at the bank or held in other ways).

Liabilities include current liabilities and provisions.

- **Current liabilities** are the organisation's creditors: money that it owes.

- The balance sheet might also include **provisions** for recurrent costs such as property maintenance or replacing essential equipment. This means that the balance sheet makes allowance for, say, one-fifth of the cost of redecorating premises every five years. The treasurer and auditor will agree how these provisions are worked out.

Balance sheets can be quite complex but the principle is straightforward. The **bottom line** shows whether the organisation's total assets (including fixed assets) are equal to or more than its total liabilities. The **net current assets** show whether current assets are equal to or more than its current liabilities.

If current assets are more than current liabilities, the surplus is called **reserves** or **accumulated fund**. Provision might be made for the reserves to be used in certain ways, such as 'staff contingency fund'.

If current liabilities are more than current assets the points raised above under 'Cashflow' must be considered. If the organisation has fixed assets it may need to consider selling them.

PREPARING FOR AUDIT

An audit is an independent report which covers:

- how much money the organisation received and spent in the financial year, and what for;

- whether the money was spent in accordance with the constitution, decisions of the management committee or other governing body, and funders' requirements;

- whether the accounts were properly and honestly kept;

- the value of its assets;

- how the financial record-keeping systems could be improved.

The person who does the audit must not be actively involved in the organisation, and should not be a relative or close associate of anyone actively involved in the organisation.

If the organisation is incorporated (as a limited company or an industrial and provident society), or if it is an unincorporated charity with an annual income over £100,000, the audit must be done by a qualified auditor. Qualified auditors use the initials CA, ACA, FCA, ACCA or FCCA after their name, indicating they are members of a recognised professional association. A funder which provides a substantial grant may also require an audit carried out by a qualified auditor.

If the organisation is unincorporated and does not receive a substantial grant, it will be adequate for the audit to be done by someone who is competent and is not directly involved with the organisation. The Charities Act 1992 includes new accounting requirements for unincorporated charities; see 'Legal accountability' earlier in this chapter. A funder will usually indicate whether the audit has to be done by a qualified auditor. If in doubt, ask.

The auditor is usually formally appointed at the annual general meeting. If this is not done the appointment should be formally made at a meeting of the management committee or other governing body.

As well as auditing the annual accounts, the auditor is available throughout the year for advice.

To do the audit the auditor will need to see all the financial records and documentation relating to the financial year. She or he may come to the organisation's office, or may ask for the financial records to be delivered (by hand or by courier; don't trust the post) to her or his office. Some auditors want to see everything all at once; others ask for the basics first then for specific items if they are needed.

The audit will be quicker and easier (and therefore cheaper) if the organisation's treasurer or a worker with responsibility for finance has drawn up draft annual accounts.

The audit will also be quicker, easier and cheaper if all the information is easily available. And the information will be more easily available if the organisation has good financial systems. **The time to start preparing for an audit is at the beginning of the financial year, not the end**. Ask the auditor at the beginning of the financial year what information will be needed, and in what form. Use the checklist below as a starting point.

Find out from the auditor if photocopies are acceptable, or if she or he must have original documents. **Keep photocopies of any documents you will need to use or refer to while the originals are with the auditor**. Provide all documents in tidy bundles clearly labelled with the organisation's name.

Audit checklist

Terms and conditions for the organisation's financial dealings

For these items, photocopies are usually acceptable:

- constitution, if it is the first time the organisation has used this auditor or changes have been made to the constitution since the last audit;

- contracts, agreements or letters setting out the conditions of grants, legacies or other income received for specific purposes;

- grant application forms;

- budgets for ongoing work or special projects;

- minutes of finance and other relevant subcommittee meetings;

- minutes of decisions of the management committee or other governing body relating to finance.

Records and documentation of income and expenditure

For these items the auditor will probably want to see originals:

- analysis book(s) for income and expenditure;

- documentation (proofs, vouchers) for income, ideally cross-referenced to the income analysis book;

- receipt book(s), if the organisation issues receipts for money it receives;

- expenditure documentation, cross-referenced by cheque number to the expenditure analysis book;

- invoice book(s), if the organisation issues invoices for goods or services it provides.

Petty cash records

Mismanagement of petty cash is a frequent problem in organisations, so the auditor will want to be sure there are proper systems and controls and they are used effectively. She or he will need:

- petty cash book(s);

- petty cash vouchers and proofs, cross-referenced by voucher number to the petty cash book;

- a written statement, signed by two people (usually the finance worker and treasurer) of how much money is in the petty cash box at the end of the year. If this does not agree with the balance in the petty cash book, the discrepancy should be explained.

Bank records

Bank records provide legal proof that money has actually come into and gone out of the organisation. The auditor will need:

- statements for all of the organisation's bank accounts, for the financial year and the month immediately after the end of the financial year (this includes accounts held at banks, building societies or other financial institutions);

- the reconciliations for all the statements (a reconciliation is a way of checking the bank statement against the organisation's own records);

- the counterfoils of all completed chequebooks used during the year, and details from the counterfoils of the chequebook(s) currently in use;

- cleared cheques, if the bank returns them to the organisation;

- all paying-in books used during the year, and details from the counterfoils of paying-in book(s) currently in use;
- passbooks and other records for deposit, building society and similar accounts.

Creditors and debtors

The auditor will need:

- a list of everyone the organisation owes money to at the end of the financial year, how much it owes and what for (the organisation's creditors);
- a list of everyone who owes money to the organisation at the end of the financial year, how much they owe and what for (the organisation's debtors);
- the lists of creditors and debtors from the end of the previous financial year.

Accruals and prepayments

The auditor may ask for:

- a list of accruals: income the organisation has received for goods or services it has not yet provided (for example, a grant cheque covering the period past the end of the financial year, payments received for training courses which have not yet been held, or booking fees received for room use after the end of the financial year);
- a list of prepayments: expenditure the organisation has made for goods or services it has not yet received (for example rent paid for the period past the end of the financial year);
- lists of accruals and prepayments from the end of the previous financial year.

Wages and PAYE records

The tax year runs from 6 April to 5 April. If the organisation's financial year straddles two tax years, the auditor will need to see the records listed below for both tax years. (If the organisation's financial year runs from 1 April to 31 March, the few days overlap of the old tax year at the beginning of April can usually be ignored if workers are paid monthly, but not if they are paid weekly.)

- a list of everyone who worked for the organisation during the tax year(s), with details of starting and finishing dates if these occurred during the tax year, salary at the beginning of the tax year(s) and details of all increments or other changes during the tax year(s);
- P11s (deductions working sheets) or the equivalent computer forms for everyone who worked for the organisation during the tax year(s) for whom a P11 or equivalent computer form was used;
- details of payments to people for whom a P11 or equivalent computer form was not used (workers who earned less than the national insurance threshold);
- coding notices received from the Inland Revenue relating to the tax year(s);

- statutory sick pay and statutory maternity pay records for the period;
- wages book, copies of wages slips, or other wages records;
- the Inland Revenue paying-in book;
- end of year returns (copies of P14s, P35 and P38);
- correspondence to or from the Inland Revenue.

Financial reports

It will also be helpful for the auditor to have:

- monthly or quarterly financial reports or other management accounts;
- draft end of year accounts, if the organisation has prepared them.

Assets

To draw up the income and expenditure account and balance sheet the auditor will need to know what the organisation is worth at the end of the financial year. So she or he will need:

- details of all real property (land or buildings) owned by the organisation;
- a list of capital equipment owned (large items that can be expected to last more than a year, such as typewriters, filing cabinets, desks, photocopiers, computers or vehicles) with model name or number, serial number, date of purchase and purchase price (or value, if it was a gift);
- a list of capital equipment the organisation is buying on hire purchase or similar arrangements;
- stock records for the year;
- end of year stock check.

Covenants

If the organisation is a charity reclaiming tax on covenants, the auditor will need:

- details of covenanted income received during the year;
- claim forms for tax reclaimed on covenants during the year;
- a list of covenants received during the year on which tax has not yet been reclaimed.

Other financial documents

Because every organisation is different, auditors will need to see different documents. Some frequent requirements are:

- membership subscription book;
- bar or coffee bar takings book;
- vehicle log book(s) and insurance records for vehicles owned by the organisation;
- details of stocks and shares held by the organisation, and of dividend payments received during the year;

- VAT records;
- corporation tax and other tax records;
- any other documents relating to the organisation's financial transactions or position.

Auditor's report

The auditor will draw up a set of draft annual accounts based on this information. They will include a record of income and expenditure actually received and spent, possibly with adjustments for creditors, debtors, accruals, prepayments and depreciation on equipment or vehicles.

There may also be a draft balance sheet showing what the organisation was worth on the last day of the financial year. This shows the total value of everything the organisation owns (money, equipment, buildings) minus the total value of everything the organisation owes.

The auditor will prefix the accounts with a statement saying they have been drawn up in accordance with certain standards, based on information provided by the organisation. It may say the auditor has had to rely on statements by the organisation's elected officers to verify transactions if documentation was not available. The statement will then (hopefully) say that in the auditor's opinion, the accounts are an accurate and honest statement of the organisation's financial dealings and situation for that financial year.

The accounts should be checked by the treasurer, submitted to the management committee or other governing body for approval, and signed by the appropriate officer(s). The auditor will advise who this should be. When the accounts are signed they cease to be draft accounts and become **final accounts**.

The accounts should not be signed unless people understand them. If anything is unclear, ask the auditor for clarification. If required, the auditor will attend a meeting of the finance subcommittee or the management committee or other governing body to go through the accounts and answer questions.

The treasurer should then present the accounts to an annual general meeting for acceptance. It is good practice to include an explanation of the accounts, since many people glaze over when they look at columns of numbers. A pictorial representation (such as pie charts or other graphs) can make the accounts easier to understand, but the charts should clarify, not make the accounts even more obscure.

The auditor should be invited to the AGM and be available to answer questions.

A good auditor will recommend ways to improve the organisation's financial systems and procedures. The auditor's advice should *always* be taken seriously.

Changing auditor

The organisation's constitution may state that the auditor can only be changed by a formal resolution at the organisation's annual general meeting, another general meeting or a meeting of the management committee or other governing body. If this is the case all members and the present auditor must be given notice that the change is being proposed, and the present auditor must be told why. The present auditor has a right to attend and speak at the meeting at which the resolution is proposed. The result of the resolution must be properly minuted.

Even if the constitution does not require it, any decision to change auditors should be made by the management committee or other governing body.

Regardless of how the decision to change auditors is made, a new auditor will need to see the organisation's audit and other financial information from the previous year, for example the list of creditors and debtors at the end of the previous year. The new auditor will advise what information is required.

Funders are likely to ask why the auditor has been changed.

Chapter 21:

Managing administration and paperwork

Poor administrative systems and procedures are a frequent cause of inefficiency in voluntary organisations. Although this book cannot look in detail at administration, this chapter provides some basic pointers so that poor administrative and information systems do not interfere with management.

It includes:

- hints for managing the post and messages;
- a basic approach to information systems;
- ideas for organising files and coping with filing;
- a brief look at computerised information systems.

MANAGING THE POST

Ideally, each piece of paper should be handled only once: receive it, read it, deal with it or pass it on, and dispose of it (to the bin or the filing cabinet) in one go. Having a block of desk time (see chapter 11) each day makes this more likely, but for most people it remains a virtually impossible ideal.

There are, however, ways to manage post and incoming messages more efficiently.

- Individuals or teams should have **pigeonholes** into which all incoming post is sorted. It is not efficient simply to drop letters onto someone's desk. If necessary, implement a system to ensure pigeonholes are regularly cleared.

- **Letters** should be dealt with immediately. This means reading them, replying to them if required, entering any tasks which become necessary into the forward planning diary, workplan to-do list, and filing the letter (with a copy of the reply) or throwing it away.

- **Minutes** should be read or at least skimmed. Use a highlighter pen to note anything that must be done, and enter it into the forward planning diary, workplan or to-do list. File the minutes where they can be easily found to take to the next meeting of the group.

- **Magazines** and newsletters should be skimmed for anything essential, then passed on to the appropriate person or put aside to be read in a block of time allocated for magazines. Highlight anything of importance. Staple a small piece of paper on the cover and note anything of particular interest or anything that needs to be clipped or photocopied before the publication is thrown away or filed.

- Anything which other people will deal with should be passed on to them without delay. A list of who receives what (magazines or newsletters, for example) can be very useful.

- If correspondence, newsletters or magazines have to be passed to other workers, write their names at the top and ensure people cross off their name after seeing the document. Or photocopy slips with the names of all workers or committee members (circulation slips), and when a document comes in staple a slip to it and indicate who should see the document. (Remember to add new workers' or committee members' names.)

- **Rubbish should be thrown away**. Ask yourself: 'Do I need to do anything about this?' If the answer is 'no', pass it on to whoever does need to do something about it, or throw it away. Ask yourself: 'When and why might I ever need this piece of paper again?' If there is no answer, throw it away. Ask yourself: 'What is the worst thing that might happen if I don't have this piece of paper?' If the answer is 'nothing', throw it away. If no one knows what needs to be kept and what can be thrown away, something is wrong.

If there is never enough time to deal with the post, the only solutions are to:

- delegate responsibility to someone who has time to read and deal with it;

- manage time better, by allowing more time for paperwork and reading;

- stop getting in so much information.

MANAGING MESSAGES

Even organisations which have efficient systems for dealing with post sometimes find it difficult to cope with phone messages or notes left by visitors.

Messages of this type should generally be passed on as quickly as possible. Everyone in the organisation should be clear who has responsibility for taking messages, and how they are to be passed on: telephoned through, put in pigeonholes, personally delivered, left on people's desks, forwarded to their home address, or whatever system is appropriate for the organisation and individuals.

Everyone who answers incoming calls should be clear about what information is required. Standard telephone message slips are available from stationers; some organisations devise their own. Or the organisation might use a message book. Regardless of the system, the message should include the date and time of call, who it is for, the caller's name and phone number, and a clear message.

A message book should include a column for people to tick when they have read the message. Without this there is no way of knowing whether the person for whom a message was intended has received it.

Scribbling a message on a scrappy bit of paper and leaving it in the middle of someone's paper-laden desk is *not* an efficient way to deal with a phone call.

MANAGING INFORMATION SYSTEMS

Sensible information systems (files, library, computer storage) save everyone's time and temper. But many systems evolve over time and are never changed; the simple alphabetical system which was perfectly OK when all the files fitted into one drawer is hopelessly inadequate when they fill four filing cabinets; the computer reference system which worked when each worker had only one disk is impossible when workers have several disks and constantly swop them around.

A book such as this cannot give advice on the specific information systems appropriate to individual organisations. However, there are a few guidelines.

As with any other organisational system, the starting point is to think through why the system is needed, what it will include, who will use it and how, and when and where it will be used. These questions can be applied to four aspects of filing or other information systems:

● **collection** or **creation**: getting the information into the organisation, from outside or from within;

● **storage**: where and how the information will be kept in the short term and permanently;

● **retrieval**: getting access to the information when it is needed;

● **return**: getting the information back to its proper place after it has been used.

A good information system makes each aspect as easy as possible for the people using the system.

Collection or creation

● What information will be collected or created? Newsletters, magazines, correspondence, minutes, reports, instructions ...?

● Why is it being collected or created?

● Who will collect or create it?

● Who is expected to use it?

● How frequently will the information come into the organisation? Daily, weekly, monthly, erratically?

● Where will it come into the organisation? Via the main office, the administrative worker, other workers?

● How will it come in? Via post, regular deliveries, verbally?

Storage

● What information needs to be kept, and for how long?

● Why does it need to be kept?

● Who will put the information into the files, library or other storage place?

● When will it go into the storage place?

● How long will it be kept?

● Where is the most convenient place for storing the information?

● How can it be most effectively stored?

Just in case we throw away the wrong thing by mistake

● If it will be transferred from temporary storage (such as a display rack) to more permanent storage (files or the library), who will do this?

Retrieval

● What information will be needed in future?

● Why will it be needed?

● Who will need it?

● Who will have to get it out of the system?

● When is it likely to be needed? Soon or distant future? Frequently or only once in a while?

● Where will the information be used?

● How can the system help get information to where it is needed, when it is needed?

Return

● Who will return the information to the system?

● When will it have to be returned? How frequently?

● Where will it come from to get back into the system?

● Is anything likely to be needed by others while it is out of the system?

● How can you make it as easy as possible to get information back into the system?

MANAGING FILING

There are several different filing systems: alphabetical, categorical, numerical, alpha-numeric or colour-coded. They can be used separately or together. Regardless of which system is used, everyone involved in the organisation should understand how information is filed, why it is kept, and the importance of returning it to the right place. It is also essential to label each filing cabinet drawer, indicating broadly what it contains.

Alphabetical

Alphabetical systems are easy to set up and use, but they quickly become unwieldy. It makes no sense to have 'Cooper, Jane', 'Cooperation with other agencies' and 'Co-operative Bank account' next to each other simply because they all happen to start with the same six letters. Jane Cooper's folder should be with other workers' personnel files; 'cooperation with other agencies' is too vague a heading and should be divided into folders for each agency or type of agency; the Co-operative Bank folder should be with other financial files.

Categorical

Dividing files by category is a sensible, straightforward approach. Typical categories for voluntary organisations are:

● finance;

● funding;

● fundraising;

● legal documents;

● policy;

● management committee;

● other committees and working groups (internal);

● personnel;

● volunteers;

● staff and volunteer training;

● premises;

● vehicles;

● equipment;

● the organisation's publications and publicity;

● other organisations, outside committees and working groups;

● various aspects of the organisation's work.

The advantage of categorical files is that all information relating to a specific area of work is together. The disadvantages are that some information may need to go into two or more categories, and the categories may become unwieldy and need to be divided into subcategories.

Subcategories should usually be arranged alphabetically within categories. Individual folders should be arranged alphabetically within subcategories or categories.

As well as its own label, each folder should have on it the category and subcategory, to ensure it gets put back into the right place.

Numerical or alpha-numeric

Numerical or alpha-numeric (using letters and numbers) systems can make it much easier to get folders back where they belong. But unless the system is logically organised in categories, it can be very difficult to get information into the folders in the first place.

When setting up a numerical or alpha-numeric system try to anticipate future use and allow enough gaps for new items to be added in a logical order.

A numerical or alpha-numeric system involves keeping an up to date index of numbers and ensuring that everyone who uses the files has immediate access to it.

Colour

Using different colour folders for different categories (or a group of categories) can make it easier to get folders back into the right place. The only real disadvantages are that coloured folders are more expensive than buff ones, and stationery suppliers are notoriously inconsistent about what they have in stock at any given time. There is not much point in putting everything relating to premises in turquoise folders if no stationer in town will ever have more folders of that colour.

Historical and current files

Within each category, information can also be divided according to how it will be used. Some is used **historically**: it is past information, used perhaps for reference or reminder but not regularly needed. Other information is **current**, needed for present work. The minutes of the most recent meeting are current, because they have to be taken to the next meeting for approval. The minutes of the previous two or three meetings may be current or historical, depending on whether they are referred to. The minutes of earlier meetings are probably historical.

It can be useful to use folders of a specific colour (perhaps red or yellow, which are easily visible on a crowded desk) for all current folders, regardless of their category. This makes it easier to have quick access to precisely the information needed for current work. However, it is important to transfer the information to the historical folder as soon as possible.

New items are usually put into the **back** of historical folders, so information is arranged chronologically (oldest on top, most recent at the bottom). Items are usually put into the **front** of current folders, so the most recent information is on top. If it is too complicated to maintain two systems, make a rule that all information should be filed in the front of all folders, and put a note to this effect on the front of the filing cabinet.

When information is no longer needed it should be cleared and either thrown away or stored. Stored information should be kept in clearly labelled filing cabinets or boxes so it can be retrieved if needed.

The organisation should always have a list of what information has been stored, and where. This is especially important if information is kept away from the organisation's office. (This might be in someone's attic or basement, or somewhere more permanent. Many peace groups, for example, have lodged their historical files with the London School of Economics or University of Bradford; it is important for the groups to know what is stored there and how they can gain access to their files.)

Making filing easier

For people who find filing a chore, these ideas might help:

● label the front of the filing cabinet;

● label each folder with its name and the section it goes in (unless colour is used to distinguish sections);

● spend some time in a good stationers considering the various types of files available (folders are cheapest and easiest but offer no protection against loss; wallet folders or box files stop items from falling out; ring binders or lever arch files keep everything in order);

● the first time a piece of paper is dealt with write in the top corner the name of the file it will eventually go into or write 'bin' if it is to be thrown away (thus enabling everyone who handles the paper to know what will happen to it);

● try to file each item as soon as it is no longer needed, or if this is not possible keep all items to be filed in one place, such as a tray labelled 'filing';

● transfer information from current to historical files as soon as possible, so current files contain only information essential for day to day work;

● return files to the correct place as soon as they are no longer being used; don't let them pile up on the desk, floor or top of the filing cabinet;

● set aside a fixed time each day or week for filing, enter it in the workplan and ensure it happens;

● sort large piles into smaller ones, divided by category or by the drawer or filing cabinet they go in;

● be consistent about whether information is put into files from the front or the back;

● when a file starts bulging, subdivide it (either into sub-categories or chronologically) or transfer it all to a box file;

● set aside a period each year to clear out the filing systems, and put it in the organisation's calendar of recurrent tasks (see chapter 11);

● **do it**. Filing ten pieces of paper may be a pain, but filing 100 is a lot worse. If you have more than a dozen items waiting to be filed it is too much.

COMPUTERISED INFORMATION SYSTEMS

Will the computer solve all your information problems? Maybe, if you think through exactly what type of systems you need and can find hardware and software which will meet those needs. But computers will not, at least for the foreseeable future, replace paper.

When setting up computerised systems:

● be sure everyone is clear about the manual (paperwork) systems that will be needed for back-up;

● develop procedures for regularly copying information so there is no risk of it being lost if the computer or disk is damaged;

● find out about the Data Protection Act and register under it if you keep on computer any information about recognisable living individuals (even if people's names are not stored, individuals can be recognised from, for example, addresses, personal characteristics or job titles);

● allow enough money in the budget for proper training for everyone who will use the computer;

● ensure the organisation has, and enforces, clear policies and procedures relating to health and safety for people who use or work near computers.

Setting up computerised information systems is even more complicated than establishing and maintaining manual systems, so look on the files, the library and other paper systems as a practice run.

The London Advice Services Alliance (Universal House, 88-94 Wentworth Street, London E1 7SA, tel 071 377 2798) has a useful series of briefing sheets on buying a computer and printer, choosing software for various applications and computer health and safety.

Chapter 22:

The not-yet good enough manager

There is no magic in good management. It is based not on complex theories but on:

● common sense;

● willingness to listen, learn and change;

● sensitivity to people and their needs;

● good understanding of the organisation's objectives, history and current situation;

● willingness, time and ability to think through the issues;

● willingness, time and ability to plan;

● willingness and time to share ideas and information.

But sometimes things don't work out well. Management committee members or managers may seem incapable of managing properly, or problems may be bigger than they can handle. What happens then?

This chapter looks at:

● what management trainers and consultants can and cannot do, and what management training or consultancy might be expected to achieve;

● some causes of managerial ineffectiveness;

● how 'do it yourself consultancy' by non-managers can help if the managers refuse to recognise or deal with the situation.

MANAGEMENT TRAINING

Managers, like all workers, can benefit from training. But management training can only be effective if it is reasonably clear what managers already know and what they need to learn. Broadly, the training required for good management can be divided into:

● **general factual or technical knowledge**: financial management; legislation related to equal opportunities, employment, premises; company and/or charity law; computer awareness;

● **factual or technical knowledge related to the organisation and its work**: specific legislation, awareness of equipment and materials, awareness of the local community or client group and its needs, awareness of the organisation's history and development;

● **general and specific skills**: how to use computers and other equipment, languages, report writing, training skills, basic skills needed to provide the organisation's services;

● **strategic issues** related to the organisation, its work and the voluntary sector: the political situation, demographic changes, what other organisations are doing, meeting the needs of specific groups, developing non-oppressive perspectives;

● **organisational and interpersonal development**: project development, planning, decision-making, teambuilding, staff supervision;

● **personal awareness and development**: assertion, stress management, time management; awareness of racism, sexism and other oppressions.

Chapter 17 looks in more detail at how to find and assess training.

Where to find training

Short management courses designed specifically for voluntary sector managers are organised by:

● Directory of Social Change, Radius Works, Back Lane, London NW3 1HL (tel 071 431 1817);

● National Council for Voluntary Organisations Short Course Programme, Regents Wharf, 8 All Saints Street, London N1 9RL (tel 071 713 6161);

● InterChange Training, 5 Dalby Street, London NW5 3NG (071 267 9421);

● local councils for voluntary service, rural community councils and other local voluntary sector development agencies;

● some local colleges;

● national organisations in particular areas of work, such as National Federation of Housing Associations, Alcohol Concern, Mind.

Professional management qualifications for voluntary sector managers are increasingly being developed. Some at different levels are:

● the Royal Society of Arts (RSA) Advanced Diploma in the Organisation of Community Groups (information from RSA Examinations Board, Westwood Way, Coventry CV4 8HS, tel 0203 470033);

● the Open Business School's 'Managing Voluntary and Non-Profit Enterprises' course, leading to the Professional Certificate in Management (information from the Open University, PO Box 222, Milton Keynes MK7 6YY);

● MSc in Voluntary Sector Organisation at the London School of Economics (information from the Centre for Voluntary Organisation, LSE, Houghton Street, London WC2A 2AE).

MANAGEMENT CONSULTANCY

A management consultant is a person or agency called in to help the organisation or a team or group within it deal with management problems and develop its work. A consultant might be called in because:

- no one in the organisation has the knowledge or skills required for a particular piece of work (for example, drawing up an equal opportunities code of practice);

- no one has the time to do it;

- the organisation is considering complicated issues and wants impartial help in sorting through the complexities;

- the organisation is aware it is not operating as well as it might, and wants ideas or recommendations on how to function more effectively;

- the organisation has got itself into a mess and no one knows how (or has the authority) to sort it out.

Consultancy can enhance good management, but cannot replace it. When the consultant leaves, the organisation will have to carry on. If people in the organisation still do not know how to manage or are unwilling to, problems will emerge even before the consultant's fees are paid.

Consultancy is not the same as **training**, although they overlap. Training is a systematic approach to learning, and is oriented to individuals. Consultancy may involve some training but is a systematic approach to dealing with a particular situation or problem, and is oriented to the organisation or team.

Consultancy is not the same as **facilitation**. Facilitation is helping people listen to, communicate with and respect each other. Consultancy may involve facilitation but focuses on the situation or problem which is being communicated about. (Obviously they might overlap considerably if the consultant is called in to look at communication problems within the organisation.)

Types of consultancy

Management consultancy is expensive. So before contacting a consultant, think about what you want from the work. Be clear about whether the consultant is being called in to:

- advise on or do a specific task;

- help with strategic planning;

- help improve the way people relate to each other (process consultancy);

- advise or make recommendations on improving structures, systems or procedures;

- help the group sort out a conflict or other problem.

These may overlap but they require different approaches from the consultant.

If the consultant is being called in to help with a specific **task**, draw up a 'job description' and 'person specification'. The 'job description' can be negotiable but will enable the consultant to know what needs doing and the organisation to monitor the consultant's work. The person specification will enable the organisation to choose the most appropriate person or agency to do the work.

Be clear about when the work will be finished (give either a deadline, or a clear indication of what the task does and does not include). Sometimes consultancies drag on because the consultant does not want to 'let go' of the work, or the organisation does not want to let go of the consultant.

Think through whom the consultant will have to speak to, whether the consultant will be expected to provide training, and what will happen if the work is done unsatisfactorily.

If the consultant is being called in to help with **strategic planning**, clarify exactly what sort of assistance is required and what knowledge or awareness the consultant will need. Make a list of necessary documents and other information. Think about the advantages and disadvantages of using an outsider for this work. It may, in some circumstances, make more sense to hire someone temporarily to do some of the manager's routine work, thus freeing the manager to do the necessary reading, thinking and strategic planning.

If a decision is made to go ahead with a consultant, be clear about whether the consultant is expected to:

- facilitate discussions within the organisation to help people come up with their own ideas;

- undertake research into possibilities, and present this research to the organisation without making proposals for action;

- present proposals for action;

- make recommendations about what she or he thinks the organisation should do.

As with consultancy based on a specific task, think about the deadline, whether the consultant is expected to provide training, and what will happen if the work is done unsatisfactorily or if the proposals or recommendations are considered inappropriate.

For **process consultancy** it is essential to choose a consultant experienced in group dynamics and willing to help the group deal with its relationship problems. (Many consultants are oriented more towards specific tasks, strategic planning or organisational structures.) The consultant will probably want to meet with the whole group, or representatives of the group, beforehand to get different people's views about what is happening and what needs to be improved.

It can be very difficult or inappropriate to set predefined objectives for process consultancy. Without a skilful consultant the whole thing can degenerate into an expensive moan session which brings issues and feelings into the open without dealing adequately with them, and without providing group members with the skills or insight to follow up on them.

A consultant asked to advise on **structures, systems or procedures** will find it easier if the organisation has made a list of the basic problems, and perhaps divided them into categories. (These might be, for example, unclear objectives and priorities; unclear terms of reference, job descriptions or boundaries; inadequate information or communication; ineffective meetings.) The consultant will

only take this list as a starting point but it saves time if some of the thinking has been done beforehand.

When the list has been drawn up, clear objectives should be set. Is the consultant expected to deal with all those problems and achieve all those objectives? Which are the priorities? What can the consultancy realistically be expected to achieve?

Is the consultant supposed to help the people in the organisation come up with their own improvements? Or is she or he supposed to put forward her or his own proposals, recommend specific courses of action, draw up detailed proposals for some or all courses of action, and/or help the organisation implement new structures or procedures?

Similarly, if the consultant is being asked to help sort out a **conflict** or other muddle it will be easier if information can be presented in a clear, straightforward way, and if people are clear about whether the consultant is supposed to help people in the group sort things out themselves or is expected to come up with her or his own recommended solution.

Having done this preliminary work, read through the DIY consultancy section below, the DIY conflict resolution section in chapter 18, and other relevant sections of this book. Ask: 'Do we actually need a consultant? Could we use the time a consultancy would take to deal with this ourselves? Could we use the money to hire a temporary worker, to free some time?' By now, the organisation should be quite clear about what it wants the consultancy to achieve, and whether it actually needs someone from outside.

Finding a consultant

There is no recognised training, qualification or certification for consultants in the voluntary sector. People who become consultants may have degrees or may have done courses in relevant subjects, or may have worked in voluntary organisations or in an advisory or support role, perhaps as a local authority grants officer. They may have been community workers or community development workers, worked in a small business or cooperative, or been involved with a commercial management consultancy firm. Anyone can become a 'consultant'.

This puts considerable responsibility on the organisation to find someone appropriate. Some organisations look to commercial management consultancies which advise business, industry and statutory agencies; this can be appropriate if the consultant is given a clear brief and understands the particular (and peculiar) nature of the voluntary sector. Commercial consultants may be helpful in dealing with tasks related to fundraising or publicity, especially for larger or national organisations, but they may be less comfortable with the values and approaches of smaller community-based or radical voluntary organisations.

Partly for cost reasons and partly on ideological grounds, most voluntary organisations look for consultants with voluntary sector experience and expertise.

The starting points to be clear about are:

- whether it is important for the consultant to be aware of your particular type of work (for example housing associations, under-fives, employment creation projects) and if so what level of specialist knowledge is required, or whether a 'generalist' approach is acceptable;

- whether the consultant needs specific knowledge or skills, for example employment law or computer systems;

- whether it is appropriate (and within the law) to look specifically for a trainer from one racial or ethnic group or of a particular gender, and if so why;

- the criteria on which the consultant's suitability will be assessed;

- whether you want to contact only one consultant, or talk to several before deciding.

Names of suitable consultants can be obtained from:

- the Management Development Team or Local Development Team at the National Council for Voluntary Organisations (tel 071 713 6161);

- the Training Unit at London Voluntary Service Council (tel 071 388 0241);

- your local council for voluntary service, rural community council or voluntary sector coordinating group;

- local, regional or national umbrella groups, federations or networks for your type of work or similar work;

- the training departments of large or national organisations involved in your type of work (for example Age Concern, Royal National Institute for the Blind, Oxfam);

- local groups which have used consultants;

- funding bodies.

When contacting potential consultants, explain briefly what the organisation does, how many staff and volunteers it has, why a consultancy is being considered, what it is expected to achieve, available time and money, and when the work is to be done. At this stage it is reasonable to ask the consultants:

- whether they are interested in the work;

- whether they have done similar work, and if so the names and telephone numbers of two or three relevant organisations with which they have worked;

- what work, training or other experience they have had which is relevant to this consultancy;

- briefly, how they would approach the work;

- how they would ensure equal opportunities considerations were taken into account in planning and carrying out the consultancy;

- whether the objectives could be met in the available time;

- how much time they would anticipate it taking;

- when they would be available to start the work (a good consultant might be booked weeks or months in advance, so plan ahead);

- what kind of report would be provided at the end of the consultancy;

- whether they would provide any follow-up support;

- their fees, whether there is an additional charge for preliminary meeting(s), how expenses are charged, and whether VAT is added.

If several consultants are being considered, these points can be discussed at interviews.

The consultant chosen to do the work will arrange at least one preliminary meeting to discuss the situation and consultancy objectives in more detail and to agree fees, time scales and other specifics. The objectives and other agreed points should be put in writing (a letter or a formal contract).

One person or a small group within the organisation should take responsibility for liaising with the consultant, ensuring she or he receives the necessary documents and other information, and discussing any questions or points of dissatisfaction that arise during the consultancy.

There is no point in bringing in a consultant unless there is a commitment to cooperating with her or him and taking seriously the consultancy report and recommendations.

A WORD OF CAUTION

Neither training nor consultancy can compensate for lack of clear objectives and priorities, inadequate planning, inappropriate structures or procedures, or individuals being more concerned about getting their own way than working together for the organisation and its users or members.

Good management is the responsibility of all committee members, managers, staff and volunteers. This responsibility can never be passed on to trainers or consultants.

WHAT IF THE MANAGERS CAN'T MANAGE?

'Our management committee doesn't have a clue; all they do is rubber-stamp our decisions ...'

'Our chair thinks she has the right to overturn any decision we make if she doesn't like it ...'

'Our project director drinks so much at lunch we have to cover for him all afternoon ...'

'The people in our collective wouldn't recognise good management if it walked in the door ...'

'The general secretary never consults anyone ...'

What happens when the managers do not want to manage, do not know how or are not able to? This is one of the most difficult situations facing any organisation, and there are no easy answers.

Some of the reasons for management committee and managerial ineffectiveness are:

- committee members, managers and their organisations try to do too much;

- they do not know what management involves;

- they are afraid of being seen as authoritarian if they use their managerial authority;

- they do not know the limits of their authority, so they misuse it;

- they have a managerial style inappropriate to the organisation, its values, and the people involved;

- people look to them as authority figures and expect them to do more than is appropriate.

In a properly managed organisation, the management committee or managers would take responsibility for recognising problems, discussing them and implementing solutions. But if they are unable or unwilling to do it, someone else will have to try. This may be done from inside the organisation, even by someone who does not have explicit managerial responsibility, or an outside consultant may be called in.

A management consultant can help the group recognise the underlying factors causing its problems, and can propose ways to improve the situation. So it may seem tempting to call in an outsider, but in many cases people within the organisation are just as aware as any consultant about what is wrong and what needs doing. Or if the organisation's budget does not extend to professional fees, there may be no alternative to do it yourself consultancy.

DIY consultancy requires time, commitment and tact. But the benefits can be significant:

- the organisation is better run;

- individuals realise they can take responsibility for changing the situation, without relying on outside consultants.

DIY CONSULTANCY

When things go wrong it is easy to point the finger at the incompetence of individual managers, whether they are management committee members, senior staff, line managers or members of a collective.

Incompetent managers are certainly an important factor, and management training may be able to increase their competence. But **bad management is nearly always rooted in organisational factors which transcend individual incompetence**.

DIY consultancy starts by looking for those factors. A problem will usually show itself as an **effect** of bad management; the person who wants to do something about it must look beyond the effect to the cause. **Why** has this situation or problem arisen?

Listed below are some causes of managerial ineffectiveness, and ways they can be dealt with *by non-managers* (or by managers, of course). In some cases, all a non-manager can do is propose to the managers that they do something. If they refuse, there is little recourse except to wait and put the proposal forward again in a few months, when perhaps the managers will be less obstructive. But in many situations a non-manager can take quite significant action.

For more ideas, read through the relevant chapters in this book. (Or leave a copy strategically on the manager's desk!) And consult two other books for practical exercises and ideas for improving teamwork and management processes:

● *Planning Together: The art of effective teamwork* by George Gawlinski and Lois Graessle (Bedford Square Press, 1988; 88 pages; ISBN 0 7199 1202 4; £11.95 + £1.50 p&p from Plymbridge Distributors Ltd, Estover Road, Plymouth PL6 7PZ);

● *Getting Organised: A handbook for non-statutory organisations* by Christine Holloway and Shirley Otto (Bedford Square Press, 1985; 70 pages; ISBN 0 7199 1162 1; £4.95 + 62p p&p from Plymbridge Distributors, as above).

Unclear objectives

No one can manage effectively if objectives and priorities are unclear. If this is the underlying problem, some approaches are:

● proposing the management committee and/or staff set up a small group (which might be called a development group, strategy group or planning group) to outline what the organisation wants to achieve in the coming year, draw up a work programme to achieve those goals, submit the objectives and programme to workers and the management committee for approval, and help the people responsible for managing work to implement and monitor the work programme;

● proposing regular (annual or six-monthly) review days or strategy days for some or all management committee members, workers and users (if appropriate), perhaps led by an outside facilitator, to review achievements and set new objectives for the next period;

● asking 'why are we doing this?' or 'how does this fit into our overall objectives?' if the management committee or individual managers seem to be going off in strange directions;

● challenging new activities or ideas if there is not enough time to do them.

Unclear terms of reference and boundaries

Sometimes individuals or groups do not manage well because they are not aware they are supposed to be managing, or are not clear about what is to be managed. Ways to improve this situation include:

● proposing terms of reference be drawn up for the management committee, subcommittees and staff groups, outlining the sorts of issues they cover and whether the committee or group can make decisions or can only put forward proposals or recommendations on each issue;

● asking 'can we make a final decision or does it have to be decided elsewhere?' in meetings, if this is not clear;

● ensuring meetings decide *who* is supposed to take action on every decision made by the meeting;

● encouraging managers to clarify 'boundary disputes' about who is supposed to do what *every time* something is not done, or is duplicated, or is done by someone who should not have done it.

Ineffective and inefficient meetings

Bad management and bad meetings are inseparable. An endless cycle is created: bad management means people do not have the information or skills they need to participate fully in meetings and make appropriate decisions, so decisions are not made or are made but cannot be implemented, so the people responsible for managing do not know what they are supposed to do or are expected to do the impossible, so people at meetings do not get the information they need to make further decisions ... and so it goes on.

Breaking the cycle might involve:

● suggesting proper agendas be drawn up for all meetings (see chapter 5);

● asking for background papers in advance;

● reading background papers and doing other preparation;

● suggesting committee training for the chair, minutetaker or others, or giving them a copy of chapter 5 of this book;

● not being afraid to say 'I'm not clear what has been decided';

● suggesting subgroups be set up to do the initial reading, thinking and discussion (and perhaps also make proposals) about complex issues, so every person in the group does not feel a need to be expert in everything.

Management committee members

Committee members may be unconfident, unaware or unsure of their responsibilities, and/or overcommitted. They may not feel able to challenge or even question staff. Ways to overcome these difficulties include:

● holding a familiarisation session before people are elected to the committee, so they know what they are getting involved in and what will be expected of them;

● preparing an induction pack for all committee members (see chapter 1);

● having an annual induction/update session for all committee members (not just new ones);

- finding a way to ask committee members what they bring to the organisation and would like to contribute to it, and what they want from the organisation;

- proposing a written 'contract' for committee members (or at least a discussion) detailing what is expected from them (attendance at meetings, reading papers beforehand, participating) and what the organisation will provide (training, information before the meeting, opportunities to meet people from other voluntary organisations);

- suggesting some management committee members attend courses on management committee skills and issues, or arranging an in-house course specifically for the organisation's committee.

Unclear job descriptions and job expectations

Even a good manager cannot manage staff or volunteers well if there are confusions about what the workers should be doing. Ways to improve this situation include:

- insisting all staff get contracts and job descriptions;

- proposing an annual review for all job descriptions, so they are kept up to date;

- proposing job descriptions or contracts for regular volunteers;

- asking 'who will do it?' when new projects or tasks are taken on;

- asking 'how will we know if it is being done adequately?' or 'how will I know if I am doing it properly?' if expectations are unclear.

Inadequate supervision procedures

It is too late to intervene when a worker, whether paid or volunteer, has already botched up a job. Good management involves regular procedures for overseeing and reviewing work, discussing difficulties and clarifying how to proceed (see chapter 16). Changes in this area require managerial support and approval, but some which can be suggested by anyone in the organisation include:

- proposing a regular (perhaps monthly) opportunity for all workers to discuss their progress and problems with someone else;

- proposing regular (perhaps annual) formal reviews for all workers;

- suggesting procedures for senior managers to have similar opportunities for discussion and formal review, perhaps with an individual or small group from the management committee or with someone from outside the organisation.

Haphazard administrative systems

Without adequate information and administrative systems, good management is impossible. Filing systems, libraries, work diaries and year planners, and procedures for dealing with post, telephone calls and time off must be clear (see chapters 11 and 21). Anyone can take responsibility for improving these systems by suggesting:

- a 'clear up the filing' day every few weeks or months, when everyone gets all their filing up to date;

- improvements to information systems, instead of constantly complaining about not being able to find information;

- a blackboard or whiteboard near the reception area, where all workers indicate when they will be in;

- improvements to administrative systems, instead of constantly complaining they do not work properly;

- sheets of instructions or a procedures book, instead of complaining that people do not know how to do things correctly.

Inadequate financial management

Decisions involving money cannot be properly made if people do not have comprehensible, up to date and accurate financial information. If this is not available, the first steps to getting it include:

- reading chapter 20 to clarify problems and get ideas;

- asking for clarification about who is supposed to provide financial information, how often and in what format;

- insisting this information is provided;

- asking for explanations if information is unclear or too complicated;

- asking for financial training (or simpler presentation) if people consistently cannot understand the information.

Disagreements and conflict

Good management involves recognising, accepting and valuing differences, creating opportunities for differing views to be expressed, and dealing with conflict when it occurs. But in many voluntary organisations there is only one view which is considered acceptable, and people who disagree with or do not understand that view are excluded or made to feel stupid. All differences are suppressed so the organisation can be 'one big happy family'. Major disagreements and conflicts are ignored. Until one day ...

Workers or management committee members who feel differences and conflict are not being managed appropriately can take action by:

- reading chapter 18 to help clarify issues and get ideas;

- suggesting ways to improve meetings, to allow time for people's views to be heard (see chapters 4 to 6);

- suggesting informal opportunities, outside meetings, for discussion and debate;

- practising what they preach: listen to people and treat them with respect, even if what they are saying is difficult, unpleasant or 'ideologically unsound';

- acting as an informal mediator to help resolve conflicts within the group, or offering to do it formally.

Managerial incompetence

Incompetence may not be the only cause of managerial ineffectiveness, but it is one cause. How can the non-manager deal with it?

- A worker concerned about the competence or ability of a staff manager might, if appropriate, contact someone higher up (talk to a senior manager about a line manager, or talk to the management committee chair or personnel subcommittee chair about a senior manager). This might be done formally or informally but should be in the spirit of asking for advice and guidance, rather than in the spirit of complaining.

- Information about relevant training can be obtained and given to the manager. Or, if that is not possible, it can be left lying around in a strategic position where the manager is likely to see it.

- A supervision session, review or other discussion with the manager can be used as an opportunity to say 'I don't feel I'm getting the managerial support I need from you ...'

- Some organisations ensure each worker has a 'support person' on the management committee. This person might be able to give advice to the worker or relay information to the management committee chair or personnel subcommittee. If this happens both the worker and support person should be clear about whether the discussions are confidential, what will be reported to other management committee members and what will be reported to the manager in question.

A management committee member concerned about the competence of a staff manager has different options.

- Discuss it with the management committee chair and/or personnel subcommittee chair, and put forward proposals for dealing with the situation. The committee chair or chair of the personnel subcommittee will probably want to discuss the situation with the manager's line manager, if there is one.

- Recommend a procedure for regular discussions with the manager, and regular formal reviews of her or his work. These discussions might be with a management committee member or members, or with someone from outside the organisation. If they are with a committee member, everyone should be clear whether they are confidential and what, if anything, will be reported back to the whole committee. If they are with someone from outside, everyone should be clear whether they are confidential or whether and how information will be relayed back to the committee.

- Training on specific aspects of management may be helpful, but a short course cannot work miracles.

- The organisation's staff recruitment and selection procedures need to be examined, to try to discover why a person unable to do the job was appointed to a managerial position.

Especially in small organisations, managerial incompetence is a serious matter which can affect the stability and future of the organisation. Steps should be taken as quickly as possible to put the situation right, or at least to minimise the negative effects.

A FINAL WORD

As voluntary organisations and community groups become more professionalised, there is a risk they will become over-managed. As increasing emphasis is placed on the management of communication, planning, monitoring, record-keeping and evaluation, the primary purpose of the organisation may be lost. Finance, funding, personnel matters and legal issues come to dominate the agenda, with little time given to the development of new or improved services or activities.

The most exciting challenge for voluntary sector managers in the 1990s may be to ensure this does not happen: to create a proper and appropriate balance between effective management and responsive, creative service delivery.